TOAD® Handbook

Second Edition

Developer's Library Series

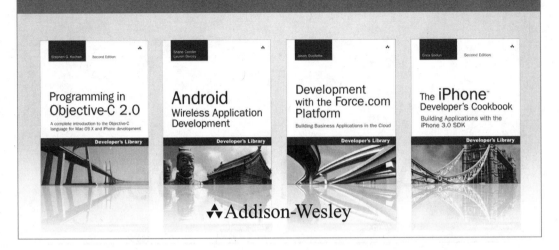

Addison-Wesley

Visit **developers-library.com** for a complete list of available products

---

The **Developer's Library Series** from Addison-Wesley provides practicing programmers with unique, high-quality references and tutorials on the latest programming languages and technologies they use in their daily work. All books in the Developer's Library are written by expert technology practitioners who are exceptionally skilled at organizing and presenting information in a way that's useful for other programmers.

Developer's Library books cover a wide range of topics, from open-source programming languages and databases, Linux programming, Microsoft, and Java, to Web development, social networking platforms, Mac/iPhone programming, and Android programming.

TOAD® Handbook

Second Edition

Bert Scalzo
Dan Hotka

⊬Addison-Wesley

Upper Saddle River, NJ • Boston • Indianapolis • San Francisco
New York • Toronto • Montreal • London • Munich • Paris • Madrid
Capetown • Sydney • Tokyo • Singapore • Mexico City

Many of the designations used by manufacturers and sellers to distinguish their products are claimed as trademarks. Where those designations appear in this book, and the publisher was aware of a trademark claim, the designations have been printed with initial capital letters or in all capitals.

The authors and publisher have taken care in the preparation of this book, but make no expressed or implied warranty of any kind and assume no responsibility for errors or omissions. No liability is assumed for incidental or consequential damages in connection with or arising out of the use of the information or programs contained herein.

The publisher offers excellent discounts on this book when ordered in quantity for bulk purchases or special sales, which may include electronic versions and/or custom covers and content particular to your business, training goals, marketing focus, and branding interests. For more information, please contact

U.S. Corporate and Government Sales
1-800-382-3419
corpsales@pearsontechgroup.com

For sales outside the United States, please contact

International Sales
international@pearsoned.com

Visit us on the Web: informit.com/aw

Library of Congress Cataloging-in-Publication Data

Scalzo, Bert.
  TOAD handbook / Bert Scalzo, Dan Hotka.—2nd ed.
      p.   cm.
  Includes index.
  ISBN 978-0-321-64910-2 (pbk. : alk. paper)
1. TOAD (Electronic resource) 2. Oracle (Computer file) 3. Application software. 4. Database design. I. Hotka, Dan. II. Title.

  QA76.76.A65S332 2009
  005.75'85—dc22
                                        2009025928

ISBN-13: 978-0-321-64910-2
ISBN-10:   0-321-64910-9

Text printed in the United States on recycled paper at RR Donnelley in Crawfordsville, Indiana.
First printing, September 2009

Editor-in-Chief
Mark Taub

Acquisitions Editor
Trina MacDonald

Development Editor
Songlin Qiu

Managing Editor
John Fuller

Project Editor
Anna Popick

Copy Editor
Jill Hobbs

Indexer
Jack Lewis

Proofreader
Simone Payment

Editorial Assistant
Olivia Basegio

Cover Designer
Gary Adair

Compositor
Kim Arney

❖

I dedicate this book to my miniature schnauzer Max,
because—as with all good dogs—Max's love and devotion
help to make me a happier and better human being.

—Bert Scalzo

❖

Contents at a Glance

Table of Contents

Acknowledgments

Bert Scalzo

I've been doing Oracle work for more than two decades, and much of what I've learned has come from other great people who were willing to share their knowledge. So rather than list a few folks and risk missing anyone, let me just say thanks to all those many people "along the way" who've helped me to learn so much. Of course, I owe a very special thanks to Oracle Corporation. To paraphrase Garret Morris as Chico Escuela on the old *Saturday Night Live*, "Oracle been berry, berry good to me." Finally, special thanks to my coauthor Dan and the many fine people at Pearson for making this book possible.

Dan Hotka

I have now been writing about Oracle-related topics for more than twelve years. What started out as something to pass the time while flying on United Airlines has turned into a rather substantial second job. I want to thank those people who have not only contributed to my work in this book but also made a positive difference in my career and life.

Special thanks go out to my wife of thirty-one years, Gail, and the rest of my family. Gail's patience, love, and understanding have allowed me to take on opportunities such as writing and the travel that come with my work. I also want to thank my children—Elizabeth (Libby), Emily, and Thomas—for giving me the foundation that continues to fuel my success.

A big "Thank you very much!" goes to Bert Scalzo for inviting me along on this book.

I want to thank the people who continue to help make my writing a success. Tim Gorman has to be the most Oracle-knowledgeable person I know. His advice and wisdom have definitely enhanced most every Oracle project I have undertaken. Other technical advice has been gleaned from (not in any particular order) Bert Scalzo, Bradley Brown, Rodney Dauphin, and Jonathan Lewis. Thank you for your technical assistance on this project and through the years.

I want to thank those managers who have helped mold my career and whose generosity led to the success that I continue to enjoy today: Karl Lenk (Sperry-Rand, Inc.), Gary Dodge (Oracle Corporation), and Deb Jenson (Platinum Technology, Inc. and Quest Software, Inc.).

I also want to thank the many friends I have met along my lifelong journey. You are too numerous to list here, but know that you have made a positive difference in my life. To you, I simply say, "Thank you."

Finally, thank you very much to my parents, Philip and Dorothy; my in-laws, Dean and Marian; my siblings, Mike and Janice; and my grandmothers, Mamie and Gladys, who will always have a special place in my heart.

About the Authors

Bert Scalzo is a database expert for Quest Software and a member of the TOAD development team. He has worked with Oracle databases for more than two decades. Mr. Scalzo's work history includes time at both Oracle Education and Oracle Consulting. He holds several Oracle Master's certifications and has an extensive academic background, including a B.S., M.S., and Ph.D. in computer science; an MBA; and insurance industry designations. Mr. Scalzo is also an Oracle ACE.

Mr. Scalzo is an accomplished speaker and has made presentations at many Oracle conferences and user groups, including OOW, ODTUG, IOUG, OAUG, and RMOUG, among many others. His key areas of DBA interest are data modeling, database benchmarking, database tuning and optimization, "star schema" data warehouses, Linux, and VMware.

Mr. Scalzo has written numerous articles, papers, and blogs, including pieces for the Oracle Technology Network (OTN), *Oracle Magazine, Oracle Informant, PC Week* (*eWeek*), *Dell Power Solutions Magazine, The LINUX Journal,* LINUX.com, *Oracle FAQ, Ask Toad,* and *Toad World.*

In addition to *TOAD Handbook, Second Edition,* Mr. Scalzo has written five books: *Oracle DBA Guide to Data Warehousing and Star Schemas* (Prentice Hall, 2003), *TOAD Pocket Reference for Oracle, Second Edition* (O'Reilly Media, Inc., 2005), *D Database Benchmarking: Practical Methods for Oracle & SQL Server* (Rampant Techpress, 2007), *Advanced Oracle Utilities: The Definitive Reference* (Rampant Techpress, 2009), and *Oracle on VMware: Expert Tips for Database Virtualization* (Rampant Techpress, 2008).

Dan Hotka is a training specialist who has more than thirty-one years in the computer industry and more than twenty-six years of experience with Oracle products. He is an internationally recognized Oracle expert, with Oracle experience dating back to the Oracle V4.0 days. Dan has written four books on the Oracle topic and has coauthored seven other popular Oracle-related books. His work is frequently published in Oracle-related trade journals, and he regularly speaks at Oracle conferences and user groups around the world. Visit his Web site at www.DanHotka.com or email him at dhotka@earthlink.net.

Introduction

This is the second edition of the first ever book to cover the very popular TOAD for Oracle database management and development tool. This book covers all of the most popular and key features of TOAD, including many features that are new additions to TOAD version 9.7. Moreover, this book offers numerous TOAD tips and tricks, with ample expert recommended advice or techniques—without focusing on any particular version of the Oracle database. Readers should be able to identify and readily adapt these "best practices" to their daily TOAD usage.

Who Should Read This Book

This book should benefit all TOAD users. It is ideal for a wide range of users, from those who are new to both Oracle and TOAD to very sophisticated or experienced users of TOAD. Furthermore, this book attempts to address the specialized needs for three key database personas: database administrators, database application developers, and data/business analysts. In truth, TOAD has so many features and offers so many benefits that no one book can realistically hope to fully cover them all. Thus each chapter focuses on a particular functional or task-related area, covering it in depth with illustrations, tips, and techniques from Oracle and TOAD experts Bert Scalzo and Dan Hotka.

This book is ideal for the following types of readers:

- The power user who wants easy access to data, help with SQL, and help with occasional coding assignments
- The user who wants to increase his or her productivity while using the Oracle RDBMS
- The IT professional who is already familiar with TOAD but needs help with its extended features
- The developer who wants to do something specific but cannot remember how
- Any TOAD user who wants to learn how to take advantage of TOAD's newly introduced features

Why This Book Is Unique

This book doesn't make assumptions about readers' prior TOAD or Oracle administrative or development background, so it presents the full range of tips and techniques applicable to these tools. The main goal of this book is to illustrate the use of TOAD and to serve as a handy reference for anyone using the TOAD database tool. To this end, the book is liberally illustrated with working examples of all topics covered.

This book is intended to be a complete, single source of information, usage, tips, and techniques for the TOAD tool. It focuses on the following topics:

- TOAD installation and setup
- Development of PL/SQL and SQL statements and scripts in an easy-to-use and intuitive environment
- Tuning SQL and debugging PL/SQL
- Modeling any user's schema
- Routine and advanced DBA tasks
- Exporting of data into various formats
- Additional features such as FTP, TKProf, StatsPack, and AWR interfaces and the ability to add your own favorite editors and programs

How This Book Is Organized

The chapters are organized as follows:

Chapter 1, TOAD Setup and Configuration, reviews the more common and critical setup and configuration steps necessary to fully maximize your initial TOAD experience. While some of these steps may seem quite simple and fairly obvious, failure to address them properly can radically reduce your initial success.

Chapter 2, Database and Schema Browsers, covers the main TOAD interface for exploring your database's structure and content (i.e., meta-data and data). This chapter explores all of the browser's advanced display options and capabilities, as well as key start-up and control options. It also explains how to filter the schemas, objects, and their data.

Chapter 3, SQL Editor, covers all of TOAD's features relevant to building and maintaining SQL and SQL scripts. This chapter explores all of the shortcuts and hot keys available, and summarizes them in convenient reference grids. Chapter 3 also explains how to build SQL with code templates and advanced topics such as "scripts that write scripts."

Chapter 4, TOAD PL/SQL Editor, covers the features available for building and maintaining PL/SQL, procedures, functions, and triggers. This chapter also illustrates just how easy it is to see the various object relationships using TOAD. In addition, it discusses use of the powerful PL/SQL symbolic debugger and PL/SQL Profiler. This chapter covers all of the shortcuts and hot keys available, and summarizes them in convenient reference grids.

Chapter 5, Database Reporting, reviews the various reports that come with TOAD, including HTML reports, the report interface, and ways to generate additional reports using the Fast Reports utility.

Chapter 6, Tuning Tools in TOAD, explores the use of the TOAD Explain Plan interface, Oracle Trace with TOAD, the TKProf interface, and newer browsers for both StatsPack and AWR.

Chapter 7, Database Management, focuses on routine DBA tasks such as checking instance status, database performance monitoring, user session monitoring and management, checking/correcting fragmentation, and creating and maintaining database objects. Anyone who has to perform database administration tasks (including power users) will find this chapter useful.

Chapter 8, Exporting Table Data, illustrates how easy it is to extract data from Oracle and import it into a variety of customized formats using TOAD. This chapter also discusses how TOAD works with existing Oracle features, such as through the Export/Import utility and the newer Data Pump alternatives.

Chapter 9, Other Useful Tools, covers the remaining features of TOAD—for example, browsing master/detail data, building SQL visually using the SQL Modeler, creating "poor man's" mini-ER diagrams via the Schema Browser hook to the SQL modeler, registering external programs for quick launch from within TOAD, visually comparing text files for differences, working with TNS Names files, making subsets of data, and managing libraries of scripts.

Chapter 10,TOAD App Designer, explores the process of creating, running, and scheduling TOAD groupings of tasks (called applications) into command-line-executable packages. Now you can record TOAD actions as macros and then execute them, thereby automating many of the TOAD tasks that you routinely perform.

We hope you enjoy using this book as much as we have enjoyed writing it.

Bert Scalzo
Dan Hotka

TOAD Setup and Configuration

Congratulations! You have just purchased TOAD, the market-leading Oracle integrated development environment (IDE) and productivity enhancement tool, and are now preparing to deploy it throughout your organization. TOAD has always adhered to one very simple mantra: to make all Oracle database interactions as easy and productive as possible. Thus, when TOAD has been properly configured, you should find it to be the single most effective and productive database tool on the market today. However, even the world's leading Oracle productivity enhancement tool requires a little attention to detail during both setup and configuration to achieve the best user experience possible. By spending just a few extra minutes wisely upfront, you should then be able to reasonably fulfill all of your various TOAD users' expectations—including database administrators (DBAs), developers, and data or business analysts.

With more than 1 million registered commercial product users, and even more freeware users, TOAD has already been deployed and utilized in just about any scenario imaginable. Regardless of whether you are working with older Oracle database versions such as 7.3 or newer versions such as 10g or 11g, you can rest assured that TOAD has seen action in those arenas. The TOAD development team takes enormous pride in supporting millions of users in a plethora of environments. You should, therefore, consider that any potential difficulties that you may encounter are most likely setup and configuration issues—and not automatically or necessarily anything particular or overly special related to your situation.

In this chapter, we review some of the more common and critical setup and configuration steps necessary to fully maximize your initial TOAD experience. While some of these steps may seem quite simple and fairly obvious, failure to address them properly can radically reduce your initial success. Once you've mastered this chapter's concepts, you should have TOAD set up properly and working ideally to support most users' needs.

Windows Platform Support

TOAD is a native Microsoft Windows 32-bit application. Such Windows 32-bit applications are very often referred to as Win-32 apps. TOAD is written in the Delphi 7 programming language, which is essentially just Object Pascal for Windows. You may have observed that some of Quest Software's newer TOAD product family members, such as TOAD for SQL Server, have been written in Microsoft C# and, therefore, require the .Net framework. But that's true only for these newer products, which don't have preexisting code bases. With nearly 2 million lines of legacy code, porting of TOAD to another language simply for the sake of porting is cost prohibitive.

As a Win-32 app, TOAD has been developed to run natively on the various Microsoft desktop operating systems, including these members of the Windows family:

- Windows 2000
- Windows XP (32 or 64 bit)
- Windows 2003 (32 or 64 bit)
- Windows Vista (32 or 64 bit)

Notice that all 64-bit versions of the various Microsoft Windows operating systems are fully supported. Microsoft created a highly compatible 64-bit environment where any well-behaved Win-32 app should run just fine within a 64-bit memory space. TOAD is no exception: It runs perfectly well on 64-bit versions of Windows. To ensure that it works, there is merely a requirement that the Oracle SQL*Net client installed for TOAD usage also be the 32-bit version. We'll cover this special SQL*Net client requirement in full detail in the next section on database connectivity.

What about older Windows versions such as Windows 95 and 98: Will TOAD run on those operating systems? The answer to this question is "probably." Unfortunately, the TOAD development team cannot reasonably or even realistically afford to undertake quality assurance (QA) testing for every possible Windows operating system version. Thus, while TOAD might function on those older operating systems, it will be more by luck than by intention. The same logic applies to newer but not yet commercially released versions such as Windows 7. TOAD may work on Windows 7 because it's based on Vista, but that platform has not yet been added to the officially supported TOAD QA list. Rest assured, however, that it will be supported once the new operating system becomes commercially available.

Another question that has come up a lot in recent times focuses on running TOAD on virtual machines that are themselves running Windows: Are there any problems with that setup? The basic answer is "no"; to TOAD, the virtual machine appears as just a Windows operating system as required. Nevertheless, we have seen some cases where memory management between the host operating system, virtualization layer, and client operating system can cause problems for applications such as TOAD. You may encounter these or other issues in your own system. For example, when scrolling a TOAD data grid all the way to the end via the slider control, TOAD may freeze up. So, when you are working on a virtual machine, keep that possibility in mind during troubleshooting efforts. The problem could be something within that technology stack.

Database Connectivity

TOAD is a database application that connects to, communicates with, and acts upon a database. As such, it requires a valid network pathway from itself to whatever target database you desire to connect to and work with. Regardless of whether that target database is on a database server on your company network or a local database running on your PC, TOAD must be able to see and communicate with it. As a consequence, database connectivity is a supremely critical aspect and step for proper setup and configuration. Figure 1.1 shows what such a valid basic network pathway should look like.

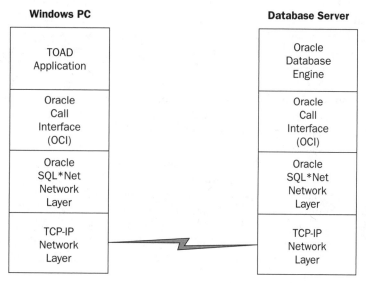

Figure 1.1   Network Pathway between TOAD
and the Target Oracle Database

For your Windows PC, where do the four key parts (i.e., the four boxes on the left side of Figure 1.1) of that network pathway between TOAD and the database come from? The TCP/IP layer will already be there from your Windows installation and network card configuration. So that part's very easy—you have nothing to do. When you install TOAD, the "TOAD Application" part of Figure 1.1 is accomplished automatically. That leaves the "Oracle Call Interface (OCI)" and "Oracle SQL*Net Network Layer" parts of Figure 1.1: Where do they come from? To implement them, you must install the Oracle 32-bit network client from the Oracle installation CD or DVD. Of course, you can also download the software from the Oracle Technology Network (OTN), but you must abide by the license agreement, which states that you have a "limited license to use the programs only for the purpose of developing a single prototype of your application, and not for any other purpose." If your target database is also running on your Windows PC, then the installation process for the Oracle database software on your PC would have already created those items for you. As a consequence, you would not need to run the Oracle software installer twice. However, if you plan to run a 64-bit database locally, then you would need to run the Oracle installer a second time to force an installation of the 32-bit client that TOAD requires.

A very common question is, Can TOAD use Microsoft's Open Database Connect (ODBC)? The answer is an emphatic "no." The data access layer component within TOAD has been designed to communicate with the database solely via the OCI API provided by Oracle. TOAD will not work with ODBC connections.

But you're not done just yet—not by a long shot. Once the pieces shown in Figure 1.1 are in place on your Windows PC (i.e., the software is installed), you still need to provide network configuration information. This type of network information tends to be very detailed and site specific, such that any database applications using this framework know how to properly navigate the network pathway. An Oracle database usually has an address and a name by which you reference it. For example, the database might be named **ORCL** and might reside at network address **192.168.1.5.** Clearly, Figure 1.1 does not show or imply how to address any of that information. In other words, the figure provides the highway infrastructure for traffic to flow, but it does not know anything about the server addresses or database names. You will have to manually configure that part of the system yourself. This step is supremely critical, as TOAD cannot talk to an Oracle database whose address and name cannot be resolved. For further reading, we strongly advise that someone at your site be familiar with the *Oracle Database Net Services Administrator's Guide.* In following examples, you'll notice that we specify port 1521: What is that and why did we use it? It's the default Oracle network port. This and a myriad of other Oracle issues are fully explained in the *Oracle Database Net Services Administrator's Guide.*

If you are working with a remote database (i.e., the database is not running on the same Windows PC as where you're running TOAD itself), then you need to configure just a single Oracle SQL*Net file: *tnsnames.ora.* It can be found in the "\network\admin" subdirectory under where you instructed the Oracle installer to install all the files for the Oracle products selected, which in our case is "C:\Oracle\product\11.1.0\db_1". Listing 1.1 shows what a basic *tnsnames.ora* file looks like to provide the information required to reach the remote database named **ORCL** and found on the server whose address is **192.168.1.5.** When asking TOAD to connect to a database, the information contained within the *tnsnames.ora* file is absolutely critical; you can't make a collect call to a person if you don't know that individual's name and phone number. The same is true for Oracle databases.

Listing 1.1   Remote Database tnsnames.ora

```
ORCL =
 (DESCRIPTION =
   (ADDRESS_LIST =
     (ADDRESS = (PROTOCOL = TCP)(HOST = 192.168.1.5)(PORT = 1521))
   )
```

```
(CONNECT_DATA =
  (SERVICE_NAME = ORCL)
  (INSTANCE_NAME = ORCL)
 )
)
```

If you're instead working with a local database (i.e., the Oracle database is running on your Windows PC where you are also running TOAD), then you have a second file that must be properly configured—the database listener file, known as *listener.ora*. Think of the Oracle listener as a "traffic cop" listening to all the network traffic that passes by his machine. If any network packets contain an address and name that resides on that machine, then the traffic cop (i.e., the listener) waves them onto that server's streets. Otherwise, all the network traffic just sails on by. So now we have two Oracle SQL*Net files to properly configure. Listing 1.2 shows what a basic *tnsnames.ora* file looks like to provide the information required to reach the database named **ORCL** that resides on the local Windows PC, which you can generally access via the network alias **localhost** or the address **127.0.0.1**. Listing 1.3 shows the corresponding *listener.ora* file. You will need both to connect TOAD to a local database; otherwise, you cannot traverse the network path even though it's all on the same machine.

Listing 1.2   **Local Database tnsnames.ora**

```
ORCL =
 (DESCRIPTION =
  (ADDRESS_LIST =
    (ADDRESS = (PROTOCOL = TCP)(HOST = 127.0.0.1)(PORT = 1521))
  )
  (CONNECT_DATA =
    (SERVICE_NAME = ORCL)
    (INSTANCE_NAME = ORCL)
  )
 )
```

Listing 1.3   **Local Database listener.ora**

```
SID_LIST_LISTENER =
 (SID_LIST =
  (SID_DESC=
    (GLOBAL_DBNAME=ORCL)
    (ORACLE_HOME=C:\oracle\product\11.1.0\db_1)
    (SID_NAME=ORCL)
  )
 )

LISTENER =
(DESCRIPTION=(ADDRESS=(PROTOCOL=tcp)(HOST=127.0.0.1)(PORT=1521)))
```

Finally, there are other mechanisms besides the *tnsnames.ora* file for resolving database addresses. For example, when using the Lightweight Directory Access Protocol (LDAP) concept, and as offered by Oracle Internet Directory (OID) or Microsoft Active Directory (AD), you will see on the TOAD connection screen that TOAD can also connect to databases using either direct connect information or LDAP-based lookup. However, both these options are beyond the scope of this book. Again, we refer you to refer to the *Oracle Database Net Services Administrator's Guide*.

Database Client Versions

Failure to install and configure the SQL*Net client will prevent TOAD from functioning. However, you must also keep in mind the version of your client libraries versus the database that you're working with. Having client libraries from an older version of Oracle and working with newer versions of Oracle is a recipe for disaster. You may well encounter Oracle OCI API error messages from within TOAD. Such a problem might well occur as TOAD attempts to call an OCI function for some feature or capability of the newer database version that the older network client library does not support.

For example, using an 8i client with a 9i database and attempting to work with columns whose data type is XMLTYPE will yield the following cryptic message:

```
OCI-21500: internal error code, arguments: [kocgpn129], [2], [], [], [], [], [], []
```

This is not a TOAD bug, nor is it a sign of lack of TOAD support for new database features; rather, it represents a simple user configuration error of trying to use an old and/or incompatible network client library version with a newer version of the Oracle database. The best advice is to always install and use the latest and greatest Oracle network client version, as it will always be fully backward compatible with prior database versions.

For the most current and authoritative reference on this issue, you should consult the Oracle metalink document **207303.1**. At the time this book was written, the document recommended Oracle client versions 11.1 and 10.2, with version 9.2 being supported in some very limited and special scenarios.

We have found version incompatibility to be one of the most prevalent problems when people report a suspected TOAD bug. Because technical support will ask you this question upfront anyway, you might as well fix compatibility problems before the call and save yourself one step in the troubleshooting process.

Which Version of TOAD to Use

This is the proverbial $64 million question. The very obvious answer is "the latest and greatest"—always. But sometimes people cannot roll out new versions across large organizations very quickly or easily. At other times people have let their TOAD maintenance contract lapse, so upgrading is no longer free unless they either renew that maintenance agreement or repurchase the product if they've been out of the maintenance loop for too long. But assuming you're current on your TOAD maintenance such that all TOAD upgrades are available to you for free, and assuming that you can deploy upgrades without restrictions or heartaches due to internal procedures, then our "latest and greatest" advice stands. Figure 1.2 shows the long TOAD versus Oracle Database version history, along with some key Oracle version support references.

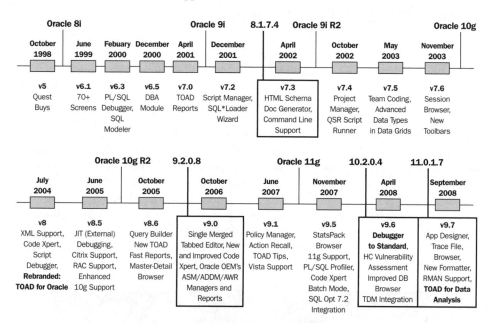

Figure 1.2   TOAD versus Oracle Version History

What, in a nutshell, does this very crowded and complex figure tell you? In short, if you're using Oracle 9.x, then you should be using at least TOAD 9.0; if you're using Oracle 10.x, then you should be using at least TOAD 9.6; and if you're using Oracle 11.x, then you should be using at least TOAD 9.7 (at the time of this writing, the current version). Anything else is like playing Russian roulette with your database work and data.

What's the logic behind our advice? Simple—much like the case with the prior section's client version advice, TOAD cannot work with database features or capabilities that came out years after the TOAD version was written. We find lots of people using TOAD 8.6 with Oracle 10g. Yes, Figure 1.2 shows that TOAD 8.6 came out after 10g Release 2 and, therefore, should support it. But Oracle often makes changes between even the minor database versions that can affect tools such as TOAD (i.e., tools that make heavy access to the internal data dictionary). For example, some Oracle data dictionary changes in version 10.2.0.2 broke a key TOAD screen. Because you should always be running the terminal Oracle release version (e.g., 10.2.0.4) for best Oracle support, then you should also choose your TOAD version based on that terminal Oracle version's release date—and not the date when the original database version itself debuted. Thus, if you're using Oracle 10g, we recommend TOAD 9.6, because TOAD 9.6 is the very first TOAD version that came out after Oracle 10.2.0.4. It's the only one for which Quest can perform QA testing and guarantee that it works.

Running the TOAD Installer

As a typical Win-32 app, TOAD provides a simple graphical installer—but you have several choices to make during that installation process. Most of these choices are quite simple and straightforward. Figure 1.3 shows the installer. There are two key items that you must decide during the installation process. First, will you be installing just TOAD by itself or will you install other members of the TOAD family of products (e.g., TOAD for Data Analysts, TOAD Group Policy Manager, TOAD Data Modeler, SQL Optimizer, Spotlight, Benchmark Factory)? The list of available programs to install will depend on which TOAD install image you download from Quest: the base install, the developer's bundle, or the DBA bundle. Second, into which directory are you installing TOAD? If you choose a new directory, that's considered a fresh install. But if you choose or let the installer choose an existing TOAD directory, then the process is actually an upgrade. You will probably want to do a fresh install in most situations so that you can keep your old version around in case you run into any problems with the newer version.

Sometimes, as with most Windows applications, you may find that your TOAD installation needs to be refreshed or removed and replaced. However, before you lay the blame

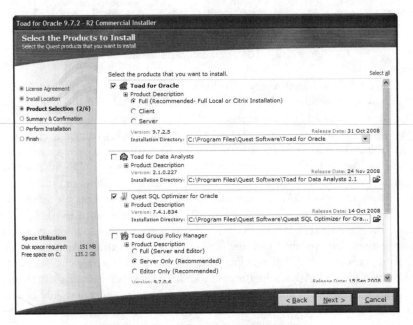

Figure 1.3   Running the TOAD Installer

on TOAD, make sure that your database connectivity is not the real issue. For example, sometimes people install Oracle updates or new tools that modify the Oracle Home setting, which is where the database connectivity information resides. In such a case, TOAD may seem to stop working. Once you're 100% sure it's not a connectivity issue related to something else and, therefore, you know you want to reinstall TOAD, then simply run the TOAD installer and uninstall TOAD.

Furthermore, TOAD creates directories in two key places. First, it places the executables under C:\Program Files\Quest Software\Toad for Oracle. You may decide to manually delete these files if the installer leaves any remnants. Second, TOAD places your custom files (i.e., those special to your Windows login) under C:\Documents and Settings\%USER%\Application Data\Quest Software\Toad for Oracle.

Copying TOAD Settings

One of the most common TOAD questions we hear is, How do I copy all my TOAD settings from one machine to another? In older versions of TOAD, that process used to be difficult, as the files were not all collected in a central location. Now it's quite simple: Just zip up the directory where all your specific settings are kept—namely, C:\Documents and Settings\%USER%\Application Data\Quest Software\Toad for Oracle\User Files.

Note that some files may be encrypted using your source machine's login information. In this case, copying the password file from one machine to another will not allow you to use those passwords unless the target machine has the same login (i.e., the directory structure is identical). Other than this exception, the remaining files and their settings should port without problem.

TOAD Adheres to Oracle Security

Probably the question most frequently asked by shops new to TOAD is, Will TOAD permit my developers to do things that they should not? The simple answer is definitely not, because TOAD cannot override or supersede Oracle's inherent security. A TOAD user has only whatever roles, system privileges, or object grants exist for the user within the database. Thus users can do no more in TOAD than they could in SQL*Plus (they simply can do it more easily and faster via TOAD). To reiterate, TOAD permits database users to have only whatever rights the DBA has granted them—there are no loopholes or exceptions.

This approach does require the DBA managing the Oracle schemas (i.e., users) to have a very firm grasp of all the privileges being handed out. For example, far too many DBAs grant the predefined roles CONNECT, RESOURCE, and DBA to their users—even though Oracle states plainly that these roles are provided merely for backward-compatibility purposes and that you should create and grant your own customized roles. Unfortunately, many people seem to have missed this fact and still overuse the predefined roles. Some DBAs do not fully realize which system privileges the predefined roles grant. For example, granting a schema the CONNECT role means that the user can create clusters, database links, sequences, synonyms, tables, and views via TOAD, because those are the privileges that CONNECT possesses. Know your predefined roles well if you plan to use them!

We recommend that you create your own custom roles and grant those to your TOAD users. Listing 1.4 shows some database roles we often create in our database for granting privileges to—and thus controlling—various TOAD users.

Listing 1.4   **Example TOAD Database Roles**

```
-- Role: Junior Developer
-- Trusted to do some things
CREATE ROLE DEVELOPER_JR NOT IDENTIFIED;
--
-- Obviously required privileges
GRANT CREATE SESSION TO DEVELOPER_JR;
GRANT ALTER SESSION TO DEVELOPER_JR;
GRANT ALTER USER TO DEVELOPER_JR;
--
-- Junior Developer privileges
GRANT CREATE PROCEDURE TO DEVELOPER_JR;
GRANT CREATE SEQUENCE TO DEVELOPER_JR;
GRANT CREATE SYNONYM TO DEVELOPER_JR;
GRANT CREATE TRIGGER TO DEVELOPER_JR;
GRANT CREATE TYPE TO DEVELOPER_JR;
GRANT CREATE VIEW TO DEVELOPER_JR;


-- Role: Senior Developer
-- Trusted to do most things
CREATE ROLE DEVELOPER_SR NOT IDENTIFIED;
--
-- Inherit All Junior Developer privileges
GRANT DEVELOPER_JR TO DEVELOPER_SR;
--
-- Senior Developer privileges
GRANT CREATE DATABASE LINK TO DEVELOPER_SR;
GRANT CREATE DIMENSION TO DEVELOPER_SR;
GRANT CREATE INDEXTYPE TO DEVELOPER_JR;
GRANT CREATE LIBRARY TO DEVELOPER_SR;
GRANT CREATE MATERIALIZED VIEW TO DEVELOPER_SR;
GRANT CREATE OPERATOR TO DEVELOPER_JR;
GRANT CREATE TABLE TO DEVELOPER_SR;
```

Another area of possible security oversight is not to forget the PUBLIC schema and its granted roles, system privileges, or object grants. For example, granting the privilege of SELECT ANY TABLE to PUBLIC (which generally isn't advisable) means that TOAD users can see the entire database's table data. Given this widespread authority of the grant, you should oversee PUBLIC rights management very wisely. TOAD will not disobey your security paradigm, but if you leave loopholes open, people generally will find and abuse them. TOAD will simply make the process of locating them easier for users by its very nature of making anything Oracle related easier.

Activating TOAD's Read-Only Mode

Most people don't realize that TOAD comes with two modes of operation entirely under their control: read/write or read-only. These modes are controlled by the license files in the TOAD install directory. When the TOAD.LIC file is a copy of (i.e., its contents are equivalent to) the FULLTOAD.LIC file (the default), then TOAD operates in read/write mode. When the TOAD.LIC file is a copy of the READONLY.LIC file, then TOAD operates in read-only mode. Here "read-only" refers to the fact that TOAD users cannot save or commit anything to the database. Read-only users are still permitted to create, modify, and save data and SQL files on their local Windows PC; they just cannot permanently affect anything on the database. Thus they cannot create objects, modify data, compile PL/SQL code, drop objects, or do anything else that would have either permanent or lasting effects on the database. For many analysts, this is a viable option.

Advanced TOAD Security Options

The approach discussed in the prior section was the original method by which TOAD supported a read-only mode of operation (and it is still used today). Over time, however, administrators asked for additional and more complex methods to control their TOAD users. And even though we always said that's what Oracle database security is for, the requests nonetheless persisted. TOAD administrators wanted to manage and control TOAD user behavior based on screens, wizards and utilities. Thus began the quest to create TOAD security.

Beginning with version 7.3, TOAD offered an advanced security management screen permitting your site's TOAD administrator to specifically define which TOAD screens, wizards, and utilities were available and executable by special TOAD security roles granted to users. Unfortunately, this TOAD security approach proved quite resource intensive, as it had to be done at the database level. Thus, for each database you manage that has TOAD users, you had to define these special TOAD roles and then define what users could or could not do within TOAD.

Beginning with version 9.5, TOAD began offering the TOAD Group Policy Manager (TGPM), which totally centralizes the implementation of this application-level TOAD security. To use this functionality, you simply install the TGPM on a Windows server that is accessible by all TOAD users, and then define your security. Think of it as an "active directory" of sorts for controlling TOAD. This highly advanced security feature is beyond the scope of this chapter's basic setup and configuration theme. Because TGPM is not required for most general-purpose TOAD usage scenarios, it is not covered in this book. TOAD's online help and www.toadworld.com provide more information if you're interested.

Customizing TOAD to User Taste

There are two key functionalities that any new TOAD user should spend a few moments investigating and adjusting to suit his or her likes or needs—because doing so will radically enhance your productivity. TOAD is shipped with many defaults chosen to apply to a universal and generic audience of millions. There's no way that you'll find all of these preselected defaults acceptable. TOAD is highly customizable, however, so it's easy to make TOAD look and work the way you prefer. This process is painless—and well worth the time spent on it.

First, the TOAD menus and toolbars can be customized by navigating to them and pressing the right-hand mouse key. You will then see a context menu that offers several choices; simply choose the "Customize…" option. TOAD will display a window that shows all the menu and toolbar icons and commands that are available. You can then drag and drop items from this customize window onto the menus and toolbars, or from the menus and toolbars to this window. Doing so will move the selected items back and forth. You can also select items on the existing menus and toolbars and move them around (i.e., rearrange them). In just a few moments' time, you can transform TOAD's primary interface into something that better fits your own personal work style.

Second, and most important, TOAD is a mature application that includes more than 10 years' worth of features. Many of those features have or offer options on how they should look and function. Again, TOAD is supremely customizable and offers you the ability to define numerous default behaviors. Simply click the toolbox icon with three check marks on the main toolbar, or choose the following items from the main menu: View → TOAD Options. Either will result in displaying the TOAD Options screen shown in Figure 1.4.

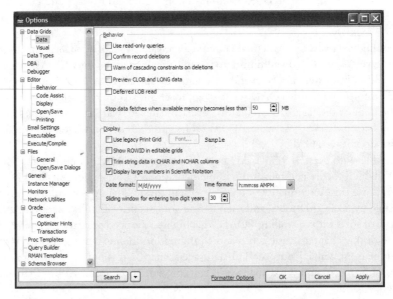

Figure 1.4   The TOAD Options Window

Take the time to navigate, learn, and set many of these values. Note that a search function is available to help you quickly locate items that you might be looking for among the plethora of choices. Use this search feature whenever necessary; it's the single best way to find things quickly. In fact, the majority of user questions about issues such as "Can TOAD do this?" and "Where do I set that?" could be answered by a quick options search. Think of this functionality as being equivalent to a Google search, and use it just as often as you do Web searches. You may need to be a little creative on what you search for, but you can also answer the vast majority of your TOAD-related questions by simply doing a search. So use the search function—you will find good things.

Summary

In this chapter we reviewed the bare essential TOAD setup and configuration issues that you should address to maximize your TOAD experiences. Once issues such as database network connectivity and client setup are handled properly, running the TOAD installer successfully, running the TOAD product, and making user customizations are fairly straightforward. This chapter's content is critical to making that process simpler and more productive. Once TOAD's prerequisites are handled properly, you should see wonderful productivity gains from using this application.

2

Database and
Schema Browsers

There are numerous Oracle database tasks that TOAD simplifies and, therefore, for which it enhances end-user productivity. Given this fact, it's difficult to state that any feature of TOAD is the most important. At its heart, however, TOAD makes short work of browsing database objects and their data, and manually querying those items. The latter task is covered in the next two chapters on SQL and PL/SQL editing, and for many is arguably the most strategically important TOAD feature. This chapter focuses on the first task—being able to simply and quickly traverse the plethora of database objects and their associated data.

While it may not be as sexy or empowering as working with the editor, browsing databases is nonetheless one of those areas people often take for granted, or merely expect to be quick and easy. If you watch people, they actually spend the majority of their time reviewing the objects and their data, and then drill deeper into that content using the complex queries they write in the editor. In this way, browsing serves as a critical prerequisite or precursory activity that helps define the context of what you do next. Browsing is actually a very critical aspect of general-purpose database work that just does not get the recognition it probably deserves. TOAD makes this highly important, yet often undervalued task much simpler.

So why title this chapter "Database and Schema Browsers? The answer is quite simple: because TOAD now has two substantially different browsers that address the unique needs of the two radically different personas that might browse a database—those users who are more interested in the database structure (e.g., DBAs) and those users who are more interested in the actual data (e.g., developers and analysts). In prior TOAD versions and the freeware, there was simply the "Schema Browser." But as we learned more about the personas using TOAD and their highly specialized needs, Quest added the "Database Browser" to complement the Schema Browser. In fact, the Database Browser can often serve as the 50,000-foot view of the database for the DBA and can serve as a front end that contextually drills down into the Schema Browser where needed. Ultimately, these two browsers are quite complementary in nature. Plus, as you will also see in this chapter's screen snapshots, they share much of the same basic look and feel (as well as underlying code). Hence they're covered together here—and prior to the chapters on editing.

You might be inclined to skip or glance over this chapter because both TOAD browsers are nothing more than explorer-like interfaces that we all use every day. In reality, because the Database Browser and Schema Browser have so many features and capabilities that people often never find, skipping this one chapter could substantially reduce your overall TOAD productivity. During most "TOAD Tips and Tricks" presentations, this topic alone seems to generate the most comments along the lines of "Wow—I didn't know TOAD could do that!" So please read on.

Auto-Start a Browser

As noted in Chapter 1, TOAD offers you numerous ways to customize its behavior to your needs. Because browsing in general tends to be such a high-frequency activity, you might like for TOAD to launch (i.e., for start-up) with the selected browser as your initial screen. Furthermore, you might want to extend this concept to any new database connection, and the screen that automatically opens with any new database connection. Either way, it's quite simple to do. Open the TOAD "Options" screen either by clicking the tool-box icon on the toolbar, or choose Main Menu → View → TOAD Options. This will open the option dialog window, shown in Figure 2.1.

Notice along the left-hand side of the screen that you must scroll down to the "Windows" section. In much older versions of TOAD, the auto-launch screen idea was controlled via a drop-down box in the "Start-Up" section. In the past, TOAD automatically listed the screens you'd most likely desire. As the number of screens increased and users' needs increased, however, we found that this concept needed to be moved to its own options area—hence the "Windows" section.

In Figure 2.1, I have set the Database Browser to be my initial screen; only one screen is permitted per database connection, and the auto-launch screen remains on top. The last item deserves explanation. If you choose to have TOAD open several screens on start-up (i.e., if you check multiple auto-open check boxes), then you can instruct TOAD which one of those is at the forefront. For example, you might open a Schema Browser and an Editor and have the browser on top as your initial entry point—but with an editor already opened and ready to go.

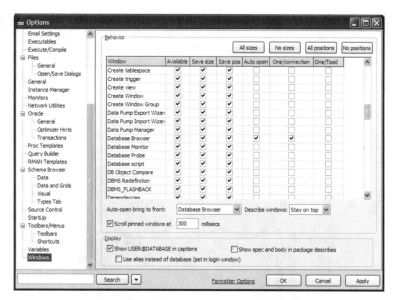

Figure 2.1   TOAD Options: Windows Section

Database Browser

The Database Browser is a relatively new addition to TOAD (having debuted with TOAD 9.5). It is available in TOAD only when you purchase the optional Database Admin Module. The idea behind this browser's development was to create a less cluttered Schema Browser like interface that would appeal to DBAs, who need a panoramic view of all the database objects, and especially those objects that are not owned by a schema (hence they are truly database-level objects, such as tablespaces, roles, directories, and users). You could argue that all these objects are also available in the Schema Browser and simply show up with no owning schema (e.g., PUBLIC). However, as you'll soon see, the Database Browser offers many other options that are not available in the Schema Browser.

You open a TOAD Database Browser screen either by clicking the database icon with glasses over it on the toolbar, or by choosing Main Menu → Database → Monitor → Database Browser. This will open the Database Browser window, shown in Figure 2.2.

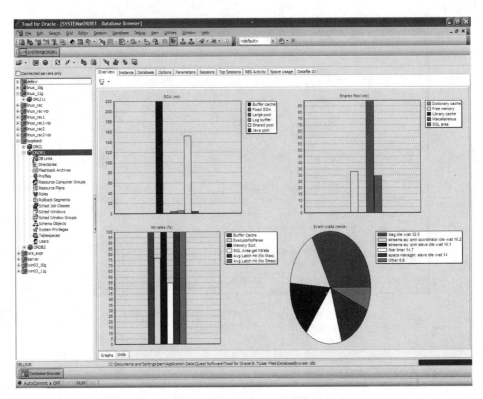

Figure 2.2   TOAD Database Browser Screen

The Database Browser is a very rich screen that offers several user perspectives and interactions. You should spend the proper time to master and benefit from them all. We will now investigate each of the major and distinct functional areas.

The tree view on the left-hand side of the Database Browser screen presents DBAs with a nice, single portal by which to simply navigate and connect to the many databases that they typically manage. It's essentially a quick entry to the TOAD connection process (without having to open the base connection screen) built directly into the Database Browser.

The tabs that appear on the right-hand side of the screen when you've selected a tree-view node for a specific database display various high-level database performance metrics. The summarized, read-only information presented in these tabs is quite often available elsewhere within TOAD with more details and capabilities. For example, the Database Browser's "Sessions" tab displays a nice summary of what's contained in the "Session Browser" screen (covered in Chapter 7) and shown here in Figure 2.3. Note,

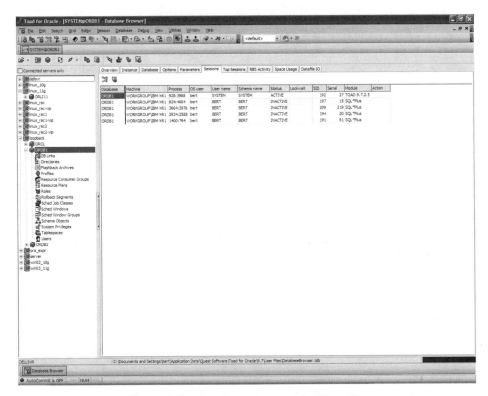

Figure 2.3   Database Browser: Sessions Tab

too, that this tab includes toolbar icons that can send you directly to the session-related screens such as the "Session Browser" and "SAG Trace/Optimization" screens. All the tabs offer contextually useful quick launch points to the detailed screens that would be your next logical step.

But here's where the Database Browser begins to demonstrate its special and useful features. What if you wanted to know about all the active sessions for all the databases on your server—how would you view all of that information in one spot? To do so, you would either multi-select all of the desired databases on the tree view or choose the server node. Now the TOAD Database Browser will display the aggregated information for that selected tab, as shown in Figure 2.4.

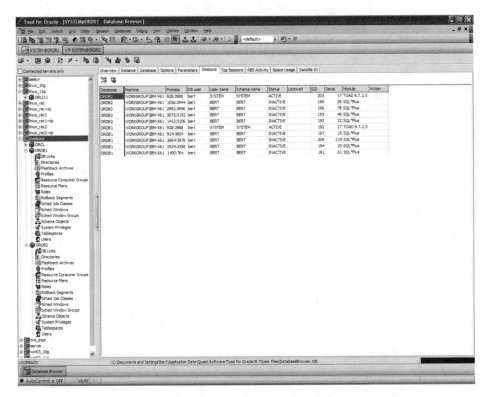

Figure 2.4   Database Browser: Sessions Info Aggregated

Note how you can now see all your database sessions across all the selected databases; this is the only place in TOAD where you can do any such cross-database analysis and investigation. This aggregation capability works across all of the TOAD Database Browser tabs—and on some tabs adds even more information. For example, the "Space Usage" and "Data File IO" tabs will present a special summary total at the bottom of the tab, as shown in Figure 2.5.

So far, we've covered the most basic items that the TOAD Database Browser has to offer. Now it's time to move into the real meat of this function—the really cool stuff that's going to make your database administrative life much easier. One of the chief complaints over the years with TOAD has been the seemingly over-complex (or convoluted, depending on who you ask), ever-growing, and ever-changing list of menu items on the main menu. Basically TOAD has become a Swiss Army knife with so many blades that the

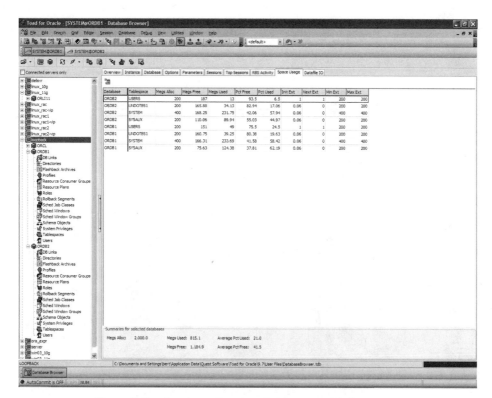

Figure 2.5   Database Browser: Aggregates with Summaries

interface to choose among them has become overwhelming. Even though (as was pointed out in Chapter 1) TOAD users can customize all of the menus and toolbars, users still expressed a desire for some simplification of the workflow (i.e., not having to connect, then navigate the main menu every time they wanted to do something).

The Database Browser addresses this problem as well. In fact, you should be able to almost forgo the main menu once you begin routinely navigating via the Database Browser. As was mentioned in connection with Figure 2.3, the various tabs offer toolbar icons to send you to the contextually related, full-powered screens—but that's still too cumbersome. The real useful power lies back in the tree view for the database nodes, which offer a right-mouse menu providing all the key screens one might need, as shown in Figure 2.6.

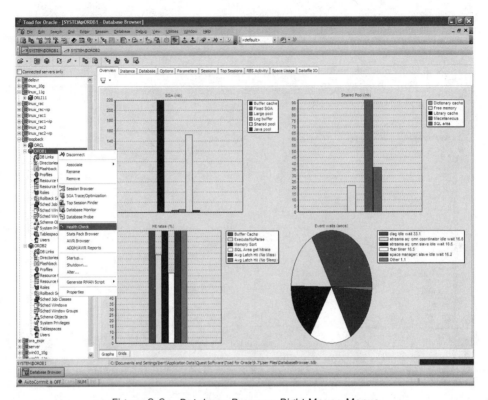

Figure 2.6   Database Browser: Right-Mouse Menus

Armed with this powerful capability, you should find yourself navigating to the Main Menu → Database area much less frequently (if at all). This one time saver alone will pay for itself in short order. But we're not quite done yet—there's one final useful Database Browser capability to examine.

Often while browsing their managed databases, DBAs need to focus on or concentrate on true database objects and their management. The Database Browser addresses this need as well. When you select a database object on the tree view as shown in Figure 2.7, the Database Browser displays just a subset of the Schema Browser on the right side for that specific object type. This display is not meant to entirely replace the Schema Browser for DBAs, but rather to augment their 50,000-foot, rapid database viewing and navigation portal with just the basics needed for typical DBA-type object maintenance.

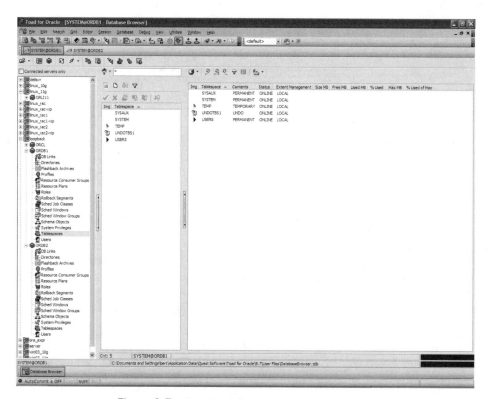

Figure 2.7   Database Browser: Database Objects

Schema Browser

No matter whether you're a DBA, a developer, or an analyst, the TOAD Schema Browser is a powerful and functional interface for exploring all your database objects. Not only does the Schema Browser permit you to very quickly and easily navigate all the complex database structures, but it also enables you to manage and control them (where granted Oracle privileges permit) as well as to view their data. So extremely useful is this one screen that when you're not coding or debugging, you'll most likely be exploring your database objects and their content via the TOAD Schema Browser. It is located off the main toolbar, appearing as a database icon with a little "org chart" above it; in addition, it is available via the Main Menu → Database → Schema Browser. The TOAD Schema Browser, shown in Figure 2.8, is an enormously robust and powerful screen, offering even more features and user customizations than the Database Browser. And because everyone will be using this "champion of browsers" screen, you really must take the time to review all that follows.

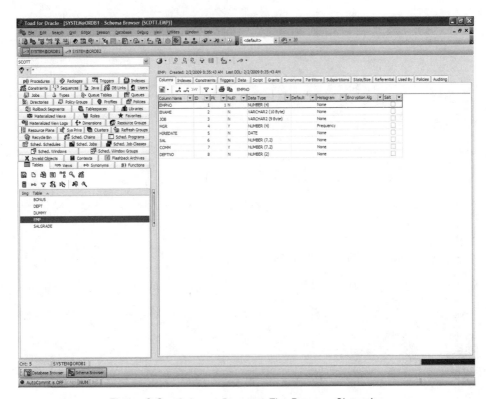

Figure 2.8   Schema Browser: The Browser Champion

While many of today's Windows tools utilize tree views for their explorer GUI design, TOAD pioneered and adopted a tabbed GUI design. The problem with tree views is that you end up scrolling far too much when there is lots of information to display. For example, opening a tree-view node for a user's tables might well display dozens of nodes and cause the tree view to scroll numerous other items of interest out of the main viewing area. With the tabbed approach, less scrolling is generally required. Returning to the prior example, choosing a user's tables via the tables tab does not cause your other main object categories (i.e., tabs) to scroll off anywhere. While it may initially take some time to get used to this interface, TOAD's novel tabbed GUI design is infinitely more productive in terms of eliminating wasted scrolling efforts—and time is money.

It may seem like an odd place to start, but you need to first decide on just how you want the Schema Browser to look and feel. As a consequence, we must start with a very detailed discussion revolving around its general appearance. Later, we'll investigate the numerous functionalities that it provides.

Some people on competing product discussion boards say things like "TOAD's Schema Browser is far too overwhelming, with too many tabs and images sucking up all the precious real estate." As with anything else in TOAD, if you don't experiment with and utilize all the cool options it offers, you could very easily arrive at this quite mistaken conclusion. Here we examine just how you configure the Schema Browser for your specific or specialized needs. It's so easy that you'll probably feel like doing your Homer Simpson "Doh" impression when we're done.

Let's start with the default TOAD Schema Browser in all its glory—with all of the possible tabs displayed and with icon images turned on as shown in Figure 2.8. We fully agree that this presentation is overwhelming and occupies far too much real estate. You can configure the Schema Browser to appear however you prefer by simply clicking on the Schema Browser window's drop-down toolbox icon (not the one on the main menu, but the one on the schema browser RHS toolbar), which enables you to adjust all of the Schema Browser-specific display options. When you open this configuration drop-down box, you'll see the simple choices shown in Figure 2.9 for adjusting the major behavioral characteristics of the Schema Browser's display.

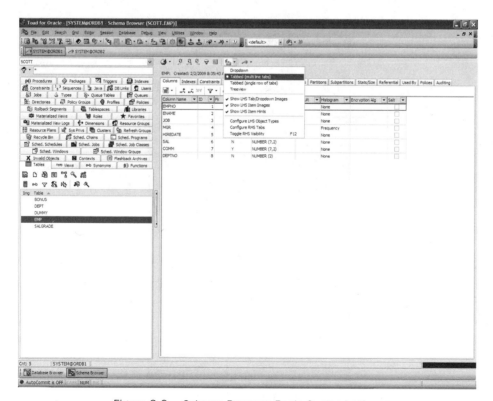

Figure 2.9   Schema Browser: Basic Customizations

We will keep the multiline tabbed style (my personal favorite), but will turn off all of the left-hand side (LHS) images and hints. Did you notice that TOAD can do a tree view just like Quest's SQL Navigator and Oracle's SQL Developer? So if you ever wondered if TOAD has feature X, the basic answer is "yes"—always look to TOAD's many options. Thus, just like the old Ragu spaghetti sauce television commercial claimed, "It's in there."

Next we will open the "Configure LHS Object Types" screen, which permits you to turn on/off the various object types displayed, rearrange their relative order, and define your own personalized captions for those objects. Figure 2.10 shows this screen.

Let's assume that you're setting up TOAD for use by a developer. In this case, you will not need to display many of the database object choices, because they may not apply to the developer job function. You might choose to turn off all the superfluous objects, shorten the remaining captions to further conserve space, and arrange their order to suit your taste. The result for what we chose is shown in Figure 2.11. Wow—we got the display back down to just one tab line. There's very little wasted screen real estate now; we just had to do our homework to get it the way we liked—and so will you. We find that many DBAs and developers opt for the drop-down list style for the Schema Browser because it avoids this real estate issue altogether and allows for very quick navigation/selection.

Figure 2.10   Schema Browser: LHS Customizations

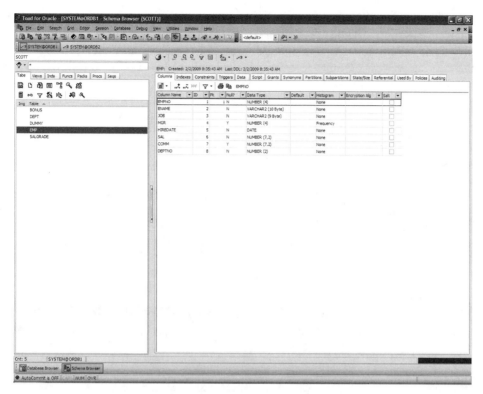

Figure 2.11   Schema Browser: Customized to Taste

Now that you have the Schema Browser looking just the way you like, let's delve into its numerous capabilities.

Any time you navigate through a database via the Schema Browser, most of the database objects will belong to a schema (i.e., user). Look once again at Figure 2.11; in the upper-left corner of the screen above the tabs, there are three controls that you will want to understand and master. The first is the drop-down box for selecting which schema or user's objects to display. In this case, even though we're connected to the database as SYSTEM, we have asked TOAD to display the objects owned by the SCOTT schema (user). Of course, we must have the proper database rights to see other users' objects. Most DBA accounts have SELECT ANY TABLE privileges, so when you're logged into such super-accounts, you'll be able to make extensive use of this drop-down box. However, many TOAD users may be able to see only their own objects and maybe a few others specifically granted to those users. If you choose a schema to which you have no rights, then all the Schema Browser tabs will appear as empty. That's not a TOAD bug per se, but rather TOAD adhering to your database security scheme. Although that behavior is a good thing, it can seem a little odd the first time your encounter it. You should also refer to the Oracle manuals to learn more about database object security and access privileges, as these settings may vary by Oracle version. For example, SELECT_CATALOG_ROLE may be the preferred method of accessing data dictionary objects owned by other SYS and SYSTEM users.

Just below this schema filter drop-down box and to the right is a text entry field known as the TOAD "Quick Filter." It is populated by default with an asterisk (*). This is simply a filter applied to the name of the objects that will be displayed under a given tab. This filtering is performed on the client side (i.e., performed by TOAD, and not the database). Let's assume that we wanted to see just those tables under my SCOTT schema whose names include the letter M. To obtain this list, we would modify the quick filter to be "*M*", as shown in Figure 2.12. In this type of filter, you can use wildcards consisting of either the asterisk or the percent sign. The asterisk is accepted because that is what many applications use; the percent sign is accepted because that is how it's done by the Oracle database.

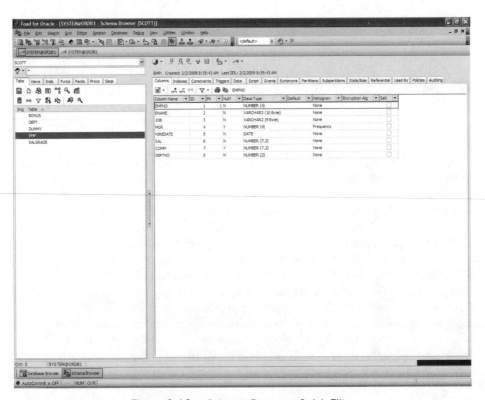

Figure 2.12   Schema Browser: Quick Filter

Just below this schema filter drop-down box and to the left is a funnel icon with a blue book in it that enables you to utilize a TOD project file definition as the filter for the Schema Browser.

Suppose you would like to filter the objects by something other than just a simple name basis as provided by the quick filter. TOAD provides a custom—and very capable—filtering mechanism for each object tab, which appears as the gray funnel toolbar icon in Figure 2.12 just above the DUMMY table's second "M." When the funnel is gray, the filter is inactive (i.e., has nothing to be applied to the search sent to the database). When the filter is red, as shown in Figure 2.13, an additional filtering context has been defined and is active. Many times people will call tech support to say that TOAD is broken because the Schema Browser tab is empty even though the user knows that something is out there. The first question is always, What color is your funnel icon?

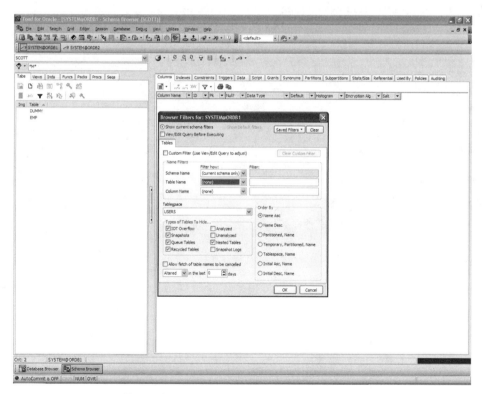

Figure 2.13   Schema Browser: Complex Filter

Note that the filter pop-up window varies by database object type (i.e., tab) because the data dictionary meta-data and contextual content differ across those database types. Even so, they all work in the same way. You make some choices that activate the filter, and the funnel turns red to indicate that the filter is active. All the filter logic that you define is appended to SQL queries sent to the database, so these complex filters (unlike quick filters) reduce the actual workload submitted to the database server. Just remember to take a quick glance at the funnel icon so you know what's going on.

There is one last item on the left-side display to be displayed, and then we'll finally look at all the tabs on the right side. Sometimes you'll want to display more information on the left side than the single column shown by default for each tab. In Figure 2.14, a right-mouse action in the tab for the tables grid area enables you to see a drop-down list of the additional display columns available. Because "Tablespace" and "Num Rows" are checked in the figure, the LHS grid now shows three columns for each table. The "Num Rows" choice works off the statistics collected for each table, so it does not generate any extra database server load by counting the rows on the fly.

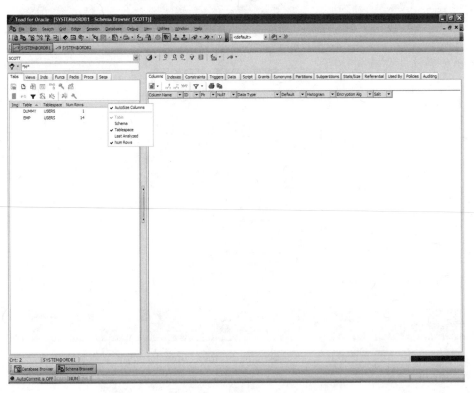

Figure 2.14   Schema Browser: Extra Columns Displayed

When you select a specific database object on the LHS, the right-hand side (RHS) tab display area will be populated with data. In Figure 2.15, the EMP table is selected under the "Tables" (or "Tabs") tab. That selection causes the RHS display to show all of the RHS tabs that go with the database object of the type table; furthermore, those RHS tabs are loaded with the meta-data or data for that specific object. As with filter pop-up windows, because all the database objects have different properties, the RHS tabs displayed will vary by object type. Hence an index object will have different RHS tabs than, say, a table or a view.

Just like the LHS tabs, the RHS tabs can be customized. You can modify which tabs are displayed, in which order, and what their captions are simply by pressing the right mouse button when your cursor is sitting atop any of the RHS tabs. Look again back at Figure 2.15: Did you notice the "Configure" option that appears just below the RHS "Partitions" tab? We pressed the right mouse button to get that menu; when you choose the configure menu option, you see a pop-up window for controlling all aspects of the RHS tabs, shown here in Figure 2.16. It works much the same way as the LHS configure menu shown in Figure 2.10.

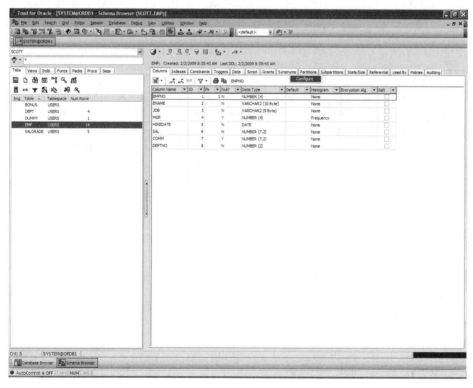

Figure 2.15   Schema Browser: RHS Display Area

Figure 2.16   Schema Browser: RHS Customizations

Okay—so now you have your Schema Browser looking just the way you like, and possibly filtering the amount of meta-data or data that it displays. At this point, we need to look into the usage of the information displayed. Much of the Schema Browser interface may seem fairly self-explanatory, but there are some real nice semi-hidden gems in there that you will want to know about and use. These little tricks should quickly become your most valuable productivity enhancers when using the Schema Browser.

Often you will want to perform some kind of database action on either the object itself (LHS) or something associated with that object (RHS). For example, you might want to truncate a table or add an index to it. When you need to perform such actions, there are generally three places to look, and all three can be seen in Figure 2.8. On the LHS, there are toolbars under each tab for the various object types. Just like the complex filter pop-ups, the toolbar icons under each LHS tab will vary depending on the database object type. While "truncate table" may make sense for a table, for instance, that action makes no sense for an index. Hence the toolbars will vary across the tabs. The same is true for the RHS tabs. If we're focused on tables for the LHS and choose the EMP table, then the RHS tabs for indexes refer to the indexes for that table. Likewise, the RHS tab toolbar icon actions will generate actions to be performed on those objects or meta-data associated with that table. Thus, under indexes, we might add or drop an index or the EMP table, we might add or drop columns to that table under the "Columns" tab, and so on.

As is often true within TOAD, you should always try pressing the right-hand mouse (RHM) button. For example, as shown in Figure 2.17, when you RHM on an object in the LHS, TOAD brings up a substantial context menu of all the things you might want to do to that object. In my tables, notice that all of them except BONUS seem to have their statistics collected (because they all show Num Rows except BONUS). If we want to analyze that table and collect the statistics so that it, too, shows a Num Rows amount, then we simply RHM on the BONUS table to open the context menu and then select "Analyze Table." That will bring up the Analyze Objects screen (Main Menu → Database → Optimize → Analyze All Objects) with the contextually correct preselected database objects (in this case, the BONUS table and indexes).

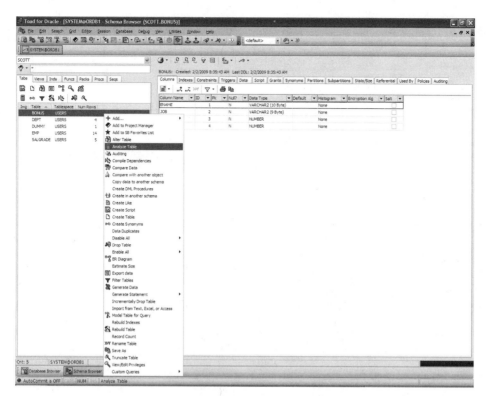

Figure 2.17   Schema Browser: RHM Context Menu

One of the most useful and often overlooked toolbar icons is the toolbox on the RHS "Script" tab, shown in Figure 2.18. This tab displays the Oracle SQL or DDL statements necessary to create the object focused on the LHS. Of course, no two people want to see the code output in the same way. The DBA might care more about structural issues such as tablespace placement, whereas the analyst or developer might be more interested in the data that goes with the object. Have no fear—TOAD can do it all. When you click the toolbox toolbar icon, the pop-up window shown in Figure 2.18 appears and permits you to make several dozen DDL generation customizations. Notice that I chose to have the data included as SQL INSERT statements, all the various constraint types are included (i.e., primary, unique, and foreign keys), and each constraint is to have its own SQL ALTER statement rather than being buried inside the SQL CREATE TABLE statement. You can quickly and easily customize the various SQL generation options to suit any need. Of course, the more items you select, the longer the script generation can take. TOAD has to read numerous Oracle data dictionary tables and views to reconstruct the original DDL—so choose wisely.

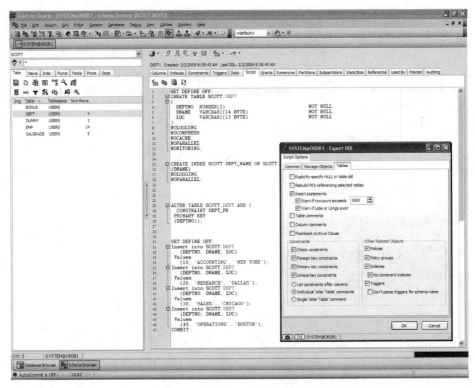

Figure 2.18   Schema Browser: Customizing Script Generation

One of the least obvious, but often most useful Schema Browser features is the ability to jump around between related items—plus the ability to have TOAD track that history and provide a Web browser-like capability to jump backward and forward among your choices. In Figure 2.19, the EMP table on the LHS and its indexes on the RHS are selected. Now we want to navigate the Schema Browser to look at the EMP table's DEPT_PK index. We could go to the LHS, choose the indexes tab, and then scroll down until we find the desired index. But that's far too much manual effort. Besides, what if the index were located in another schema? We would have to do a lot more manual navigation among possibly multiple schemas until we found the right index. Instead, we can simply perform a RHM key on the DEPT_PK index on the RHS and then choose the "Jump To" option (also available by pressing Shift + F4). That selection would instantly jump on the LHS tab to index for the right schema and index definition. Also take note of the sundial toolbar icon on the RHS above all the tabs. This drop-down menu item lists all the items that you've jumped to; thus you can go backward and forward to these items, just like you would in a Web browser. Knowing about and utilizing this feature can save you literally hours of Schema Browser navigation steps.

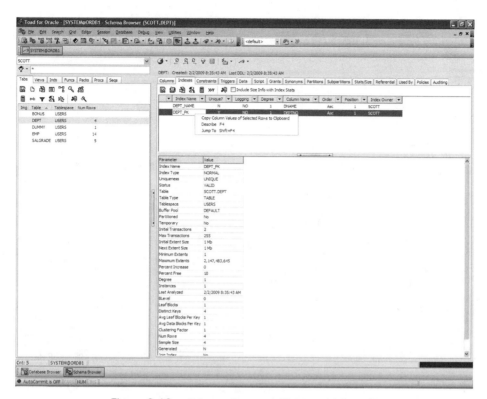

Figure 2.19   Schema Browser: History and Jump-To

Finally, we all generally browse the database objects with the eventual and ultimate intention of browsing the data associated with those objects. The Schema Browser's RHS "Data" tab serves that purpose, and has numerous features to make browsing both easy and productive. Remember, TOAD lets you browse and potentially modify only data that you have privileges to, so don't mistake the Schema Browser's wonderfully simplistic, yet amazingly powerful interface to that data as a means to somehow circumvent the database's security. If TOAD allows you to perform some action on the object or its data while browsing, then two things are true. First, you were doing more than simply browsing. Second, the DBA has given you the required rights to complete that action; otherwise, TOAD would have issued a database security violation error.

With that caveat clearly spelled out, let's examine just what the Schema Browser can do when working with objects' data in the "Data" tab. Look very closely at Figure 2.20, because we're going to refer to it repeatedly in the next few paragraphs. While the point of this screen may seem obvious, it has many cool things that you might not necessarily find easily on your own.

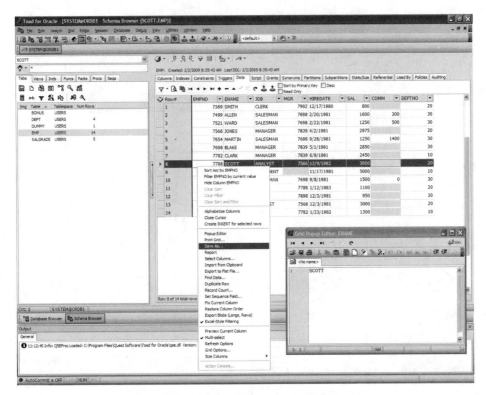

Figure 2.20   Schema Browser: RHS Data Tab

When you click on the Schema Browser RHS "Data" tab, TOAD initially loads the data grid you see with the first *N* rows (where *N* depends on your TOAD options setting for the data grid fetch size) of data for that database object (e.g., for the table). We will examine five areas of this tab in more detail.

First, notice the toolbar on the Schema Browser RHS "Data" tab. Much like as in the Schema Browser LHS, a funnel icon appears (gray when inactive and red when active) when you are defining a filter for a query sent to the database server to populate the grid. There are also some VCR buttons for moving the record location (e.g., next record, last record) and some check boxes to indicate whether to append a sort clause to the query sent to the database server or whether to make the data grid content read-only. In other words, even though you may have database privileges to modify the data, do you want TOAD to respect or override that privilege?

The second key area is the data grid's column headers. You can drag-and-drop them to reorder the headers as you prefer (they are initially displayed by default in table order, unless you've previously recorded a preferred ordering). You can perform sorts on the columns (done on the client side by TOAD); in fact, you can do most of the same things with these columns as you can in Microsoft Excel with its columns, including anchoring a column so that as you scroll left and right it persists in your viewable area. This point actually segues quite nicely into the next section.

The third major area is the RHM menu (remember, when in TOAD try RHM whenever you're looking for features). Thus, for the previously mentioned column anchoring to take effect, you would simply choose the RHM options for "Fix Current Column." We recommend that you try out the following options at a minimum, as they are amazing productivity enhancers:

- Save As: permits you to write the data to your local hard drive in several dozen file formats, including comma delimited, Access Database, Excel, XML, HTML, SQL statements, and SQL Loader data files.

- Print Grid: permits you to print both the SQL that fetched the data grid and the data grid's contents, using all normal Windows print-type capabilities such as preview, set properties, print, and so on.

- Report: imports the data grid query into the TOAD "Fast Reports" report writer tool. Think of this amazing option as being akin to having a complete report writing tool like Crystal Reports built into TOAD for free.

- Import from Clipboard: provides a nice little wizard to help you take tabular type data in the Windows Clipboard and append it to the data grid.

The fourth area on the Schema Browser RHS "Data" tab is simply the data grid itself. Look back at Figure 2.20 and focus on just the data grid from the EMP table; ignore the distractions from all the other stuff crammed into this figure. If we click in a column like HIREDATE, a drop-down arrow form appears on the left side of the text field. If you click on that form, it opens a calendar GUI—which means you don't have to deal with Oracle date-type formats. If you instead click on a foreign key (FK) column such as DEPTNO, and if the proper options are set, you'll see a pop-up editor-like window for reviewing and choosing the legitimate parent table values. If you double-click on a cell (or choose "Popup-Editor" in the RHM menu), then the "Grid Popup Editor" shown in the lower-right corner of Figure 2.20 appears; it is our fifth and final item on the "Data" tab.

Note that the data grid in the Schema Browser has all the same capabilities and functionalities as the data grid in the Editor. Thus, once you have learned and mastered one data grid, you're ready to use any other data grid. We might even go so far as to say that the data grid is what makes TOAD unique and so well loved. Once you have found the data you're keenly interested in, TOAD helps you to modify, export, print, report on, and perform all the other truly business-oriented tasks that you will need to do with the data. The only real difference between data grids worth mentioning is that the Schema Browser data grid has read/write privileges by default, whereas the Editor data grid is read-only. As noted in Chapter 3's discussion of the Editor, that grid can function as read/write, too—with some input from you.

Schema Browser Options

As with anything else in TOAD, there are many different ways that people might want a certain feature to operate or look. Quest tries very hard to select those options that will serve most people well right out of the box, but there's no way we can pick the right settings for 2 million people. Instead, you can take advantage of numerous Schema Browser options to increase your productivity and satisfaction with the user experience, assuming you have to take enough time to set them. Don't fret—it's actually quite easy.

Simply click the toolbox icon with three check marks on the main toolbar, or choose Main Menu → View → TOAD Options, and navigate to the Schema Brower section, as shown here in Figure 2.21. There are four subsections of settings, but we will examine only the first two, as they provide many of the key items sought by most users. On your own, you should take the time to review and set the settings across all four subsections.

The "Data" subsection of the Schema Browser options shown in Figure 2.21 defines certain high-level, behavioral properties. For example, should the LHS tabs' contents be refreshed automatically after a new database object is created and/or after an existing database object is dropped? If this option unchecked, then you'll need to click one of the Schema Browser refresh toolbar icons (the three icons located just to the left of the sundial for jump-to history): either refresh LHS only, refresh RHS only, or refresh both. Note the radio group with the user or schema options. Why have the schema drop-down list on the LHS show users who have no objects? Perhaps choosing the second option, "show only users who own objects," will make you more productive. There are many options here that you should set to meet your specific needs and likes.

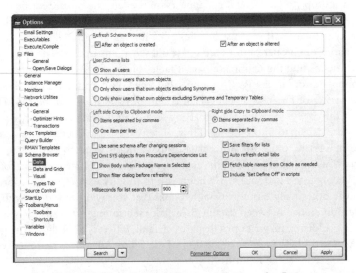

Figure 2.21   Schema Browser: Options for Data

The second subsection, shown in Figure 2.22, displays a host of options more closely related to the RHS data grids. Remember how we said earlier that the column reordering could be retained with the proper options set? See the check box for "Save layouts"? If you want your reworked column settings to persist, then you need to select this option. What about the FK lookup we mentioned earlier? Once again, it is an option—the "Enable FK Lookup." Three other highly useful options worth noting are outlined here:

- Limit the fetch to N: This option enables you to tell TOAD that because this is a true browsing experience, users may need to view only N rows (i.e., TOAD will fetch only that many rows from the server, thereby limiting or reducing server workload). Users really should go to the editor or somewhere else within TOAD when they want to perform more massive data-intensive operations.

- Use NOPARALLEL Hint: Non-DBAs will not know (or often care) too much about Oracle being able to perform work in parallel on the server. Under some database configurations, however, the TOAD browser can hold excessive resources when its work is done in parallel. This option provides a simple way to disable that functionality, thereby avoiding the performance issues that can sometimes occur.

- Auto-Size columns: This option is really self-explanatory, but is sometimes better done manually or by permitting overrides.

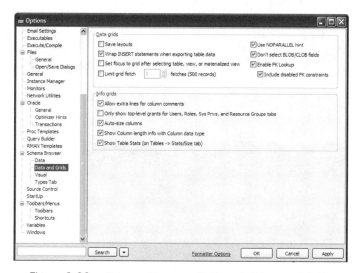

Figure 2.22   Schema Browser: Options for Data and Grids

Summary

For many TOAD users, this chapter covers arguably the single most important functional aspect of TOAD—the process of browsing database objects and their data. Because we cannot write queries or administer databases without some insight into what the objects are and what data they contain, the importance of browsing cannot be underestimated. TOAD's Database Browser and Schema Browser are very robust and fairly straightforward to use. To achieve the most productive database and actual data browsing experience, you need to know the tips and tricks detailed in this chapter, which are some of the best found in the entire book.

3

SQL Editor

The SQL Editor is the original development area of TOAD. This window allows you to type, execute, run, save, reload, examine the explain plan, and tune SQL statements. In this chapter, you will learn how to use TOAD to create and execute SQL scripts, and save both the scripts and the output. This chapter discusses and illustrates the major options available in the SQL Editor.

Basic Concepts of the SQL Editor

TOAD makes SQL development easy in a number of ways:

- Keyboard shortcuts
- Table and column pick lists
- SQL templates
- Ability to create/execute SQL scripts
- Ability to review/edit/save result-set data
- Compatibility with SQL*Plus

The Editor window is the basis of the entire TOAD tool, giving you the ability to create, edit, execute, format, and save both individual SQL statements (possibly to be inserted into applications) and scripts that contain multiple SQL statements. Figure 3.1 shows the basic SQL Editor window.

Figure 3.1 shows the default values for SQL Editor. Notice the buttons at the top of the screen that perform numerous functions (including executing the current SQL, saving the current SQL query, and so on). There are three rows of buttons, which are actually displaying the seven default TOAD toolbars, as shown in Figure 3.2. The toolbars can be toggled on and off via the right mouse menu. Hover the mouse over a button and a balloon will appear with a message about its use.

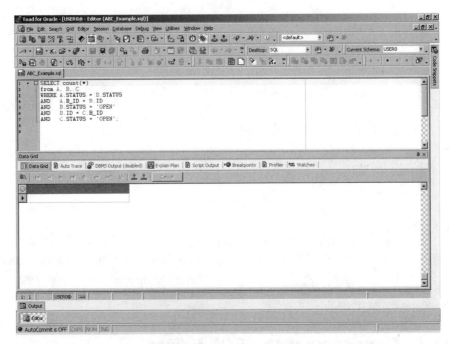

Figure 3.1   TOAD SQL Editor Screen

Figure 3.2   TOAD SQL Editor Screen Toolbars

A shortcut is a keystroke or keystrokes that perform a certain function. Pressing the F1 key, for example, brings up TOAD's help facility. There is a button on the toolbar for most every shortcut. The savvy TOAD user makes extensive use of the shortcuts.

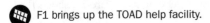 F1 brings up the TOAD help facility.

The first toolbar allows easy access to the main TOAD browsers and editors as well as the save functions. Some additional TOAD features also appear on this toolbar.

First toolbar (left to right):

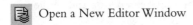 Open a New Editor Window

Open a New Schema Browser Window

Open a New Database Browser Window

Open a New Session Browser Window

Open a New SQL Modeler Window

Master Detail Browser Window

Project Manager Window

Open an Output Window

AppDesigner

Find Object

Search Knowledge Base

Script Manager

Configure/Execute External Tools

Configure TOAD Options

Save All Options

Toggle PL/SQL Profiling

Toggle Compiling with Debug

Commit

Rollback

New Connection

End Connection

Display Tip for Active Window

The second toolbar focuses on retrieving and saving code. It allows you to save code, access other Quest Software tools, and load code into the environment via a number of methods.

Second (middle) toolbar (from left to right):

Change Session for This User

Create a New Tab Using the Default Style

Close the Active Editor Tab

Load from File

Load Object from Database

Save

Save As

Save All Tabs

Reload from Disk

Reload Object from Database

Print

Optimize SQL

Profile Code

Execute Quest Code Tester

Make Non-SQL Code Statement from SQL

Strip SQL from Non-SQL Code

Navigate Back

Desktop: Change Editor Desktop

 Save Desktop

Delete Desktop

Current Schema: Performs Alter Current Schema

The third and final toolbar focuses on code execution, the script and PL/SQL debugger, and standard windows operations such as cut and paste, clear, and so on. This toolbar also allows you to obtain information on specific objects.

Third toolbar (from left to right):

Execute Statement

Terminate Execution

Execute as a Script

Execute Explain Plan for Current Statement

Compile Dependent Objects

Execute PL/SQL with Debugger

Set Parameters for Use with Debugger

Step Over

Trace Into

Trace Out

Run to Cursor

Toggle Breakpoint

Add Watch

Attach Debugger to External Session

Cut

Copy

Paste

Select All

Clear All

Find Text

Find Next

Replace Text

Undo Edit

Redo Last Undo

Convert to Uppercase

Convert to Lowercase

Check File Out of Source Control

Undo Checkout (Lose Changes)

Check File into Source Control

Get Last Version from Source Control

It is easy to customize these toolbars. Each has a "More Buttons" option, as shown in Figure 3.3. Existing buttons can be displayed or hidden using this pop-up box. The "Customize" option allows for more buttons to be added to any part of that particular toolbar using a drag-and-drop operation. Figure 3.4 shows the "Execute Code Snippet" button—a favorite button of the author—added next to the Statement Execution button.

Figure 3.3   TOAD SQL Editor: Customizing the Toolbar

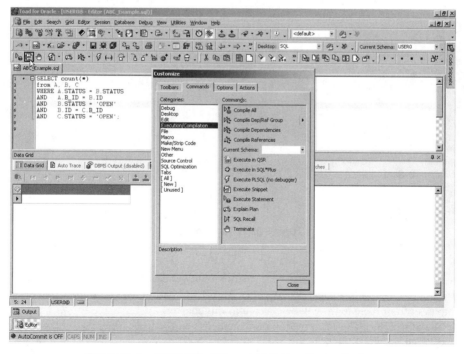

Figure 3.4   TOAD SQL Editor: Add Button Customization

The first shortcut is F2. It toggles the bottom output window or, put more accurately, it toggles the edit window to become a full-screen view. Shift + F2 toggles the grid output (on the bottom) to become a full-screen view. Figure 3.5 shows the SQL Editor with the output toggled "off," or the full-screen grid. This option is helpful when you are working on longer SQL statements or SQL scripts. You can easily toggle "on" the output tabs when you desire to see the output.

F2 toggles on/off the full-screen editor.

Shift + F2 toggles on/off the full-screen data grid.

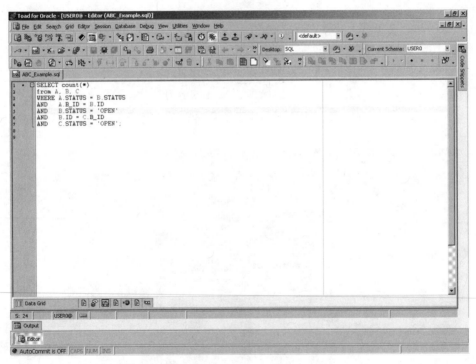

Figure 3.5   TOAD SQL Editor Screen: Full-Screen Grid

The lower section, or data grid, contains the result-set data from the query, the explain plan used to retrieve the data, code statistics, Auto Trace output, DBMS output, and Script output. Each of these items will be covered in this chapter.

The SQL Editor also has a plethora of parameters and settings. Figure 3.6 shows the TOAD options for this editor. Just about anything having to do with the content of these

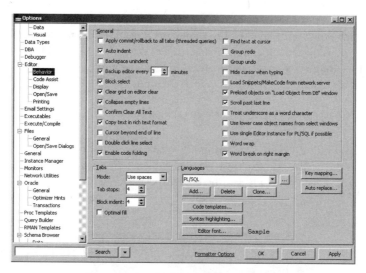

Figure 3.6   TOAD SQL Editor Options

tabs can be modified—from the text colors, auto-save, and auto-commit, to printing and about any display option. Notice that the SQL syntax appears (along with any other Oracle reserved words) in blue, whereas the supplied columns, table names, and other variable syntax appear in black. Comments appear in green. These color patterns are controlled by setting the Editor Options. To do so, click the TOAD Options button on the first toolbar or select the appropriate menu item: View → TOAD Options.

Although TOAD has only one editor, it supports six coding styles:

- SQL Style (covered in this chapter)
- PL/SQL Style (covered in Chapter 4)
- Text Style
- HTML Style
- Hex Style
- RMAN Style

The availability of these coding styles allows TOAD to assist you when you are using a particular coding style for the script/code task at hand, supporting the particular formatting and special features for each style. The single-editor approach makes it easier for all of the features to be shared across the supported coding styles. Choosing TOAD Options Editors → Behavior, then the "Language" area (see Figure 3.6), allows for specific coding styles to be viewed and maintained for each style.

The TOAD Options Executables allows for the definition of an external editor to be used with each editor tab. Ctrl + F12 will copy the code from the tab into this external editor. Notepad is the default editor for a Microsoft Windows TOAD installation. If Notepad does not meet your needs for an external editor, you can direct TOAD to your editor of choice: Toad Options → Executables → Editor.

Ctrl + F12 accesses a previously defined external editor.

Each TOAD Editor session supports multiple tabs. As code is opened from either the file system or the database, a new tab is opened. Figure 3.7 shows the ABC_Example.sql code that was opened from a file and the LOOPING_EXAMPLE that was opened from the database.

Figure 3.7   TOAD SQL Editor: Multiple Code Tabs per Session

Figure 3.8 also shows how to open additional empty tabs in each of the editor styles. Right-mouse click on an existing tab to get the pop-up menu, and then select "New Tab" and the code style desired. This same pop-up menu allows for navigation to all open tabs, close tabs, rename tabs, and so on.

TOAD supports threads, which allows SQL statements to be canceled while they are running. The "Terminate Execution" button will "ungray," indicating that cancellation of a SQL execution, a PL/SQL execution, or a PL/SQL Debugging session is now permitted. This behavior is automatically enabled in TOAD and can be turned off by deselecting "Execute Queries in Threads" on the TOAD Options Oracle → Transactions display.

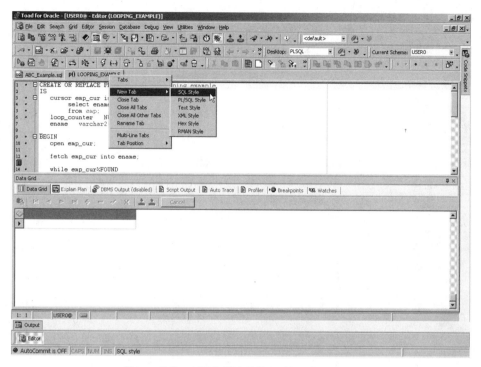

Figure 3.8 TOAD SQL Editor: New Editor Tab

There are several ways to get SQL into the SQL Editor. You can simply type in a new SQL statement. You can use the "SQL Recall" option (F8 or View → SQL Command Recall) and select a SQL statement from the stored SQL history (see Figure 3.9). Pressing Alt + Up arrow and Alt + Down arrow also walks you through the SQL statement history. In addition, you can use the File → Open (also Ctrl + O) menu, and cut-and-paste SQL statements from other applications. The "Load" option is also useful for loading SQL statements from files that appear on the pop-up menu when the right mouse button is clicked. The SQL Recall window can be auto-hidden along the edge of the TOAD screen by clicking on the toggle pushpin (next to the Close button, at the upper-right corner of the SQL Recall window). This pushpin toggles the auto-hide behavior versus keeping the SQL Recall window constantly active. If you move the mouse near the auto-hide tab, the window will reappear.

Alt + Up arrow fetches the previous SQL statement from the TOAD history.

Alt + Down arrow fetches the next SQL statement from the TOAD history.

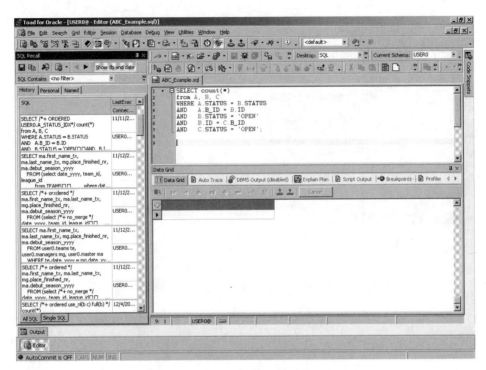

Figure 3.9   Selecting SQL from SQL Recall

SQL Recall has several configuration options, which are found on the TOAD Options →
Editor → Code Assist pane; see Figure 3.10. Notice how you can control the number of
SQL statements to be saved, and the time they are saved (e.g., before execution, only
valid SQL).

Notice the "Personal" and "Named" tabs in Figure 3.9. Right-clicking on an item in
the SQL Recall panel allows for SQL statements in the recall area to be moved to the
"Personal" tab or organized by a "name" in the "Name" tab; see Figure 3.11.

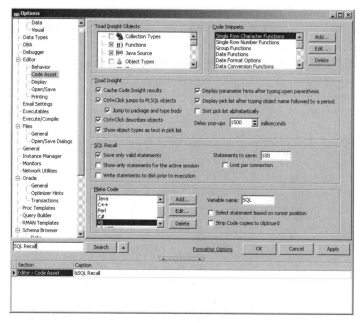

Figure 3.10   SQL Recall Options

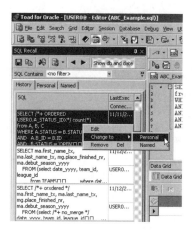

Figure 3.11   SQL Recall: Personal/Named Tabs

TOAD can also format your SQL into an easy-to-read format. Figure 3.12 shows how to access the formatter by clicking the right mouse button and selecting Formatting tools → Format code. Figure 3.13 shows how TOAD formats the SQL.

The TOAD code formatter can also be customized to suit your preferences. When accessing the TOAD formatter, notice the "Formatter Options" (see Figure 3.12). Figure 3.14 shows the various options and a sample window that will display the result of applying the selected option on some sample code.

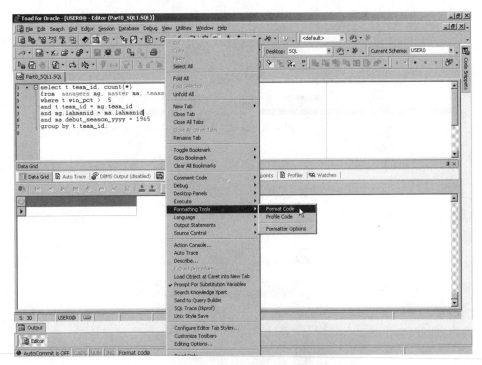

Figure 3.12   Accessing SQL Formatter

Figure 3.13   TOAD-Formatted SQL

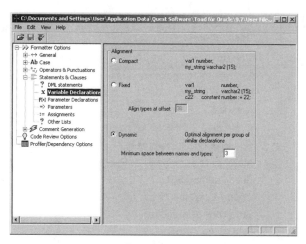

Figure 3.14   SQL Formatting Options

This overview section has covered some of the basic concepts and features of the SQL Editor. The remainder of this chapter focuses on specific topics related to the SQL Editor.

Predefined Shortcuts

Keyboard shortcuts is one of the features that makes TOAD so powerful and easy to use. TOAD comes with a host of predefined shortcuts. These shortcuts, which save keystrokes and mouse actions, perform a variety of tasks such as issuing a "describe" on the current highlighted object. This section highlights all of the shortcuts available for TOAD 9.7. The shortcuts differ slightly between the various editors. Table 3.1 shows all the shortcuts in keystroke order; Table 3.2 presents them in description order. This section focuses on the shortcuts for the SQL Editor only.

Table 3.1   **Shortcuts by Keystroke**

Shortcut	Description	Illustration
Shift + Ctrl + R	Alias replacement	
Alt + Down arrow	Display next statement (after Alt + Up arrow)	
Alt + Up arrow	Display previous statement	
Ctrl + .	Display pop-up list of matching table names	
Ctrl + A	Select all text	
Ctrl + C	Copy	
Ctrl + E	Execute explain plan on current SQL Statement	Figure 3.36
Ctrl + End	In the data grid: goes to the end of the record set	

continues

Table 3.1   **Shortcuts by Keystroke,** *continued*

Shortcut	Description	Illustration
Ctrl + F	Find text	
Ctrl + F12	External editor, pass contents	
Ctrl + F9	Verify statement without execution (parse)	
Ctrl + G	Goto line	
Ctrl + Home	In the data grid: goes to the top of the record set	
Ctrl + L	Converts text to lowercase	
Ctrl + M	Make code statement	
Ctrl + N	Recall named SQL	Figure 3.11
Ctrl + O	Opens a text file	
Ctrl + P	Strip code statement	
Ctrl + R	Find and replace	
Ctrl + S	Save file	
Ctrl + space	Code templates	
Ctrl + T	Columns pick list	Figure 3.18
Ctrl + Tab	Cycles through the collection of MDI child windows	
Ctrl + U	Converts text to uppercase	
Ctrl + V	Paste	
Ctrl + X	Cut	
Ctrl + Z	Undo last change	
F1	Windows help file	
F10 or Right mouse	Pop-up menu	Figure 3.4
F2	Toggle full-screen editor	Figure 3.5
F3	Find next occurrence	
F4	Describe table, view, procedure, function, or package	Figure 3.21
F5	Execute SQL as a script	Figure 3.27
F6	Toggle between SQL editor and results panel	Figure 3.5
F7	Clear all text	
F8	Recall previous SQL statement	Figure 3.9
F9	Execute SQL statement	Figure 3.26
Shift + Ctrl + S	Save file as	
Shift + Ctrl + T	Columns pick list, no alias	
Shift + Ctrl + Z	Redo last undo	
Shift + F3	Find previous occurrence	
Shift + F9	Execute current SQL statement at cursor	

The competent TOAD user uses the Shift + F9 shortcut to execute SQL statements one at a time out of a script, and uses the F8 button to recall the previous SQL statement. The TOAD user also makes use of the cut-and-paste technique to move code between TOAD windows.

 Shift + F9 executes single SQL statements.

 F8 recalls the previous SQL statement.

Table 3.2   Shortcuts by Description

Description	Shortcut	Illustration
Alias replacement	Shift + Ctrl + R	
Clear all text	F7	
Code templates	Ctrl + space	
Columns pick list	Ctrl + T	Figure 3.18
Columns pick list, no alias	Shift + Ctrl + T	
Converts text to lowercase	Ctrl + L	
Converts text to uppercase	Ctrl + U	
Copy	Ctrl + C	
Cut	Ctrl + X	
Cycles through the collection of MDI child windows	Ctrl + Tab	
Describe table, view, procedure, function, or package	F4	Figure 3.21
Display next statement (after Alt + Up Arrow)	Alt + Down arrow	Figure 3.7
Display previous statement	Alt + Up arrow	Figure 3.7
Display pop-up list of matching table names	Ctrl + .	
Execute current SQL statement at cursor	Shift + F9	
Execute SQL as a script	F5	Figure 3.27
Execute explain plan on current SQL statement	Ctrl + E	Figure 3.36
Execute SQL statement	F9	Figure 3.26
External editor, pass contents	Ctrl + F12	
Find and replace	Ctrl + R	
Find next occurrence	F3	
Find previous occurrence	Shift + F3	
Find text	Ctrl + F	
Goto line	Ctrl + G	
In the data grid: goes to the end of the record set	Ctrl + End	

continues

Table 3.2   Shortcuts by Description, *continued*

Description	Shortcut	Illustration
In the data grid: goes to the top of the record set	Ctrl + Home	
Make code statement	Ctrl + M	
Opens a text file	Ctrl + O	
Paste	Ctrl + V	
Pop-up menu	F10 or Right mouse	
Recall named SQL	Ctrl + N	Figure 3.11
Recall previous SQL statement	F8	Figure 3.9
Redo last undo	Shift + Ctrl + Z	
Save file	Ctrl + S	
Save file as	Shift + Ctrl + S	
Select all text	Ctrl + A	
Strip code statement	Ctrl + P	
Toggle between SQL editor and results panel	F6	Figure 3.5
Toggle full-screen editor	F2	Figure 3.5
Undo last change	Ctrl + Z	
Verify statement without execution (parse)	Ctrl + F9	
Windows help file	F1	

User-Defined Shortcuts

TOAD is completely configurable. You can easily add or change the keystrokes used for existing shortcuts. To do so, access TOAD Options → Editor Behavior → Key mappings (lower-right corner of this panel). Figure 3.15 shows how the shortcut keystrokes can be easily modified. Access the Editor Options menu with a RHM click or press the F10 key and select "Editing Options." To change an existing keystroke assignment, select "Key Assignments," locate the particular assignment, make the appropriate change, and click the OK button, as illustrated in Figure 3.15.

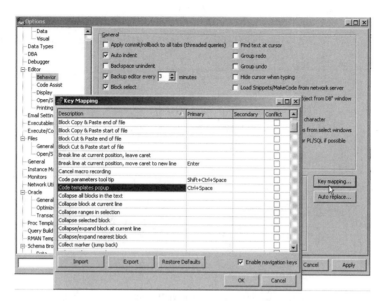

Figure 3.15   TOAD Change Shortcut Keystroke Assignments

Using Bind Variables

TOAD supports all kinds of SQL statements and scripts, from all kinds of applications. If you were to bring in SQL from, say, a SQL*Forms application, it will contain bind variables. Bind variables are used to supply SQL with data at execution time. As a consequence, applications can use the same SQL statement to select and manipulate different data, depending on the data supplied to the bind variables.

 Bind variables makes efficient use of the Oracle RDBMS SQL pool, as the SQL will not be reparsed when you use bind variables. The text of the SQL remains the same, so Oracle will reuse the same execution plan, making for a more efficient database environment.

When TOAD encounters bind variables, it will prompt you to supply their values, as shown in Figure 3.16. The "Scan SQL" option will check for any missing bind variables—a particularly useful step if you are adding and changing bind variables in this interface.

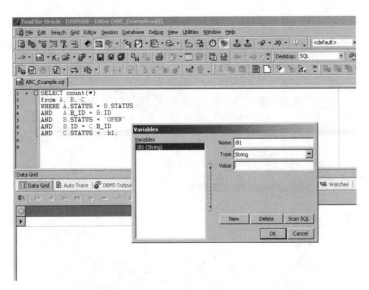

Figure 3.16   Resolving SQL Bind Variables

In TOAD, substitution variables work the same way as bind variables do. Remember that substitution variables are resolved into SQL text at parse time, but bind variables won't change the actual SQL text (which greatly facilitates SQL reuse in the Oracle SQL pool). TOAD will prompt for the data for each substitution variable, just as it does for bind variables.

Table and Column Name Select Lists

TOAD makes it easy to find and work with tables and columns. Figure 3.17 illustrates use of the Object Palette window. Access Main Menu → View → Object Palette to display a panel of available tables for this particular user. If the user has privileges for other schemas, then the pull-down menu can be changed to that of the schema owner; those objects will then appear in the select list. Double-clicking on the selected object adds the selected table where the cursor was last positioned in the SQL Editor.

Similarly, you can add columns to the SQL Editor via the "Show Column Select Window" option. Figure 3.18 illustrates the use of this window to add three columns— EMPNO, ENAME, and JOB—to the SQL query being built in the SQL Editor.

 TOAD will automatically provide a column select list when you type or select a valid schema table name that is followed by a period ("."). Wait a second, and the column pick list will appear as illustrated in Figure 3.16!

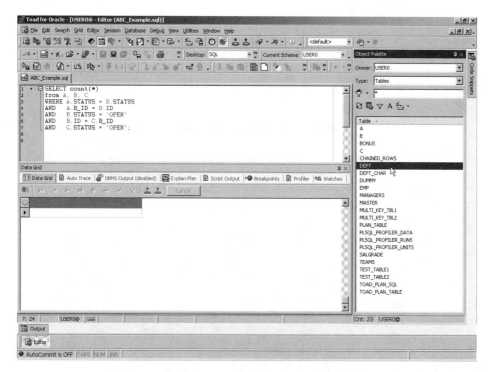

Figure 3.17   Object Palette Select List

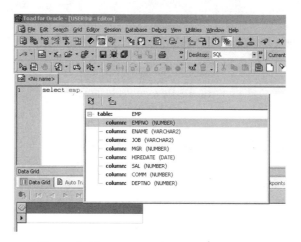

Figure 3.18   Automatic Column Pick Lists

Double-click on a column in this pick list to select it. To select multiple columns at once, use the Shift + click or Ctrl + click combinations to select several columns at one; press the Return (Enter) key to add the columns to the SQL Editor screen.

 This feature, which is called "insights," is controlled by the path TOAD Options → Code Assist. Notice that the options in Figure 3.18 allow you to control the amount of time before the pop-up list appears, the order of the items in the pick list, and more.

Figure 3.19 shows the TOAD Options screen that controls the insights illustrated in Figure 3.18. Using the options in the center of the panel, you can control the amount of time before the insights pop-up appears, determine whether it is to appear at all, and set the order in which things in the pick list will appear, among other things.

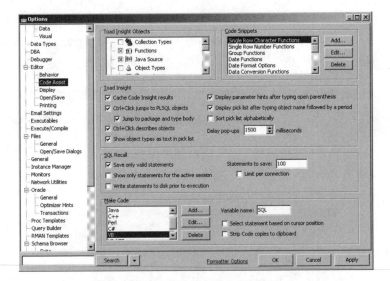

Figure 3.19   Column Pick List Options

TOAD Table Aliases Substitutions

TOAD supports the use of its own alias names. Aliases act like the previously mentioned insights and are a convenient way to shorten keystroke sequences, give short names to rather long table names, or give a short name to a line of syntax. These aliases are signaled by a period (".").

There is no way to add or maintain these aliases using TOAD, however. Instead, you must make sure TOAD is not running and edit the ALIASES.TXT file in the TOAD home directory User Files folder. The TOAD home directory is usually found in the folder \Program Files\Quest Software\TOAD for Oracle\ . Enter lines into this file in the following format: table_name=alias. When the alias is entered followed by a single period, the alias name will be substituted for the table_name.

Use Shift + Ctrl + T (or Edit → Pick-list drop-down no alias) to ignore the alias and get the correct list of columns.

Shift + Ctrl + T ignores the alias request.

Auto-Replacement Substitutions

TOAD comes with a variety of automatic replacement items, such as those designed to correct common typing errors and SQL syntax errors. This mechanism is activated by using the space bar. For example, if you enter "teh," TOAD will automatically replace this text with "the" when you press the space bar.

Auto-replace items are easy to set up using TOAD Options → Editor Behavior → Auto replace… (found on the lower-right side of this options panel). The left side of Figure 3.20 shows several syntax errors and aliases; the right side of the figure shows what will be substituted when these errors/aliases are entered and the space bar is pressed. Use the "Add" button to add your own syntax accessed by short keystrokes. For example, as Figure 3.20 shows, the author of this book has set up an auto-replace called "pl" that will replace a DBMS_OUTPUT.PUT_LINE syntax.

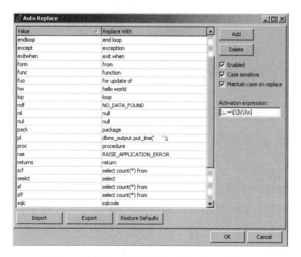

Figure 3.20   TOAD Auto Replace Setup

SQL Templates

TOAD can easily format a SELECT, INSERT, or UPDATE statement for any data-oriented object (view or table). Simply place the cursor on the object desired and press F4. This action will perform a "describe" operation on the object, as illustrated in Figure 3.21. Notice in Figure 3.21 that everything you need to know about the object appears in this window. This describe window gives information very similar to that found in the Schema Browser (see Chapter 2). Specifically, all of the same data grid options are available. Column names can be added to the SQL in the SQL Editor window via a drag-and-drop mouse operation.

The "Scripts" tab will create the syntax necessary to re-create this object.

 It is particularly nice to have TOAD build a script that creates the object. This information comes from the data dictionary and accurately reflects the object that you are working with. I have used the "Scripts" tab to develop and save create statements for tables and indexes of interest to me (i.e., test data).

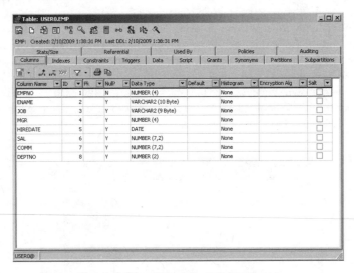

Figure 3.21   Object Description Panel

Right-click on the "Columns Name" column of the "Columns" tab and select "Generate Statement" from the pop-up context menu (see Figure 3.22). Notice that you have a choice of an INSERT, SELECT, or UPDATE boilerplate template that will include the columns for this object. Figure 3.23 shows the template that the SELECT statement option generates.

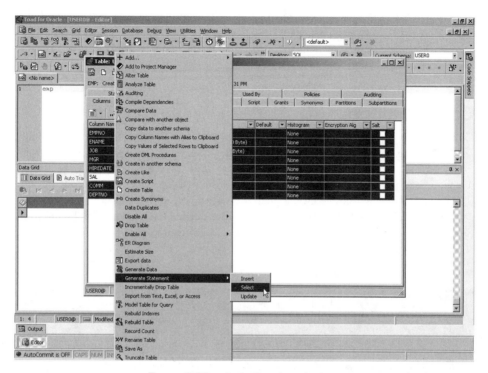

Figure 3.22   Code Template Options

Figure 3.23   Generated SELECT Code Template

 F4 describes the object.

Click on a column in the "Columns" tab and select "Generate Statement."

TOAD also provides boilerplate code templates called Code Completion Templates. These templates are generally intended for Oracle-supported programming languages such as PL/SQL and can be used in the SQL Editor as well. Chapter 4 covers the use and maintenance of TOAD Code Completion Templates.

Code Snippets

Code Snippets are code templates such as date formats, tuning hints, functions (including single row, date, and group by functions), and other code templates. They are accessed via the menu: View → Code Snippets. TOAD can auto-hide this panel along the edge of the screen, or it can be unpinned to keep it visible on the desktop. Accessing the code in Code Snippets entails a simple mouse drag-and-drop operation.

In Figure 3.24, a Code Snippet was added to the SELECT statement from Figure 3.22. Notice the categories in which the Code Snippets are organized.

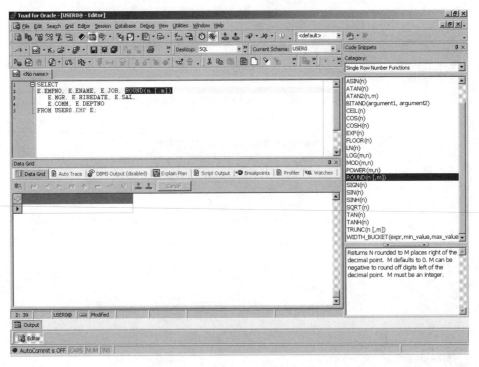

Figure 3.24   Code Snippets in Action

Code Snippets are maintained using TOAD Options → Editor → Code Assist. In Figure 3.25, notice how the upper-right corner allows for additional Code Snippet categories to be added or deleted. When one category is edited, the Code Snippets themselves can be maintained (changed, adding of your own, and deleting ones you will never use, perhaps).

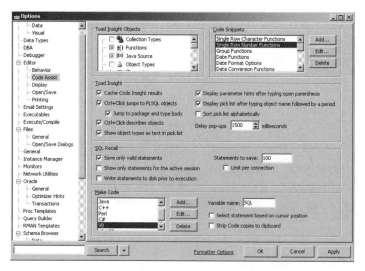

Figure 3.25   Code Snippet Maintenance Options

Executing SQL Statements

TOAD not only allows you to easily edit and create SQL and scripts containing SQL, it allows you to execute the SQL, review explain plans, and examine/edit/change the result-set data, track SQL execution times, and more.

The easiest way to execute SQL is with the Execute SQL button, the leftmost button on the third toolbar (execute SQL statement). Using this button executes the statement and returns the data when in full-view mode. Remember that F2 toggles between just the SQL Window and the results panel.

The "Execute SQL" button executes all SQL that is in the window. Some people highlight the code that they want TOAD to execute. Others simply place the cursor on the SQL statement and use the "Execute Snippet at Cursor" button (added to this display in a prior example; the second button on the third toolbar), whereas others use the "Execute as Script" button (found to the right of the "Halt" button). Clicking either button will display the output in the "Script Output" tab.

F9 also executes the SQL statement. Likewise, the SQL–Window → Execute SQL All does the job, as illustrated in Figure 3.26.

F9 executes the current SQL statement.

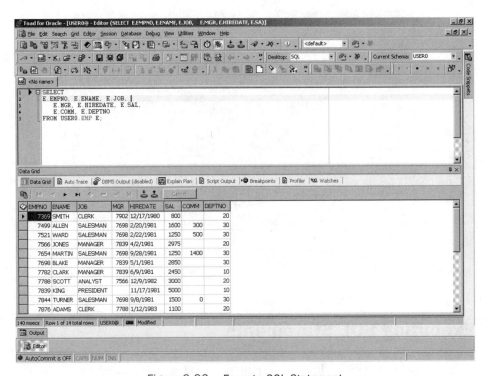

Figure 3.26   Execute SQL Statement

If you are working with SQL in a script, highlight the SQL in the script and press F9 to execute the single SQL statement only, or use the "Run as Script" button.

Executing SQL Scripts

TOAD allows you to execute individual SQL statements and entire SQL scripts as scripts. This will display the output of the script in the "Script Output" tab in the results panel (see Figure 3.27). This ability might be convenient when you are working with scripts, because you don't have to exit the TOAD environment to run scripts in SQL*Plus, for example.

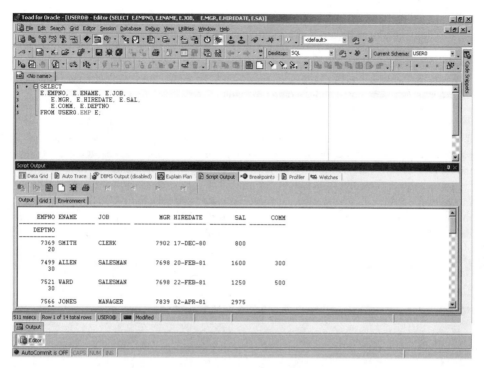

Figure 3.27   Execute SQL*Plus SQL Script as a Script

> If any of the tabs discussed here do not appear on your TOAD, simply right-click in the SQL Editor window, select Desktop Panels, and click the desired tab. The Editor → Desktop Panels menu item also gives access to displaying these tabs. The Desktop Panels option can also be used to hide unwanted/unneeded tabs.

> F5 executes the current SQL statement as a script.

The script output gives you the output that the script will produce, not just the data. Figure 3.27 shows a short SQL*Plus script and its output with column headings. SQL*Plus compatibility with TOAD is discussed later in this chapter. Notice the options available on the "Script Output" tab. TOAD provides the character–mode output (similar to that of SQL*Plus), a data grid of the data found, and the parameters used to run the SQL.

Editing Result-Set Data

TOAD allows you to change the data that appears in the data tab of the results panel. Notice the red button found at the bottom of the data grid display in Figure 3.26.

Selecting ROWID in the SQL (see Figure 3.28) will change the color of this button to green, allowing data to be modified directly from this data grid.

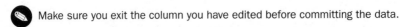 TOAD provides the keyword "edit," where you can type in "edit emp" or "edit scott.emp" where ename = 'SMITH'; when you enter such a command, the green button will also appear in the data grid and the data tab results panel.

Notice the toolbar that has appeared along the top of the data grid tab in Figure 3.28. This toolbar allows you to change fields, navigate around the data grid, and commit/roll back any changes made. Right-mouse click and select Pop-up Editor to put any individual item in its own edit window. Date fields can pop up a calendar panel as well.

To save the data changes, click the "Commit" key on the third toolbar or use the commit button on the data grid toolbar (it appeared when you selected ROWID). This data maintenance ability also works the same way as in the data tab of the F4 object describe as well as the data tab for a table in the Schema Browser (see Chapter 2).

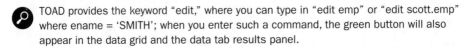 Make sure you exit the column you have edited before committing the data.

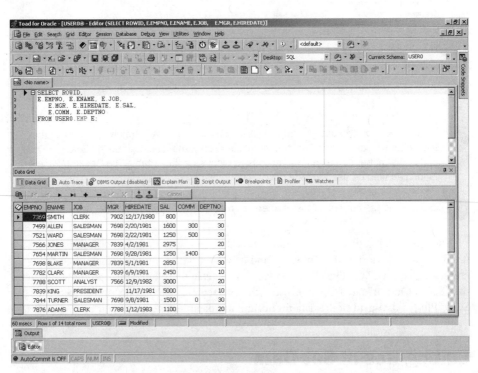

Figure 3.28   Changing Data Values in the Results Panel

You can also sort the data in the data grid by simply left-mouse clicking on the columns and making your sort-order selections.

TOAD allows you to view all the data for a particular row. Click on the "book"-looking button (found in the upper-left corner of the data grid, left of the data grid column headings) and the current row in the data grid will appear in a pop-up box. Figure 3.29 shows the data in the pop-up. Notice that the mouse cursor is pointing to the icon that make the pop-up appear. Also notice that this data applies to the first row in the data grid as it is marked as the current row.

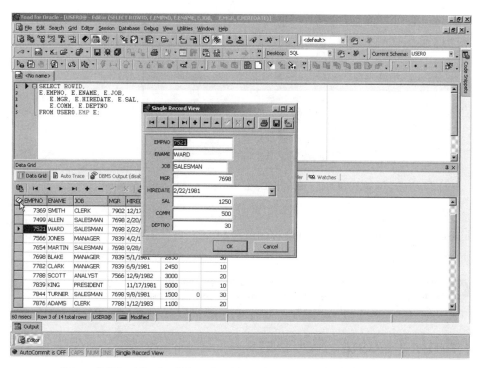

Figure 3.29   Viewing/Changing Single-Row Data Values in the Results
Panel

Saving Result-Set Data

The data in the results panel data tab can easily be saved in a number of formats. Right-mouse click on the data grid and select "Save As ..." from the pop-up menu. Notice all the options available in Figure 3.30. You can create a delimited file, XML-formatted file, and

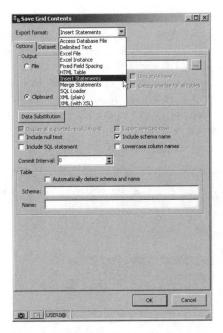

Figure 3.30   Saving Data Values in the Results Panel

insert statements (useful to create test data) and/or copy the results to the clipboard or to a named file. The TOAD team is always adding more options to this part of TOAD as well.

 This "Save As" option appears wherever there is a data grid, including the F4 describe screen and even the data grids in the master/detail browser!

Printing Result-Set Data

TOAD makes it easy to format the data grid into an attractive report. Select the print grid by right-mouse clicking on the data grid and selecting "Print Grid…". TOAD supports the old "Legacy Print Grid," a character-mode output that is easy to adjust. TOAD also supports "Fast Reports" for reporting; this feature is covered in detail in Chapter 6. Figure 3.31 shows the use of the path TOAD Options → Data Grids → Data. Notice that the "Use Legacy Print Grid" option is checked; it enables use of the simple character-mode report output when the "Print Grid" option is selected.

 Clicking on the data grid gives many options, including "Print Grid…".

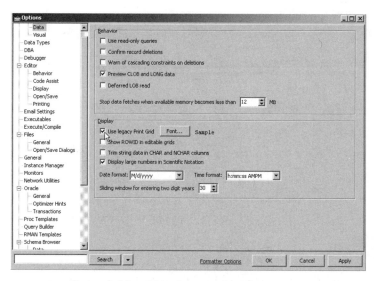

Figure 3.31   TOAD Data Grid Display Options

Figure 3.32 shows the panel used to adjust the headings of this report. Figure 3.33 shows the columns and their options. Headings can easily be changed by executing a single click on the columns and making changes to the appropriate boxes.

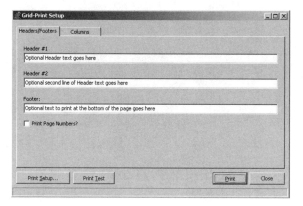

Figure 3.32   Legacy Print Grid Heading Options

If column totals are desired, select the column in the report to print the display as shown, and then check the "Total this column" check box.

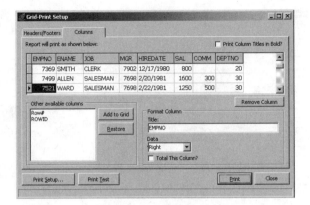

Figure 3.33   Legacy Print Grid Column Options

The non–Legacy Print Grid is simple to set up as well. Using TOAD Options, uncheck the previously mentioned "Legacy Print Grid" option. When the "Print Grid…" option is selected, the setup screen shown in Figure 3.34 appears. It offers a bit more of a graphical display. Colors can be changed, there is a bit more control over the page size, and the query used to populate the report can be adjusted as well. Figure 3.35 shows the Print Preview view of this report.

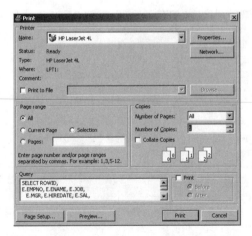

Figure 3.34   TOAD Print Grid Display Options

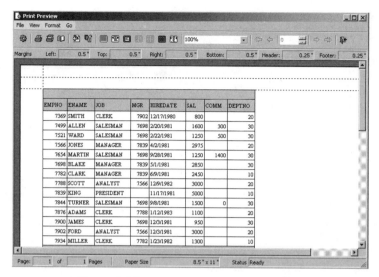

Figure 3.35   TOAD Print Grid Print Preview

Examining Explain Plans

TOAD allows you to easily see the explain plan for the currently executed SQL state-ment. Clicking the Explain Plan button on the third toolbar will produce an explain plan. This is visualized on the "Results Panel, Explain Plan" tab. Figure 3.36 illustrates a rather simple explain plan.

 Ctrl + e also runs and displays an explain plan.

 It is beyond the scope of this book to provide the background necessary for understand-ing explain plans, and for understanding the various features of the rule- and cost-based Oracle optimizers. TOAD does support changing the Optimizer Mode by right-mouse click-ing on the SQL statement and selecting the "Optimizer Mode" option. Cost-based hints can easily be added via the Code Snippets → Optimizer Hints option (discussed earlier in this chapter).

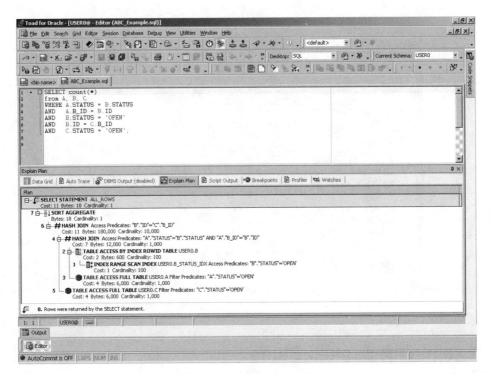

Figure 3.36   TOAD Explain Plans

If you get the error "ORA-02404 Specific Plan Table Not Found," then either the TOAD server-side objects setup has not been run as described in Chapter 1 or the TOAD explain plan table has been renamed. The solution is to run the TOAD server-side setup as defined in Chapter 1, which, among other things, builds the TOAD_PLAN_TABLE. If you choose to use the Oracle RDBMS plan table (found in <Oracle Home>\RDBMS\ admin) in file utlxplan.sql (this file is executed for each schema owner), then click the TOAD Options button, and under the Oracle part, change the explain plan table name to "PLAN_TABLE" (removing "TOAD_" from the beginning), as illustrated in Figure 3.37. This will allow TOAD to find the explain table for your schema. Figure 3.37 shows the TOAD option that controls this plan table name; it is located in the pathway TOAD Options → Oracle → General.

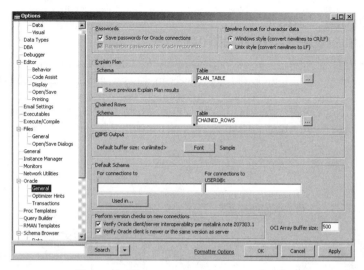

Figure 3.37   TOAD Explain Plan Options

The explain plan in TOAD is very adjustable. Right-mouse click on the explain plan panel and select "Adjust Content." This panel, as shown in Figure 3.38, allows you to adjust the displayed content of the "Explain Plan" tab. Chapter 6 covers these options in a bit more detail.

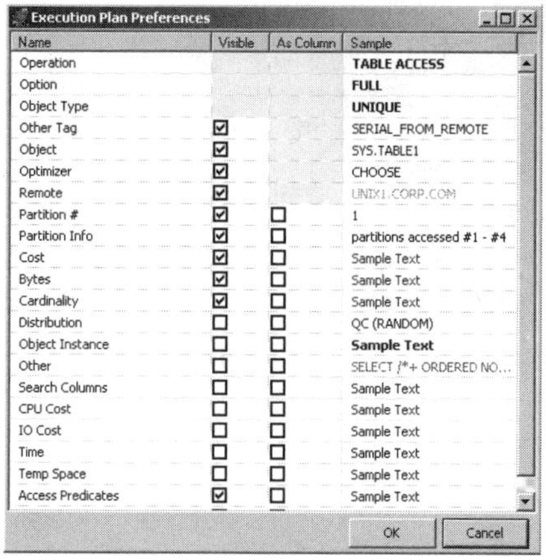

Figure 3.38   TOAD Explain Plan Adjust Content Panel

Examining Basic Performance Information

TOAD tracks basic information about the execution of the SQL statement or scripts. This information might be helpful in debugging certain issues with the SQL statement itself.

To populate this panel, right-click on the SQL Editor window and select "Autotrace" (it's a toggle option); see Figure 3.39. Then execute the SQL statement. The panel will be populated with database statistics associated with this execution, as seen in Figure 3.40.

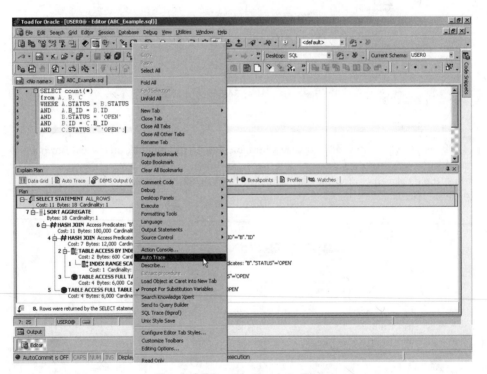

Figure 3.39   Starting Auto Trace

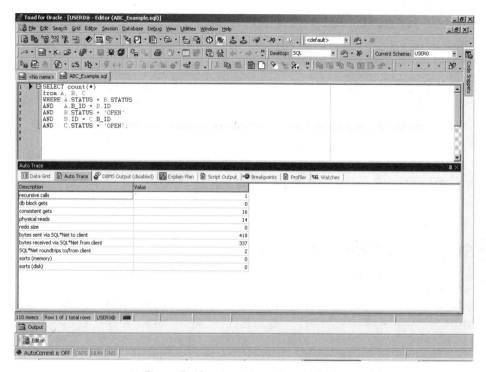

Figure 3.40   Auto Trace Statistics Tab

It is beyond the scope of this book to go into great depth regarding the meaning and interpretation of these various statistics.

- Recursive calls: Oracle sometimes issues additional SQL statements on behalf of the running SQL statement; that is, it executes recursive calls. Reasons for employing recursion include the existence of many extents on the object, dynamic space allocation (with an insert), and dictionary cache misses. The trace facility also generates recursive calls.

- Db block gets: This is the number of database block gets; it can be either physical or logical reads.

- Physical reads direct: This is the number of block fetch requests issued by Oracle.

Other Result Output Tabs

There are several more output tabs supported by TOAD. Most of these tabs will be covered in other chapters in this book as noted.

- DBMS Output: displays DBMS_OUTPUT (covered in Chapter 4).
- Query Viewer: tracks execution times of the same SQL (covered in Chapter 8).
- Profiler: displays output from the PL/SQL Profiler (covered in Chapter 4).
- Breakpoints, Watches, Navigator, and Call Stack: are associated with the PL/SQL Debugger (covered in Chapter 4).
- Code Expert: gives SQL coding suggestions.
- REF Cursor Results: are associated with PL/SQL Package output.

SQL*Plus Compatibility

SQL*Plus is used for a variety of tasks in the Oracle environment. In the early days (Oracle version 5 and earlier), SQL*Plus was also used as an administrative tool. Those administrative actions were performed using the Server Manager role before Oracle Enterprise Manager (OEM) came into being. Today, SQL*Plus has taken back the Server Manager role, allowing for administrative syntax to be processed from a script via SQL*Plus. SQL*Plus has always been a good character-mode reporting tool, a tool used to create SQL-creating-SQL (the next topic in this chapter), and more. It offers quite powerful formatting and file creation functions (spool commands) to perform a variety of tasks in the Oracle environment.

TOAD is an excellent tool to create and maintain these SQL*Plus scripts. The "Script Output" tab in the results panel, for example, allows you to see what the script has produced without having to leave TOAD and run the script in a separate window with SQL*Plus.

TOAD primarily supports the reporting features of SQL*Plus and not the administrative functions that have been given back to SQL*Plus.

 Make sure to run any SQL*Plus script as a script!

TOAD supports the following SQL*Plus commands:

@ ("at" sign)
@@ (double "at" sign)
& (ampersand)
&& (double ampersand)
/ (slash)
ACCEPT
BREAK
BTITLE

CLEAR (partially—a few variants are not supported)

COLUMN (partial support, including for ALIAS, NOPRINT/PRINT, and NEW_VALUE)

COMPUTE (partial support, including SUM, MIN, and MAX)

CONNECT

DEFINE

DESCRIBE

DISCONNECT

EXECUTE

EXIT

HEADING

HOST

JUSTIFY

MERGE

PAUSE

QUIT

PASSWORD

PRINT

PROMPT

REMARK

REPHEADER

REPFOOTER

SET (TOAD supports nearly all the SET command's many variants/options, with the few exceptions that are listed in the following subsection.)

SHOW

SPOOL

START

STORE SET

TTITLE

VARIABLE

WHENEVER OSERROR

WHENEVER SQLERROR

UNDEFINE

TOAD simply ignores these SQL*Plus commands:

SET ARRAYSIZE

SET AUTORECOVERY

SET BLOCKTERMINATOR

SET CMDSEP

SET COMPATIBILITY

SET CONCAT

SET COPYCOMMIT

SET COPYTYPECHECK

SET DESCRIBE

SET EDITFILE

SET EMBEDDED

SET FLAGGER

SET FLUSH

SET INSTANCE

SET LOBOFFSET

SET LOGSOURCE

SET MARKUP

SET PAUSE

SET SHIFTINOUT

SET SQLBLANKLINES

SET SQLCASE

SET SQLPREFIX

SET SUFFIX

SET TAB

SET TIME

The following SQL*Plus commands are not supported in TOAD:

APPEND

ARCHIVE LOG

ATTRIBUTE

CHANGE

CLEAR BUFFER

CLEAR SCREEN

CLEAR SQL

COPY

DEL

EDIT

GET

HELP

INPUT

LIST

RECOVER

RUN

SAVE

SHUTDOWN

STARTUP

SQL-Creating-SQL

Sometimes, even in today's world of super-GUIs, a SQL script is still the best way to do something. Plus there are always those people who steadfastly prefer working on the command line to working with a GUI, no matter what. Can TOAD accommodate—and even facilitate—these needs?

The example presented in this section shows how to turn on and off the referential integrity within an entire schema—whose list of table names can and will change over time. The fact that the list of table names can change adds another level of complexity or challenge. How can we write a one-time solution that will handle this dynamic list of table names. The answer: with Quest's TOAD, plus using the technique of dynamic SQL scripting.

Dynamic SQL scripting is a very old and powerful trick. You write a SQL script that will both generate and then execute the real SQL script. The primary enabling technologies have always been the Oracle data dictionary and certain SQL*Plus commands—namely, SPOOL and EXECUTE. Because TOAD has always strived to support a majority of SQL*Plus commands, TOAD can be used to build and run all such dynamic SQL scripts.

Let's return to the example, in which we need scripts to dynamically turn on and off foreign keys for a schema. Here is the script for the first half, turning off the referential integrity (the reverse solution is left for you as an exercise):

```
-- ri_off.sql
set pagesize 0
set feedback off
set term off
spool c:\temp\ri_off.tmp
select 'alter table '||owner||'.'||table_name||' disable constraint
'||constraint_name||';'
  from user_constraints
  where constraint_type = 'R'
  and status = 'ENABLED';
spool off
set term on
set feedback on
set echo on
@c:\temp\ri_off.tmp
```

Figure 3.41 shows this dynamic SQL file opened in TOAD's editor and then executed as a script (i.e., F5—with output displayed in the script output tab). No matter how the schema may change (i.e., tables be may created or dropped), this dynamic SQL script should always function as intended. As stated earlier, the two primary enablers are the Oracle data dictionary and TOAD's support for SQL*Plus commands, especially SPOOL. The algorithm is pretty straightforward: disable formatting and feedback, spool output to a temporary file, query the data dictionary to create the real SQL command for each row returned, terminate spooling, enable formatting and feedback, and finally execute the temporary file, which should now contain the dynamically correct SQL.

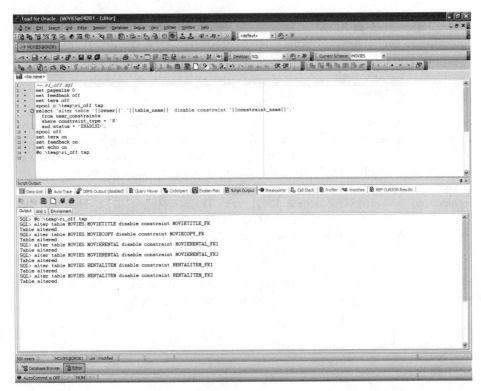

Figure 3.41   Script to Create a Script

Summary

This chapter covered use of the TOAD SQL Editor, illustrating most of the features available. The real power in using TOAD becomes available when you get comfortable with the various keyboard shortcuts and set up appropriate aliases and auto-replacements to facilitate the development cycle for SQL statements and SQL scripts.

The next chapter covers the TOAD PL/SQL Editor. Some of the features may appear similar to the TOAD SQL Editor features discussed in this chapter. In fact, some of the features really *are* the same or similar. This book will make the distinction clear and provide examples that are appropriate for whichever editor that the developer is using.

4

TOAD PL/SQL Editor

The PL/SQL Editor is a better editing environment for PL/SQL procedures, functions, packages, and database triggers than the SQL Editor described in Chapter 3. This editor contains a PL/SQL debugger, which is a full-featured symbolic debugger, and a profiler, which tells how long each line of PL/SQL code took to execute (critical information when you are tuning PL/SQL).

The PL/SQL Editor enables you to develop, save, run, debug, profile, and tune PL/SQL wherever it appears in applications or the database.

Basic Concepts of the PL/SQL Editor

TOAD provides a number of features that make PL/SQL development easy:

- Keyboard shortcuts
- Table and column select lists
- PL/SQL templates
- Options for creating and executing PL/SQL procedures or parts of procedures
- Complete debugging capabilities
- Complete source code control

The PL/SQL Editor is accessed by opening a new editor tab with the PL/SQL coding option selected (see Figure 4.1) or by opening a PL/SQL object from the database (see Figure 4.2).

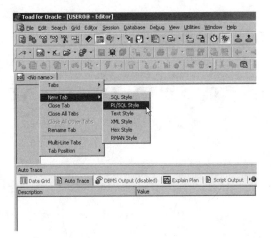

Figure 4.1   Opening a PL/SQL Editor Tab

Figure 4.2   Opening a PL/SQL Object

The PL/SQL Editor window gives you ease and flexibility in both creating new PL/SQL objects and editing existing PL/SQL objects from the database. The PL/SQL Editor recognizes when you are working with packages and splits the code into two tabs: one tab for the package specification and one tab for the package body. TOAD also does this kind of recognition when you open a text file that contains PL/SQL code, as long as there is either a PL/SQL package specification and body or more than one PL/SQL procedure or function. Figure 4.3 shows the dual tab TOAD opened when accessing a pack-age. Code can be written from scratch and code can be loaded into this editor from the Schema Browser as well.

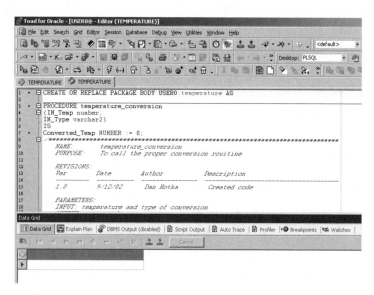

Figure 4.3   Opening a PL/SQL Package into Two Editor Tabs

Many of the same features described in Chapter 3 for the SQL Editor work with the PL/SQL Editor as well—features such as auto-replace, snippets, insights, and so on. Figures 4.1 through 4.3 show the default settings for the PL/SQL Editor. The various buttons at the top of the screen perform just about any function (including executing the current SQL statement or script, saving the current SQL statement or script, and so on). There are three rows of buttons, organized into three TOAD toolbars. When you hover the mouse over a button, a balloon will appear with a description of its use.

These toolbars are easily turned on and off via a right mouse click on the toolbar. TOAD is completely customizable.

A *shortcut* is a keystroke or series of keystrokes that performs a certain function. Pressing F1, for example, brings up the TOAD help facility. There is a button on the toolbar for just about every shortcut. The savvy TOAD user makes extensive use of these shortcuts.

F1 brings up the TOAD help facility.

The first two toolbars in the PL/SQL Editor are the same as the toolbars in the SQL Editor (discussed in Chapter 3). This chapter focuses on the PL/SQL Editor and primarily just the third row of buttons.

The third toolbar has buttons for actions that are specific to the PL/SQL Editor, such as compiling, debugging features, and source-code check-in/check-out:

Execute Statement

Terminate Execution

Execute as a Script

Execute Explain Plan for Current Statement

Compile Dependent Objects

Execute PL/SQL with a Debugger

Set Parameters for Use with a Debugger

Step Over

Trace Into

Trace Out

Run to Cursor

Toggle Breakpoint

Add Watch

Attach Debugger to External Session

The first shortcut is F2, which toggles the bottom output window between the full-screen view and the view displaying the bottom output grid. Figure 4.3 shows the PL/SQL Editor with the output toggled off—that is, the full-screen grid. This view is helpful when you are working on longer SQL statements or SQL scripts. You can easily toggle on the output tabs when you want to see the output.

F2: Toggles Output Window

Shift + F4: Toggles Action Console (displays compilation errors)

F9: Compile

Ctrl + S: Save

F11: Run

Shift + F9: Set Parameters

F8: Step Over

F7: Trace Into

Shift + F8: Trace Out

F12 Run to Cursor

Ctrl + F5: Add Watch

The PL/SQL Editor has several parts. The main edit window enables you to edit multiple PL/SQL objects at the same time. Each object will have its own tab along the top of this section. See the LOOPING_EXAMPLE tab in Figure 4.4. Pressing Shift + F4 will activate the Action Console (it can also be activated by following the path Edit → Action Console) so that it displays any compilation errors encountered by the PL/SQL compiler. Notice the lower-right status line, which displays the message "Syntax errors" in Figure 4.4; it can also show error counts and warning counts.

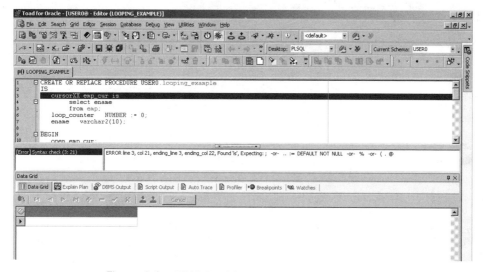

Figure 4.4   TOAD PL/SQL Action Console with Errors

Notice the line numbers in the gutter along the left side of the screen. The "+" and "-" symbols in this column allow for code groupings such as IF THEN ELSE, BEGIN and END, and the like to be expanded and condensed as needed. As a consequence, you can easily display the code of interest while hiding other, nonessential code. The lines marked with a period (".") contain executable lines of code. They are of particular interest during debugging, a topic that will be revisited later in this chapter.

Bookmarks allows for easy navigation to various parts of PL/SQL code. Lines of code can be "bookmarked" so that they can easily be navigated to during editing sessions or at later points in the future. Notice the numbered boxes in the left gutter of the screen shown in Figure 4.5. Right-clicking in the editor window and selecting "toggle bookmark" will place a bookmark on the line the cursor is on. Likewise, right-mouse clicking and selecting "goto bookmark" allows for easy navigation to the bookmarks. There is also an option to clear all the bookmarks simultaneously.

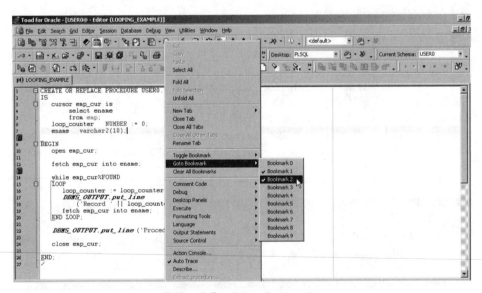

Figure 4.5   Editor Bookmarks

The bookmarks in the PL/SQL Editor work the same way in the other editors. TOAD also remembers where the bookmarks were placed from prior TOAD edit sessions.

The lower section of the screen contains various tabs and enables you to set and see the breakpoints for the debugger, the debugger watches, the call stack (which objects have called other objects), and the DBMS_Output. These tabs are of great interest to the PL/SQL Editor. Chapter 3 discussed all of these various output tabs. Recall that pressing F2 toggles to the full editor screen or a half screen displaying these tabs. When you right-mouse click on these lower tabs, you will have the option to toggle additional tabs on and off as needed.

TOAD 9.7 includes six editors: SQL Editor (covered in Chapter 3), PL/SQL Editor (covered in this chapter), Text Editor, HTML Editor, Hex Editor, and RMAN Editor. The editor environment applies its options to all six editors. In addition, TOAD allows you to copy code to an external editor of your choice. For example, TOAD defines Notepad as its external editor of choice in a Windows environment. To change the default for the external editor, use the TOAD Options → Executables panel and change the "External Editor" option found at the bottom of the panel.

To use an external editor, press the key combination Ctrl + F12. If your current session has not been saved, you will be prompted to save it. Also, upon exiting your external editor, you will be prompted to reload your work from the saved file. Figure 4.6 shows some work loaded into the Notepad editor.

 Ctrl + F12 accesses a previously defined external editor.

```
LOOPING_EXAMPLE - Notepad
File  Edit  Format  View  Help
CREATE OR REPLACE PROCEDURE USER0.looping_example
IS
    cursor emp_cur is
        select ename
        from emp;
    loop_counter  NUMBER := 0;
    ename    varchar2(10);

BEGIN
    open emp_cur;

    fetch emp_cur into ename;

    while emp_cur%FOUND
    LOOP
        loop_counter := loop_counter + 1;
        DBMS_OUTPUT.put_line
            ('Record ' || loop_counter || ' is Employee ' || ename );
        fetch emp_cur into ename;
    END LOOP;

    DBMS_OUTPUT.put_line ('Procedure Looping Example is done');

    close emp_cur;

END;
```

Figure 4.6   Using Notepad as an Editor in TOAD

There are several ways to get PL/SQL code into the PL/SQL Editor. You can simply type in a new SQL statement, or create a new work area for a new SQL or PL/SQL block using the "Create New PLSQL Object" button. You can load SQL or PL/SQL from a file using the "Load File" button; this button has a drop-down menu that contains the history of loads. You can check out code from the source code using the "Check File Out of Source Control" button. You can also load the code from the database using the "Load Source from Existing Object" button, which has a drop-down menu that contains the history of selected objects. Finally, you can load code from other applications by using the cut-and-paste technique.

Figure 4.7 illustrates the process of loading code from a file. Notice that the drop-down menu from the "Load File" button shows a history of files accessed by TOAD. Loading code from the database is just as easy when you use the "Load Source from Existing Object" button; it has a similar drop-down menu of a history of objects accessed by TOAD.

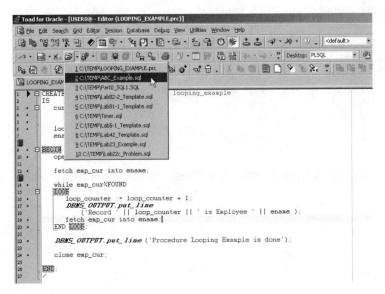

Figure 4.7   Loading Code into the PL/SQL Editor

Formatting PL/SQL Code

TOAD can quickly transform your PL/SQL into an easy-to-read format. Figure 4.8 shows how to access the formatter by right-clicking in the edit window and selecting Formatting Tools → Format Code from the context menu. This context menu contains several options that you can choose to configure how the formatting occurs. Figure 4.9 shows the result—that is, how TOAD formats the SQL. Notice that TOAD puts a comment line in the code, indicating that it has been formatted. You can adjust the TOAD formatter to match your local coding standards by accessing View → Options → Formatter Options.

Now you've learned some of the basic concepts and features of the PL/SQL Editor; the remainder of this chapter covers specific topics related to this editor.

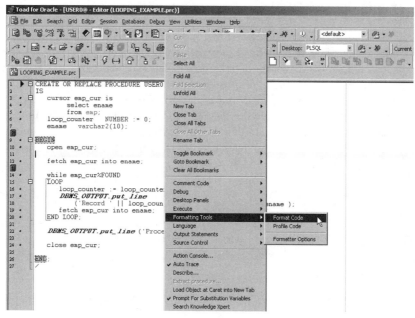

Figure 4.8   Accessing the PL/SQL Formatter

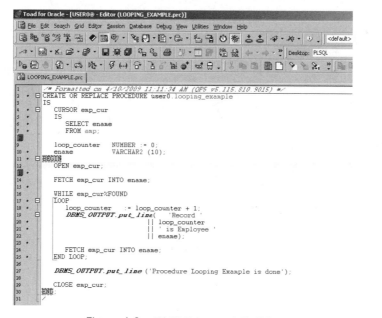

Figure 4.9   TOAD-Formatted PL/SQL

Predefined Shortcuts

Keyboard shortcuts are one of the features that make TOAD so powerful and easy to use. TOAD comes with a host of predefined shortcuts. These shortcuts save keystrokes and mouse actions and perform a variety of tasks, such as issuing a "describe" on the current highlighted object or completing a "find" operation (find next, find previous, and so on). This section highlights all of the shortcuts available for TOAD 9.7. Be aware that the shortcuts available differ slightly between the PL/SQL Editor and the SQL Editor (covered in Chapter 3). This section focuses on the shortcuts for the PL/SQL Editor only.

Tables 4.1 and 4.2 are handy cross-references for all of the PL/SQL Editor shortcuts. Table 4.1 shows the shortcuts arranged by keystroke, and Table 4.2 shows the shortcuts arranged by description. The third column refers you to the figure in this chapter where the shortcut is illustrated.

F2 or Shift + F2: Toggles output window

F9: Compile

Ctrl + S: Save

F11: Run

Ctrl + F9: Set Parameters

F8: Step Over

F7: Trace Into

Shift + F8: Trace Out

F12: Run to Cursor

Ctrl + F5: Add Watch

Table 4.1   **PL/SQL Editor Shortcuts by Keystroke**

Shortcut	Description	Illustrations
F1	Windows help file	
F2	Toggle output window	4.2
F3	Find next occurrence	
Shift + F3	Find Previous .occurrence	
F4	Describe table, view, procedure, function	3.21
F5	Set/delete breakpoint	4.22
Shift + F7	Trace Into while debugging	4.20
Shift + F8	Step over while debugging	4.20
F9	Compile	4.14
Ctrl + F9	Set code execution parameters	4.15
Shift + F9	Execute current source without debugging	4.14
F10 or right-mouse	Pop-up menu	
F11	Execute current source with debugging	4.20
F12	Execute current source to cursor with debugging	
Ctrl + F12	External editor, pass contents	
Ctrl + A	Select all text	
Ctrl + Alt + B	Display breakpoint window	4.22
Ctrl + C	Copy	
Ctrl + D	Display procedure parameters	
Ctrl + Alt + D	Display debugger in DBMS output window	
Ctrl + F	Find text	
Ctrl + G	Go to line	
Ctrl + L	Convert text to lowercase	
Ctrl + M	Make code statement	
Ctrl + N	Recall named SQL statement	
Ctrl + O	Open a text file	
Ctrl + P	Strip code statement	
Ctrl + R	Find and replace	
Ctrl + S	Save file	4.16
Shift + Ctrl + S	Save file as	4.16
Ctrl + Alt + S	Display call stack window	4.26
Ctrl + T	Columns drop-down	
Shift + Ctrl + R	Alias replacement	
Shift + Ctrl + T	Columns drop-down, no alias	

continues

Table 4.1   **PL/SQL Editor Shortcuts by Keystroke,** *continued*

Shortcut	Description	Illustrations
Ctrl + space	Code templates	4.11, 4.12
Ctrl + U	Convert text to uppercase	
Ctrl + V	Paste	
Ctrl + Alt + W	Display debugger watches window	4.20
Ctrl + X	Cut	
Ctrl + Z	Undo last change	
Ctrl + .	Display pop-up list of matching table names	
Shift + Ctrl + Z	Redo last undo	
Ctrl + Tab	Cycles through the collection of MDI child windows	

Table 4.2   **PL/SQL Editor Shortcuts by Description**

Description	Shortcut	Illustrations
Alias replacement	Shift + Ctrl + R	
Code templates	Ctrl + space	4.11, 4.12
Columns drop-down	Ctrl + T	
Columns drop-down, no alias	Shift + Ctrl + T	
Compile	F9	4.14
Convert text to lowercase	Ctrl + L	
Convert text to uppercase	Ctrl + U	
Copy	Ctrl + C	
Cut	Ctrl + X	
Cycles through the collection of MDI child windows	Ctrl + Tab	
Describe table, view, procedure, function, or package	F4	3.21
Display breakpoint window	Ctrl + Alt + B	4.22
Display call stack window	Ctrl + Alt + S	4.26
Display debugger in DBMS output window	Ctrl + Alt + D	
Display debugger watches window	Ctrl + Alt + W	4.20
Display popup list of matching table names	Ctrl + .	
Display procedure parameters	Ctrl + D	
Execute current source to cursor with debugging	F12	
Execute current source with debugging	F11	4.14
Execute current source without debugging	Shift + F9	4.14
External editor, pass contents	Ctrl + F12	
Find and replace	Ctrl + R	
Find next occurrence	F3	

Table 4.2   **PL/SQL Editor Shortcuts by Description,** *continued*

Description	Shortcut	Illustrations
Find previous occurrence	Shift + F3	
Find text	Ctrl + F	
Go to line	Ctrl + G	
Make code statement	Ctrl + M	
Open a text file	Ctrl + O	
Paste	Ctrl + V	
Pop-up menu	F10 or right-mouse	
Recall named SQL	Ctrl + N	
Redo last undo	Shift + Ctrl + Z	
Save file	Ctrl + S	4.16
Save file as	Shift + Ctrl + S	4.16
Select all text	Ctrl + A	
Set execution parameters	Ctrl + F9	4.15
Set/delete breakpoint	F5	
Step over while debugging	Shift + F8	
Strip code statement	Ctrl + P	
Trace Into while debugging	Shift + F7	
Toggle output window	F2	4.2
Undo last change	Ctrl + Z	
Windows help file	F1	

Using Aliases, Pick Lists, Shortcuts, Snippets, and Auto-Replacement Substitutions

The PL/SQL Editor also supports the following features:

- User-defined shortcuts: You can easily add or change the shortcut keystrokes for existing shortcuts.
- TOAD aliases: You can give short names to rather long table names or give a short name to a line of syntax.
- Column pick lists: Also called TOAD insights; when you enter a table name and a period ("."), a column pick list will appear.
- Snippets: These predefined bits of code are used via a drag-and-drop mouse operation.
- Auto-replacement substitutions: You can use the auto-correct feature of TOAD to assign a short key sequence to an entire line of syntax, for example.

User defined shortcuts, TOAD aliases, column pick lists, snippets, and auto replacement substitutions are all described in detail in Chapter 3.

TOAD snippets also include a couple of categories specifically geared toward the PL/SQL Editor. Figure 4.10 illustrates the "Defined Exceptions" attributes. Another type of snippet that is convenient for cursor coding is the "Cursor Attributes" category.

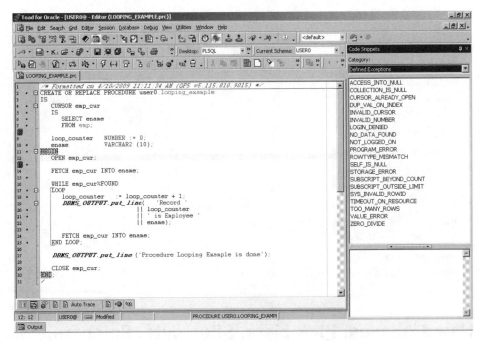

Figure 4.10   Snippets PL/SQL Categories

PL/SQL Object Templates

Code completion templates are boilerplate syntax where you type in a template name and key sequence, and a code template is inserted automatically. These templates can have substitution variables—that is, variables where you substitute a more appropriate value customized to your code.

TOAD supplies a number of these code templates. This section describes how to modify these templates and even add your own code templates.

The PL/SQL object templates are stored in TOAD and are easily visualized and modified via the pathway TOAD Options → Editor → Behavior (or right-click in the editor window and select "Editor Options"). The lower-right part of the panel displays PL/SQL in the Languages window; you click the "Code Template" button to access the desired template.

Figure 4.11 shows the Cursor Loop template. To use this template, enter "crloop" and then press the key combination Ctrl + space. Notice the "&" variables in this template. The single vertical bar is where TOAD will place the cursor after inserting the code into the editor. Notice Figure 4.12 shows a pop-up menu for the substitution variables embedded in this template. Figure 4.13 shows the code after its insertion in the PL/SQL Editor, with the substituted code being highlighted to indicate its location.

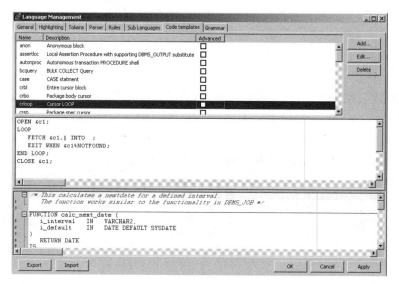

Figure 4.11   PL/SQL CRLOOP Code Template

To add your own template, click the "Add" button visible in Figure 4.11. This action opens a line in the template window. Enter your template label (which will be used when you access the template with the Ctrl + space key combination) and then enter your code.

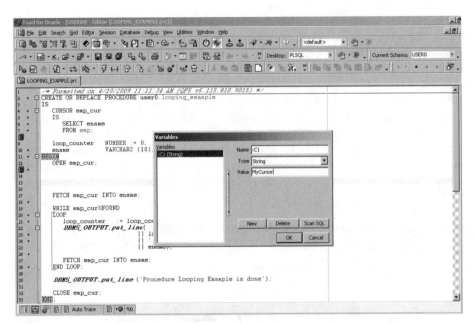

Figure 4.12   PL/SQL Code Templates in Action

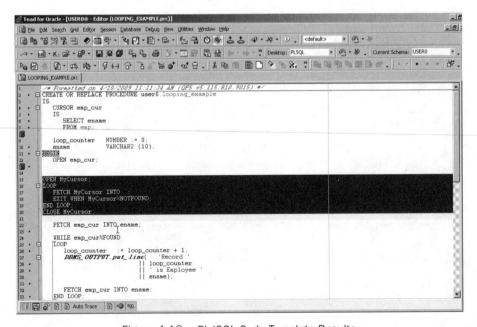

Figure 4.13   PL/SQL Code Template Results

Compiling PL/SQL Code

Compiling code in the PL/SQL Editor window is easy. Simply click the "Compile" button (leftmost button on the third toolbar) or press F9.

 F9: Compile

The compiled code is shown in Figure 4.14. The error panel was discussed earlier in this chapter. Notice the message line near the bottom of the screen: It shows no errors or warnings, which indicates this procedure compiled without syntax errors and is ready to be executed.

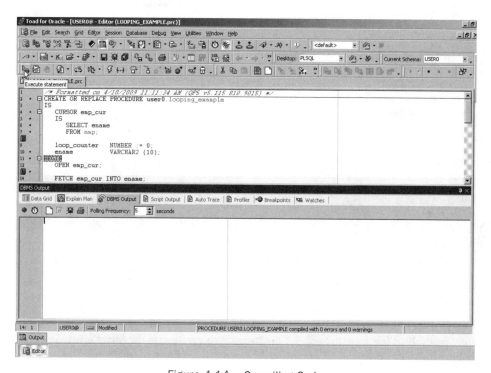

Figure 4.14   Compiling Code

Executing PL/SQL Code

TOAD enables you to develop and run code without having to leave one environment and go to another (as you would using an editor and SQL*Plus, for example). Code can easily be run by clicking the "Run" button or pressing the F11 key. Figure 4.15 shows the "Set

Parameters and Execute" pop-up panel, where you can enter any required parameters. The parameter button or the key combination Ctrl + F9 can also be used to define parameters.

 F11: Run

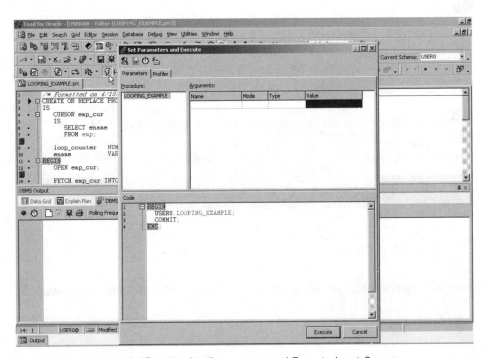

Figure 4.15   The Set Parameters and Execute Input Screen

Figure 4.16 shows the results of the execution. This particular PL/SQL code has DBMS_OUTPUT, so the "DBMS_OUTPUT" tab is displayed. The DBMS_OUTPUT must be enabled (click on the red dot to change it to green) and the DBMS_OUTPUT polling frequency time can be moved up. The contents of this tab can be saved, printed, and cleared as necessary.

 To see the DBMS_OUTPUT, make sure the output option on the "DBMS_OUTPUT" tab is turned on. This is the equivalent of setting *serveroutput on* in SQL*Plus.

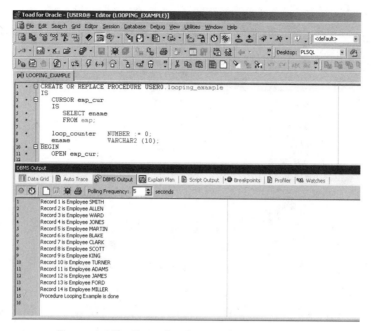

Figure 4.16   Executing Code with DBMS_OUTPUT

Saving PL/SQL Code to Files

Saving your work to operating system files is easy. Just click the "Save As" button (see the mouse cursor in Figure 4.17) and pick the location where you would like the code to be created. When you achieve a clean compilation of the code, it is also stored in the database in the schema to which you are currently connected. Figure 4.17 shows the Save to File function. Pressing Ctrl + S will save the code in the original file it was created as; pressing Shift + Ctrl + S will perform the same task as clicking the "Save As" button. Notice there is a "Save All" option that will prompt and save the contents for all editor tabs.

 TOAD remembers the last computer folder that files were opened from or saved to.

You can also right-click on the tab of the item you want to save or close. If the file has been changed since it was opened or created, you will be prompted to save the file before TOAD closes the tab.

Notice in Figure 4.17 that TOAD will pick the appropriate file suffix for the code it notices. This default can be easily changed via the drop-down context menu.

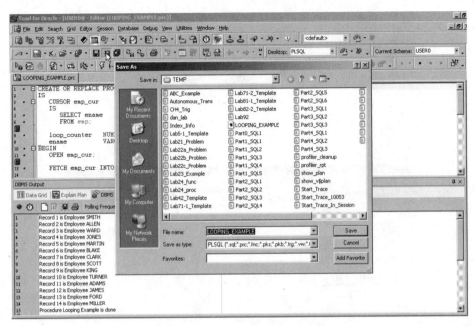

Figure 4.17   Saving Code to a File

Ctrl + S: Save file with its current name (Save)

Shift + Ctrl + S: Save file with a different name (Save As)

Debugging Setup, Requirements, and Parameters

TOAD contains a powerful debugger that enables you to traverse code, view variable content, start or stop execution of code, step in and out of called procedures, and change variable content during code execution. This kind of code debugging is known as *symbolic debugging*.

In the past, access to the TOAD Debugger required the purchase of an additional license. The TOAD Debugger is now included as a standard feature in TOAD. You can check whether a logged-in user has the necessary debug execution privileges by accessing the Help → Toad Advisor menu option.

Basic Debugging PL/SQL Code

The TOAD debugger is easily accessed by using the nine buttons on the right side of the PL/SQL Editor toolbar (third toolbar); see Figure 4.18. These same functions are also accessible from the Debug menu (see Figure 4.19). All of the functions have corresponding shortcuts as well.

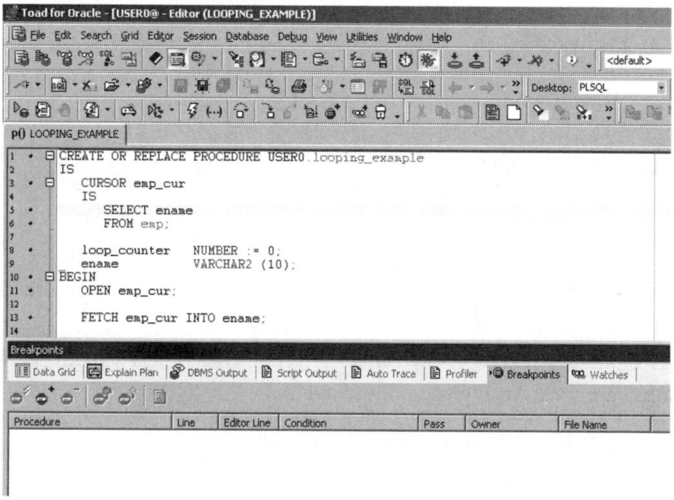

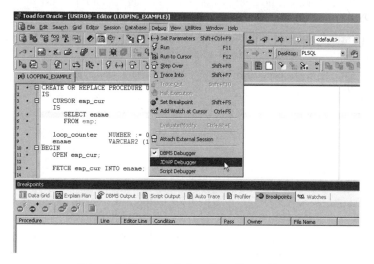

Figure 4.18   The Debug Toolbar

Figure 4.19   The Debug Drop-Down Menu

The following keystrokes also access many of the TOAD Debugger features:

F11: Run

Shift + Ctrl + F9: Set Parameters

Shift + F8: Step Over

Shift + F7: Trace Into

Shift + F10: Trace Out

Shift + F12: Run to Cursor

Shift + F5: Add Breakpoint

Ctrl + F5: Add Watch

The TOAD debugger relies heavily on certain functions. These functions, described in the following list, are used throughout this section:

- Set Parameters: Allows you to set any input variables.
- Run: Executes the procedure or function.
- Run to Cursor: Executes the procedure or function until the line containing the mouse cursor is reached.
- Step Over: Executes one line of code at a time but does not go into any called procedures or functions.
- Trace Into: Executes one line of code at a time and goes into any called procedure or function, executing its code one line at a time as well.
- Trace Out: Returns execution to the calling routine, stopping on the next line of code after the call statement.
- Halt Execution: Stops debugging or stepping through the lines of code.
- Set Breakpoint: Stops the debug process at the line with the breakpoint.
- Add Watch at Cursor: Watches allow for the contents of specific variables to be monitored during the debugging process. This key allows you to add additional variables to be monitored.
- Evaluate/Modify: Allows for "watched" variables to be visualized and changed on the fly.
- Breakpoints: A breakpoint stops execution at the line containing the breakpoint. This key allows you to add, change, or delete breakpoints.

- Call Stack: Displays the call stack, or an ordered list of procedures or functions that were called to get to this particular procedure or function.

- Watches: Displays the variables currently being monitored. This window also allows you to add, change, or delete watched variables.

- DBMS Output: Displays any DBMS_OUTPUT generated by the procedure or function.

DBMS_OUTPUT is not displayed until the procedure or function completes its execution or until you click the Halt button.

Let's walk through a simple debugging session using TEMPERATURE.PKG, which contains a procedure and its related functions.

These procedures and functions are available in the "Downloads" tab of this book's Web site, located at www.informit.com/title/9780321649102.

The debugging process relies heavily on the Oracle Probe API. As a consequence, the TOAD debugger cannot see any of the code variables until the code is actually executing.

The two buttons most users work with when going through the code are "Trace Into" and "Step Over." "Trace Into" stops on each line of code. "Step Over" does the same thing, except it does not follow the lines of code into a called procedure or function; instead, the code is executed and the debugger simply stops on the next line of code in the current procedure.

This discussion focuses on named buttons, but TOAD often provides a shortcut and/or keystroke combination to access the same function.

You can set "watches" to review and edit the content of variables. Watches enable you to see how the contents of the variables change as the code is being debugged, with the values appearing in the tab at the bottom of the screen (see Figure 4.21). You can also hover over a variable with the mouse to display the variable's contents as well.

The TOAD debugging environment takes advantage of three output-related tabs:

- Breakpoints: Allows you to see breakpoints and set breakpoint options.

- Watches: Allows you to see and modify data.

- Call Stack: Allows you to visualize the module relationships during execution.

If these tabs are not visible on your screen, right-click in the editor window and select them from the "Desktop Panels" item in the pop-up context menu.

The output tabs can be organized via a drag-and-drop operation, easily turned on and off using the "Desktop Panels" menu item, and toggled to display the full-screen editor. You can display these tabs along the bottom of the TOAD screen by pressing the F2 button.

There are several ways to initiate a debug session:

- Put the cursor in the code and click on the "Run to Cursor" button
- Set a breakpoint to stop the execution at a desired point, and then click the "Run" button
- Click the "Trace Into" button to start debugging and stop at the first executable line of code

To begin a debugging session, load TEMPERATURE.PKG, click the "Trace Into" button, and click "Yes" in response to the dialog box question, "Do you want to compile reference objects with debug information?"; see Figure 4.20. This series of steps inserts the necessary debug information into the appropriate procedures and functions. In the "Set Parameters and Execute" box, highlight "Temperature_Conversion" on the left and set variables *IN_TEMP* and *IN_TYPE* to 10 and C, respectively. Finally, click "OK."

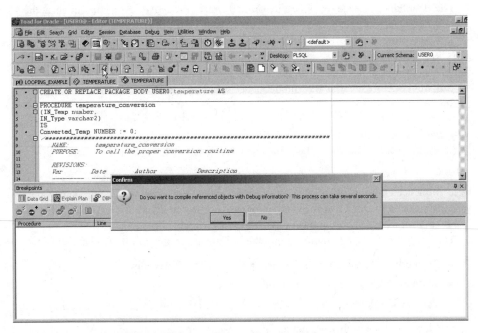

Figure 4.20   Compile with Debug Information

Now set a watch on *Converted_Temp*; the debugger should have stopped on this first line. You can perform this task in various ways—for example, by clicking the "Add Watch" button on the toolbar; using the "Watches" tab line and clicking the "+" button; by right-clicking on the variable name; or by pressing Ctrl + F5. Notice that the "Watches" tab (see Figure 4.21) has added the *Converted_Temp* variable and that its value is NULL. TOAD has not executed this first statement, so the variable is not yet set to 0. Press Shift + F7 or click the "Trace Into:" button, and you will be able to watch the value of the *Converted_Temp* variable change.

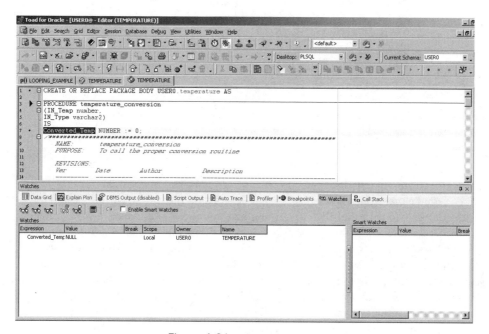

Figure 4.21   Setting a Watch

You can walk through the code, see the content of variables anywhere they appear, and change the contents of the variables on the fly by selecting the variable in the "Watches" tab and clicking the "Evaluate/Modify" button (see Figure 4.22). This function enables you to change the contents of a variable right before you begin a critical check or initiate a procedure for testing purposes. Click the "Modify" button on the top of this dialog panel to change the variable's value.

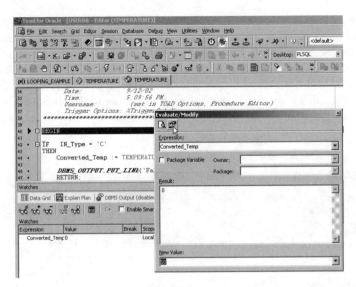

Figure 4.22   Changing Variable Content

Rather than stepping through code one line at a time, you might want to run a bunch of code and either stop at a designated point (a breakpoint) or at the cursor's position in the code. You can click the "Run to Cursor" button or press F12 to execute the code until it reaches the line where the mouse cursor is located. You can set a breakpoint in a number of ways (by clicking just to the left of the line where you want the breakpoint, as shown in Figure 4.23; by using the "+" button on the "Break Points" tab; or by pressing Shift + F5). This allows you to execute the code by clicking the "Run" button or pressing F11; the debugger will stop when it gets to this line. Later in this chapter, you will learn how to set conditional breakpoints, so that the debugger will stop on a line only when certain conditions exist (such as when a loop has been executed 10 or more times). Stopping the code at convenient times enables you to evaluate variable content at critical points in the code. Clicking the "Halt" button will stop execution of the code at any time.

Notice the dots in the left gutter, along with the line numbers and line condensing symbols (and bookmarks, if used). These dots indicate executable lines of code. You can set breakpoints on these lines.

Debugging triggers differ from debugging procedures. The *INSERT INTO*, *UPDATE .. SET*, and *DELETE* trigger code is not available to the debugger until the values have been entered.

When debugging a loop such as *FOR LOOP_COUNT IN 1..500 LOOP ...*, set a watch on the *LOOP_COUNT* variable. Use the "Evaluate/Modify" function to change this variable's value to 499 so you don't have to manually walk through the loop 500 times to see the code exit the routine.

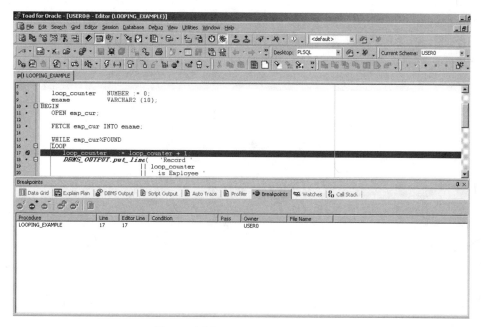

Figure 4.23   Setting Breakpoints

Debugging Breakpoint Options

The previous section described how you would set breakpoints to stop the code at prede-termined lines of code. TOAD also allows you to set "conditional" breakpoints.

The steps to set breakpoint options are as follows:

1. Establish a regular breakpoint where the code is to be stopped.
2. In the breakpoint tab, highlight the breakpoint to be adjusted, and click the "Edit Breakpoint" button in this same tab.
3. Notice that a breakpoint can be stopped at a certain variable condition or by the number of passes (i.e., loops) that code execution went past this breakpoint.

Figure 4.24 illustrates how to set a breakpoint so that execution stops after 10 times through the loop. The breakpoint turns blue when the breakpoint has stopped the pro-cessing of the code. Press F11 to execute the procedure. Notice in Figure 4.25 that a watch was placed on the *loop_counter* variable and that the *loop_counter* has a value of 9. Thus the loop is on its tenth iteration and the variable *loop_counter* (where the breakpoint is set) has not been incremented yet.

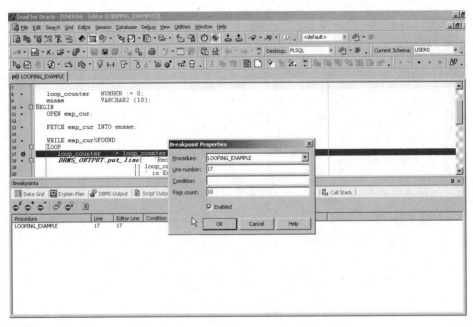

Figure 4.24   Setting a Conditional Breakpoint

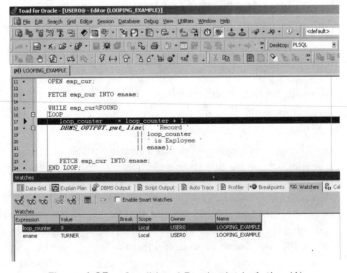

Figure 4.25   Conditional Breakpoint in Action (1)

Figure 4.26 illustrates how to set a conditional breakpoint on a particular condition such as *ENAME = SMITH*. When running the procedure now, position the mouse over *rec.name* on line 11; you will see that the code did stop executing when the *ENAME* of *SMITH* was located. If you check the *loop_counter* variable, you will notice that it is at 0, so *SMITH* just happens to be the first row returned.

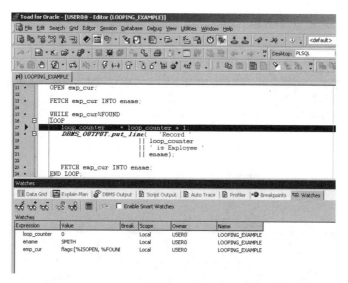

Figure 4.26   Conditional Breakpoint in Action (2)

Advanced Debugging PL/SQL Code

The "Call Stack" tab is handy to see which routine you are in and at which line number. Notice that Figure 4.27 names the Temperature package twice. This is because at line 44, you entered the *Celsius_to_Fahrenheit* function (at line 61). This call stack allows you to see the tree structure of called routines based on code execution.

TOAD also allows watches to be set on implicit variables and even record types. Notice in Figure 4.28 that a watch placed on the *rec* implicit variable (implicit variables are not defined in other places in the procedure) displays all of the columns in the EMP table for the row containing the conditional breakpoint! You can also position the mouse over the *rec* variable type to display all of the current column data.

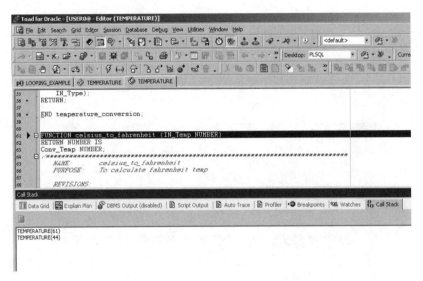

Figure 4.27   Call Stack Information

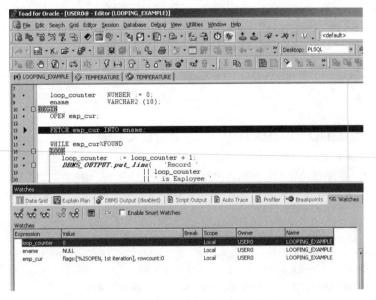

Figure 4.28   Implicit Variable Watch

TOAD allows for code to be debugged from a live transaction environment. This technique is known as "just in time" (JIT) debugging. To follow this approach, the PL/SQL code needs to be in the editor, compiled with debug information; you then click the "Attach debugger to external session" button.

A bit of setup is required for this kind of debugging. The application from the live environment needs to enter the following commands:

- ALTER SESSION SET PLSQL_DEBUG=TRUE
- id := dbms_debug.initialize('TOAD')
- dbms_debug.debug_on;

Then, in TOAD, make sure the code to be debugged is in the PL/SQL Editor with a breakpoint set. Enter the same initialization string (*TOAD*, in this example) when attaching to external session, as shown Figure 4.29.

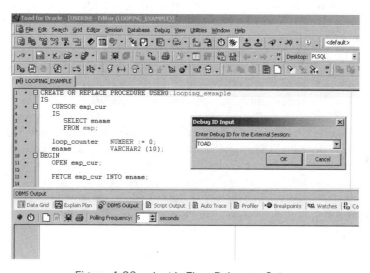

Figure 4.29   Just-in-Time Debugger Setup

When the application is then executed and the PL/SQL code is executed, the application will appear to be hung. In reality, it is working in DEBUG mode inside TOAD at that point. The end result in TOAD should look like Figure 4.26.

Once the PL/SQL routine has terminated, be sure to enter *dbms_debug.debug_off;* in the live environment. Otherwise, the next time the application is executed, it will again appear hung while waiting for TOAD's debug session to commence.

Profiling PL/SQL Code

Profiling PL/SQL allows you to see how long your code took to execute and how long each line of code took to execute. This information is important when you are tuning PL/SQL code or a complete set of related routines.

Starting with version 8i, Oracle can track statistics on the execution of SQL, including procedures and functions. TOAD interfaces with the DBMS_PROFILE package, giving you an easy way to track and compare your program statistics. This package then populates three tables in the user's account:

- PLSQL_PROFILER_RUNS
- PLSQL_PROFILER_UNITS
- PLSQL_PROFILER_DATA

If the "Stop Watch" button on the top toolbar or the "PL/SQL Profiling" and "Profiler Analysis" buttons (on the Database menu) are grayed out, run the script *<Oracle Home>/ RDBMS/admin/profload.sql* while working as the SYS user. You will also need to navigate to Database → Administer → Serverside Objects Administration and select the SQL Profiler option. This will create the three PLSQL_PROFILER tables mentioned previously.

The "Stop Watch" button on the top toolbar is a toggle switch. Click it and then run your code (click the "Execute PLSQL" button or press F11). When execution of your code has terminated, click the "Stop Watch" button again to stop profiling. When profiling is started, TOAD will put a comment into *PLSQL_PROFILER_RUNS* containing the name of the first procedure and a time stamp. TOAD will profile all code called.

TOAD version 9.6 and later includes an output tab called "Profiler," as shown in Figure 4.30. The second level of drilling shows all code that was executed. Drilling into each of these levels allows for each line of code that incurred any execution time to be seen, indicates how many times it was executed, and shows how long it took to execute. As you click on lines of information in this tab, TOAD will jump to that line of code in the PL/SQL Editor.

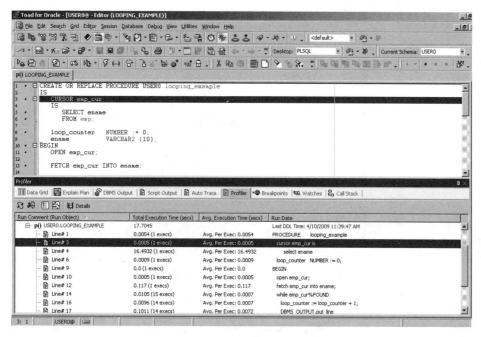

Figure 4.30   Oracle Profiler Collection

TOAD releases prior to TOAD 9.6 work a little differently. When the profiler is activated, a dialog box will appear that allows you to set the run label information (the default code name and time stamp are filled in). When you want to see how your code executions compare with each other, select the menu item Database → Optimize → Profiler Analysis (see Figure 4.31); TOAD will display similar information for each run. Double-clicking on any of the functions in the lower panel will further break down the time-related data. You can easily see which part of your code is taking the longest to execute, as shown in Figure 4.32. In addition, you can filter out particular unit types and change the graphic displaying the data into a bar chart.

 TOAD 9.6 and 9.7 both support this type of profiler analysis.

Figure 4.31   Accessing Profile Analysis

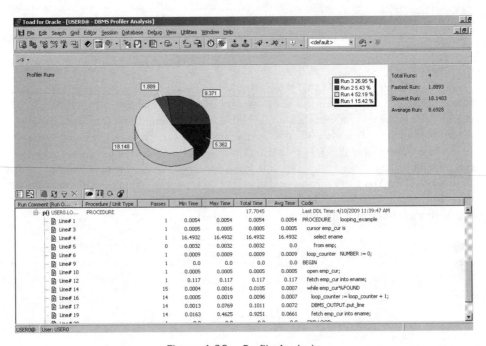

Figure 4.32   Profile Analysis

Setting Up Source Code Control

Source code control supports a systematic approach to code development, thereby ensuring that only one person makes changes to the code at any given time. Such systems also provide other benefits during code development—for example, security (only certain people can access certain code) and code change tracking. TOAD supports many source code control systems; check the TOADSoft.com site for a complete list of these systems.

It is easy to set up source code control with TOAD. Make sure your source code control software is installed and working properly. Then go to the "Source Control" category of the TOAD Options screen and fill in the appropriate options.

Using Source Code Control

TOAD allows you to check code into and out of any supported source code control package. Many source code control systems use "projects" to organize code. Pick the project with which you want to associate the code, and TOAD will then check it in. When you attempt to check out code, if someone else has it checked out, the source control package will issue a message—which TOAD will display—identifying who has the code checked out and typically when that person checked it out.

 The author does not claim to be a source code control expert.

Summary

This chapter covered the use of the TOAD PL/SQL Editor, illustrating most of the features available with this editor. The PL/SQL Editor not only enables you to easily create and work with packages, procedures, triggers, and functions, but also puts the full power of a symbolic debugger at your fingertips.

## 5

Database Reporting

TOAD contains a variety of useful reports. These reports include code advice reporting, database status reporting, and reports about any kind of object in the database (e.g., tables, indexes, code).

This chapter describes ways to modify these reports and build new ones using the Fast Reports interface (using the "Design Selected Report" option). Any TOAD data grid has a "Report" option that allows the SQL used to populate the data grid to be built into a formalized report that can then use this standardized reporting interface.

This chapter also describes how to build an HTML file that documents all objects and relationships per database schema.

The TOAD Report Manager contains a variety of useful reports that are standard parts of TOAD. It offers an easy interface with which to develop and manage (both development and execution management) nice-looking reports using Fast Reports, a graphical report development interface.

 Each new release of TOAD contains more and updated reports.

TOAD also allows for the easy generation of a related hyperlinked file that completely documents all the objects and relationships owned by a particular schema account.

TOAD Report Manager

The TOAD Report Manager can produce many useful reports—containing information about objects and useful information in the database—that are built using this report writer. The Report Manager can also store and reuse reports that were built with Fast Reports, a robust report-generating tool that will be discussed later in this chapter. The predefined reports found in the Report Manager fall into the following categories:

- Cluster Reports
- Code Xpert Reports

- DB Health/Performance Reports
- My Reports (user-defined reports)
- Schema Reports
- Sequence Reports
- Stored Program Reports
- Synonym Reports
- Table and Index Reports
- Trigger Reports
- View Reports

The TOAD Report Manager enables you to readily copy, modify, and execute these various reports. Figure 5.1 shows the Database → Reports → Report Manager menu access pathway; Figure 5.2 shows the Report Manager interface. The categories of delivered reports appear on the left side of the Report Manager screen. On the right side of the screen, the code editor displays the updatable SQL on which each report is based.

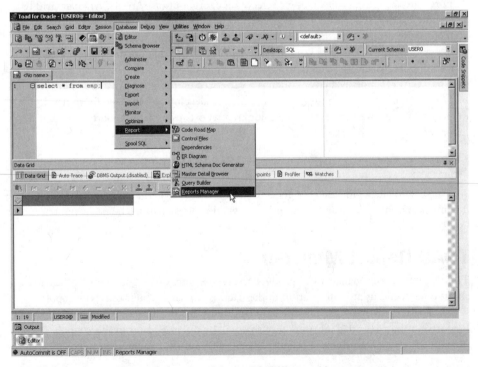

Figure 5.1   Opening the TOAD Report Manager

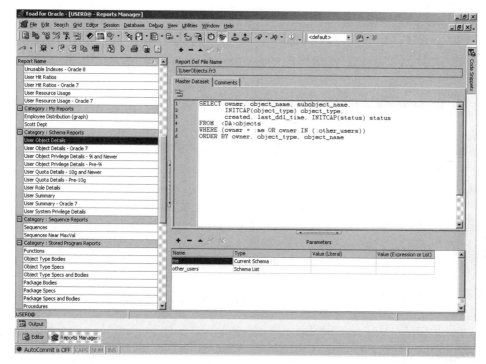

Figure 5.2   TOAD Report Manager Interface

The Report Manager toolbar allows for the report definitions to be

- Imported or exported.
- Copied.
- Renamed.
- Printed.
- Set up for external execution.
- Scheduled for later execution.

This toolbar includes the following buttons:

Export Report Definitions (drop-down options that let you manage the type of export)

Import Report Definition Files

Import All Report Definition Files in a Directory

Copy Report Definition Files

Rename or Change Category

Design Selected Report (using the Fast Reports interface)

Run Selected Report

Print Selected Reports

Generate Command Line File for Selected Reports

Schedule

Report Execution

The TOAD Report Manager interface allows you to run any report both quickly and easily. Simply click on the desired report and then click the "Run Selected Report" button. Figure 5.3 shows the execution of the User Objects report; following its execution, this report is displayed in the TOAD Previewer. Notice the toolbar that appears along the top of the display; its options enable you to print the report, save the report, and search for text strings in the report. There is also an icon to export the report to a variety of formats, including PDF, rich text, Excel, and JPG.

Clicking the "Print Selected Reports" button will display the printer selection options and printing instructions; see Figure 5.4. This type of execution will create the selected reports and send the output directly to the selected printer.

TOAD can also build a script to run these reports from a scheduler (i.e., execute the reports from outside the TOAD interface). The "Select Command Line File for Selected Reports" function will generate a .txt file with the necessary command to run the selected reports from a command-line prompt or a scheduler process, for example. Notice the various output options in Figure 5.5. If you click on the "Generate Command Line File for Selected Reports" button on the far right side of the Report Manager toolbar, TOAD will generate the code for the User Objects report, as shown in Figure 5.6.

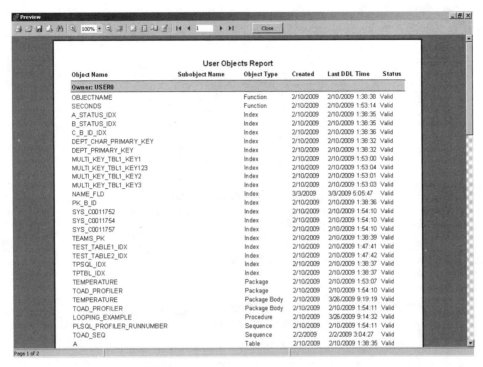

Figure 5.3   TOAD Report Execution

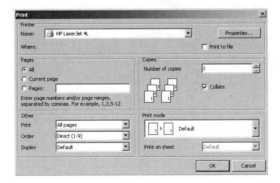

Figure 5.4   TOAD Report Printing

TOAD must be installed on the computer that is running this script.

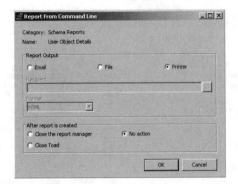

Figure 5.5   TOAD Command-Line Setup

Figure 5.6   TOAD Command-Line File Contents

Building Reports Using Fast Reports

You can also use the TOAD Fast Reports interface to format any data grid output. Figure 5.7 shows a simple query, the results of that query, and the right-click context menu with the "Report" option selected. Clicking this option will bring up the Fast Reports interface shown in Figure 5.8.

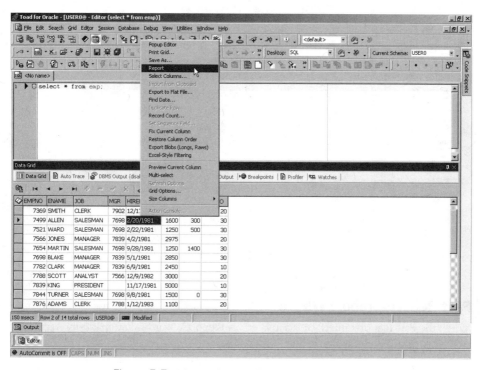

Figure 5.7   Accessing the Fast Reports Interface

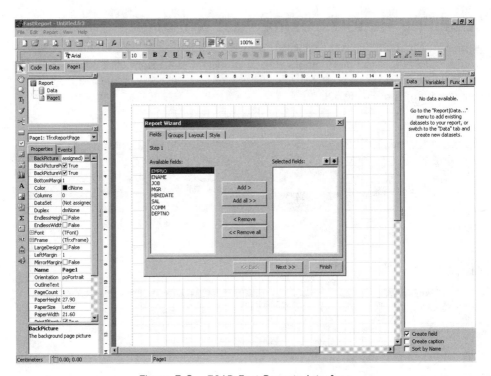

Figure 5.8   TOAD Fast Reports Interface

Fast Reports Report Wizard

When the Fast Reports interface is activated, its Report Wizard is automatically started as well. This wizard presents four tabs:

- Fields
- Groups
- Layout
- Style

This wizard allows you to organize the same results from the data grid into a nice-looking report. On the first tab, you can select the fields that should appear in the report. Figure 5.9 shows the "Groups" tab, which allows you to select control break fields. In this example, the same data grid information is displayed as in previously created reports; be aware, however, that the output of this option depends an ORDER BY clause in the SQL.

The "Layout" tab (see Figure 5.10) allows you to choose among several basic report formats. Figure 5.11 shows the basic report styles.

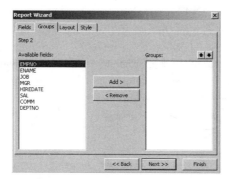

Figure 5.9   TOAD Report Wizard: Group Tab

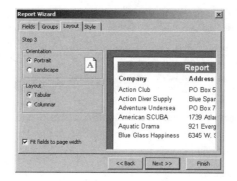

Figure 5.10   TOAD Report Wizard: Layout Tab

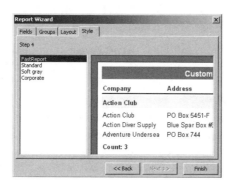

Figure 5.11   TOAD Report Wizard: Style Tab

Figure 5.12 shows the default Fast Reports layout using the fields from the data grid. Notice the data selection on the right side of the image. Also notice the properties pallet and the three tabs along the left side of the screen. The properties pallet, in combination with the button icons found along the far left side of the screen, allow you to make just about any change to this report—for example, inserting images, adding charts, using additional data sources, and changing the background. In the center of each property pallet, along the edge, is a series of small dots. Clicking on these dots hides or expands the associated pallet, giving you a larger view of the report layout.

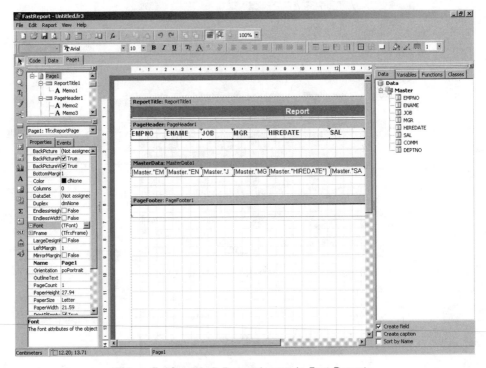

Figure 5.12   TOAD Report Layout in Fast Reports

Executing Fast Reports

To execute your report, click on the "Code" tab on the upper-left side of the Fast Reports interface. This will expose a series of buttons that make the code that executes the report visible; see Figure 5.13. Fast Reports includes a real-time debugger that supports the user's total control over and visualization of the report execution process. This execution script can be saved into various language formats. Clicking the green "Execute Report" button generates the report from this interface.

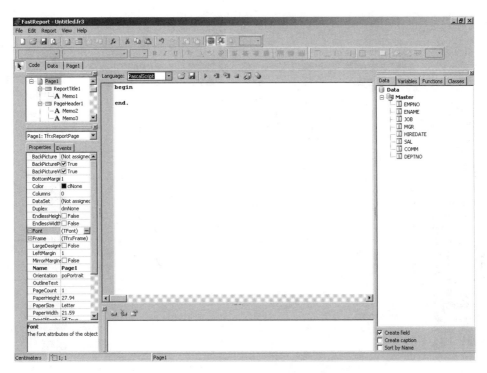

Figure 5.13   Executing Reports from Fast Reports

Figure 5.14 shows the report built using the Report Wizard within the Fast Reports interface. Click the "Close" button to close this window and return to the Fast Reports interface.

Building Fast Reports

Fast Reports is a full–featured report writer. This interface can be used to modify an existing report, modify reports generated from the Report Wizard, or build reports from scratch.

This section introduces you to the various components of the Report Writer interface and illustrates how you can change the report and column headings. The coverage here is quite brief, however: An entire book could be written on just this interface alone!

 Download the complete Fast Reports documentation file from fast-report.com/en/ documentation. This chapter provides a brief introduction to the Fast Reports interface, but the full documentation covers this interface in complete detail.

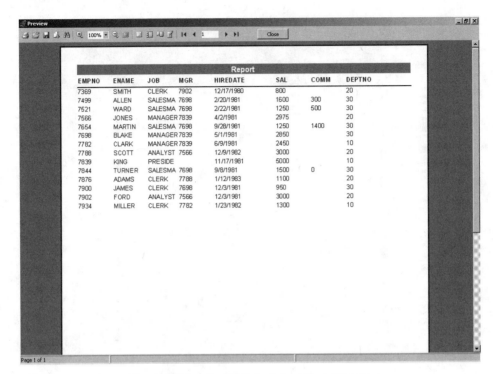

Figure 5.14   Report Output from Fast Reports

Notice the data pallet on the right side of Figure 5.12. This pallet controls the data from Oracle, any variables assigned to the report (for totals and calculations), and an entire series of functions and classes that can be applied to various parts or the entire report.

The upper-left pallet is the navigator pallet that allows you to see the various components of the report and determine which report object is currently selected. The lower-left pallet is object sensitive. In other words, it will be active for any object selected in the report, allowing for the various functions and visual attributes of that object to be added or changed.

 To select multiple objects, use the multiple-select features inherent to the Microsoft Windows environment. Click on one object, hold the Shift button down, and click on the end of a row of objects to select all of these objects simultaneously. Any changes made in the property pallet or by using the formatting buttons will be applied to all of the selected items.

Figure 5.15 shows the "Variable" tab of the data pallet. A variety of predefined variables (e.g., page numbers, date and time stamps) can be added to the report with a drag-and-drop operation, as illustrated here with the Page # column.

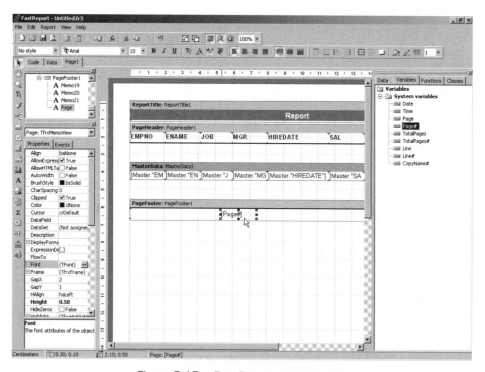

Figure 5.15   Fast Reports: Variable Tab

Two toolbars along the top of the Fast Reports interface allow for reports to be saved and opened; font color, size, and shape to be controlled; and additional items to be added to the report. The top toolbar controls various features about the report. It includes the following buttons:

New Report

Open Report

Save Report

Preview Report

New Report Page

New Dialog Page

Delete Page

Page Settings

Variables

Cut

Copy

Paste

Undo

Redo

Group

Ungroup

Show Grid

Align to Grid

Fit to Grid

Zoom

The second toolbar mostly controls the appearance of items in the report. It includes the following buttons:

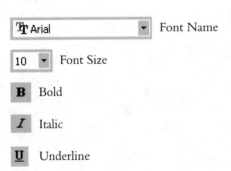

Font Name

Font Size

Bold

Italic

Underline

Tr   Font Settings

A   Font Color

ab   Highlight

Text Rotation

The remaining buttons on this toolbar control the text alignment, frame outline, shadowing, frame style, and background colors.

To change any item in the report, simply click on the item and apply the changes. Figure 5.16 shows the *ENAME* heading in a memo box (double-click on any of the report items). The text of this item can be easily changed. The "Format" tab in this panel also allows you to apply various functions to this item (e.g., if it were a number, then the number could be formatted); the "Highlight" tab allows you to change the item's colors.

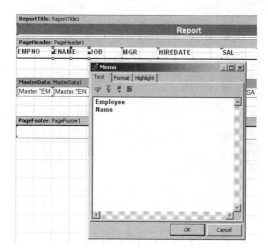

Figure 5.16   Modifying Report Fields

Clicking the "Preview" button on the top toolbar displays the report as it currently exists. Saving the report will save the report in a "Reports" folder (Documents and Settings → User → Application Data → Quest Software → TOAD for Oracle → 9.7 → User Files → Reports) along with the other reports that came with TOAD; see Figures 5.17 and 5.18.

Figure 5.17　Saving Reports

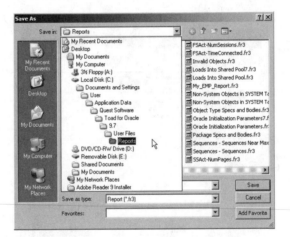

Figure 5.18　Actual Report Location

Adding Reports to the TOAD Report Manager

It is easy to add new reports to the TOAD Report Manager. To add new reports built with the Fast Reports interface, start the Report Manager using the following menu items: Database → Report → Reports Manager. See Figure 5.19.

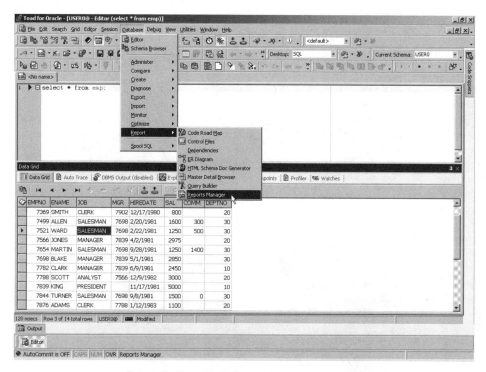

Figure 5.19   TOAD Report Manager Interface

Highlight the category on the left where the report should be added and click the "Add Report" button (in the middle above the report definition panel). TOAD will display the report category you highlighted in a dialog box; see Figure 5.20. Click "OK" if this is the category to which you want the report added. TOAD will then open a new dialog box allowing you to name the report, as shown in Figure 5.21.

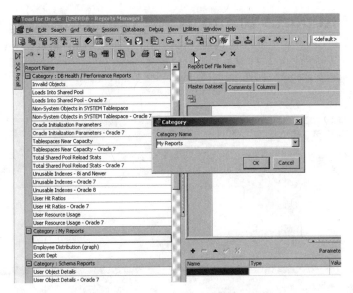

Figure 5.20   Report Category Dialog Box

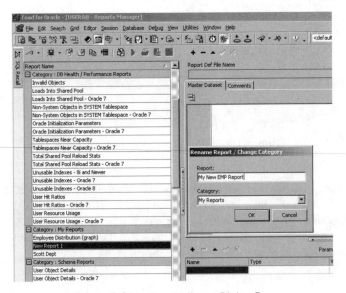

Figure 5.21   Report Name Dialog Box

You may use the copy-and-paste technique to obtain the original SQL from the SQL Editor that was used to design the report being added. Alternatively, you may enter the exact SQL again into the master data set panel; see Figure 5.22.

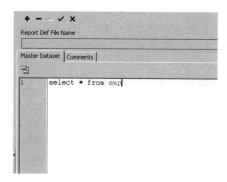

Figure 5.22   Master Dataset SQL

Next, click the "Design Selected Reports" button on the Report Manager toolbar. Open the report previously developed using Fast Reports; see Figure 5.23.

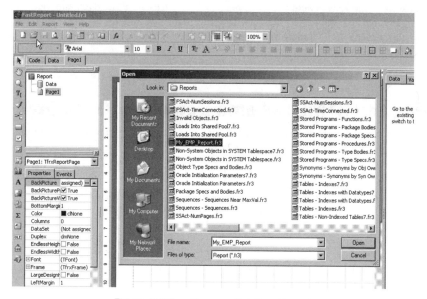

Figure 5.23   Open an Existing Report

Close the Fast Reports interface. As shown in Figure 5.24, your report definition now appears along with your SQL in the Report Manager. This report can now be run, scheduled, and modified just like any other report stored in the Report Manager.

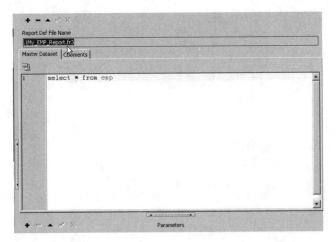

Figure 5.24   Added Report in the Report Manager

 Take your specialty scripts and build reports for them in the SQL Editor, and then add those reports to the Report Manager. Not only does Fast Reports generate a nice-looking report, but the TOAD Report Manager also provides a convenient place to organize and execute your scripts.

Using the HTML Schema Document Generator

TOAD can create a hyperlinked document for any schema in the database. This HTML document can then be viewed outside of TOAD.

To create the schema document, select Database → Report → HTML Schema Doc Generator. See Figure 5.25.

Next, select one or more schemas to be included in the report on the "Sources" tab. Figure 5.26 shows the SCOTT schema being selected.

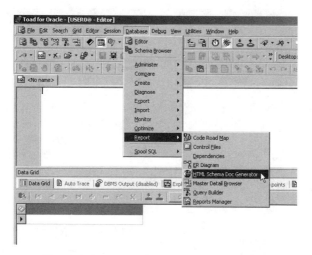

Figure 5.25   HTML Schema Doc Generator

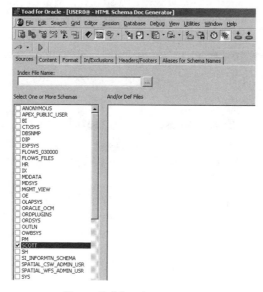

Figure 5.26   Sources Tab

The "Content" tab (see Figure 5.27) shows the various objects that can be included in the output document. The other tabs control the appearance, headings, and other attributes of the report itself.

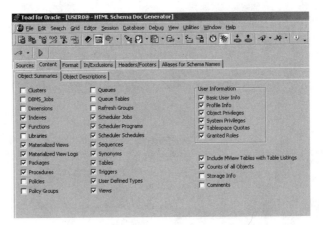

Figure 5.27   Content Tab

Click the green "Begin HTML Schema Doc Generation" button. You will be prompted for a name and a location in which to save the HTML document. Once the schema document is generated, TOAD will ask you if you wish to view the file. The HTML document can then be viewed in a Web browser, as shown in Figure 5.28.

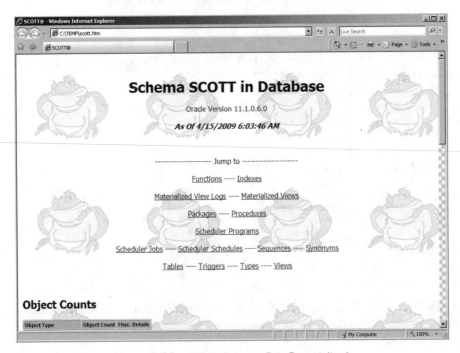

Figure 5.28   HTML Schema Doc Report (top)

Figure 5.29 shows the various information associated with this schema. You can click on the items of interest (i.e., the links found near the top of the report; see Figure 5.28) to drill into the report as illustrated in Figure 5.30.

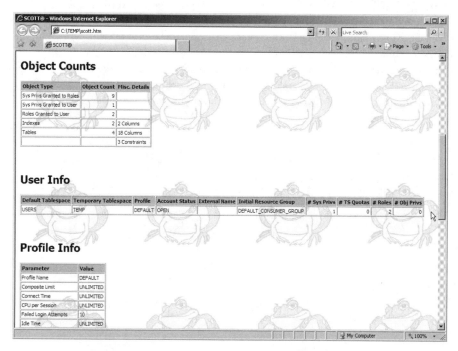

Figure 5.29   HTML Schema Doc Report (Info)

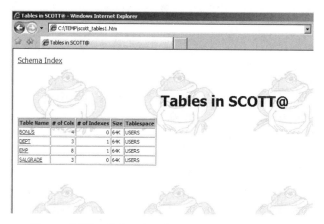

Figure 5.30   Using the HTML Schema Doc Report

Summary

This chapter covered the processes of generating, modifying, and saving the various reports that come with TOAD by using the Report Manager. Reports can be built from any data grid within TOAD, and these reports can then be added to the Report Manager for better report management and future execution. This chapter also described how you can use TOAD to build an HTML document that contains useful information about any schema account in Oracle.

Building reports based on your own scripts, then adding them to the Report Manager, will allow you to better manage and subsequently execute your own scripts. Using the HTML Schema Generator allows you to learn about your newly assigned applications and discover the intricacies of each application in an HTML format.

## 6

Tuning Tools in TOAD

The Oracle database contains a variety of useful information when it comes to SQL and database performance monitoring and tuning. This chapter focuses on a variety of useful tuning topics that are integrated into TOAD.

Oracle Tuning Using TOAD

SQL explain plans provide useful information about how Oracle will process the SQL statement and perform the requested tasks. TOAD has several options for displaying these explain plans in useful formats. Auto trace is the ability to see the statistics from Oracle that the particular SQL statement generated when executing.

The Oracle Trace facility, also known as a 10046 SQL trace (pronounced 10-046), captures all SQL (both application code and SQL generated by Oracle) for either an individual SQL statement or an entire user session. TOAD allows for this trace to be turned on and off for user sessions as well as for visualizing the contents of the trace file.

StatsPack is an Oracle database statistics collection facility. It collects statistics on a scheduled basis, with each collection called a "snapshot." StatsPack does not reference any particular interval as a standard, because the interval may change depending on usage. For instance, hourly intervals are generally good choices for showing trends, whereas smaller intervals are good options for performing more detailed investigations. TOAD has a nice interface to this facility, allowing for additional statistics collections to be performed and for the report to be viewed either singly or in a series of useful graphs.

Automated Workload Repository (AWR) is another statistical feature of Oracle 10g and later versions. It automatically collects a variety of application and database information, which it then stores for the better part of a week (unless the timing is manually adjusted). TOAD has a great facility to display this information in a variety of formats.

 Some of these features, such as AWR, require additional licenses from Oracle. Check with your DBA to make sure you are licensed to view this information.

SQL Explain Plans/Auto Trace

When Oracle processes a submitted SQL statement, it creates an execution plan—that is, the path that Oracle will follow to resolve the requested data from the SQL statement. The visualization of this execution plan is called an explain plan. TOAD displays explain plans in a variety of formats, as described in this section.

Explain Plans

The TOAD SQL Editor contains an "Explain Plan" tab (see Figure 6.1). Chapter 3 covers the buttons on the third toolbar of SQL Editor, which include the "Explain Plan" button. Clicking this button generates an explain plan for the SQL in the editor, the SQL that is highlighted, or the SQL on which the cursor is currently positioned.

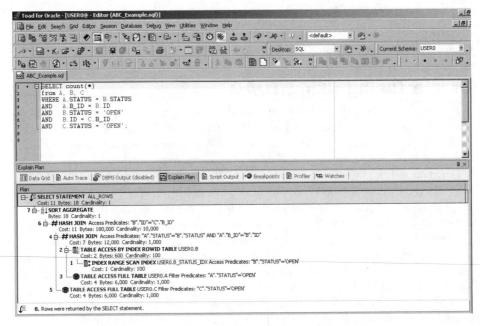

Figure 6.1   TOAD Explain Plan Tab

🔍 If the "Explain Plan" tab is not visible, right-click in the SQL Editor window, select "Desktop Panels," and click the "Explain Plan" option.

✏️ The goal of this chapter is to introduce you to the various tuning tools and performance information available within TOAD. It is beyond the scope of this chapter to discuss the contents of this explain plan or to offer any performance analysis information.

SQL explain plans indicate how Oracle will process SQL statements and script. TOAD, in turn, displays this valuable information in its "Explain Plan" tab. To adjust this display, right-click the explain plan and select "Display Mode," as illustrated in Figure 6.2. Notice the various display options in the figure.

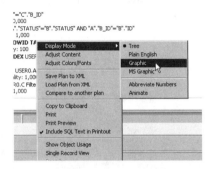

Figure 6.2   TOAD Explain Plan: Display Options

The author prefers the display of the explain plan as it appears in Figure 6.1. This view shows the join conditions and statistics, along with the explain plan text.

Figure 6.3 shows the "Adjust Content" option (right-click on the explain plan and select "Adjust Content"). In this panel, you can select the information that is displayed in Figure 6.1 and indicate whether it should appear on the same line with the other items or appear as a separate column in the same "Explain Plan" tab.

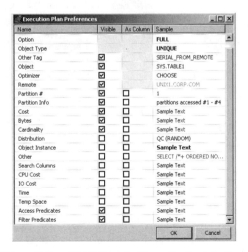

Figure 6.3   TOAD Explain Plan: Content Options

TOAD can also visualize and compare two separate explain plans. To access this view, right-click on the explain plan and select "Compare to another plan" from the context menu (see Figure 6.4). The resulting explain plan comparison will look like Figure 6.5, complete with comments. Notice the display mode in the upper-right corner. TOAD can compare the various display modes as well.

Figure 6.4   TOAD Explain Plan:
Compare to Another Plan Options

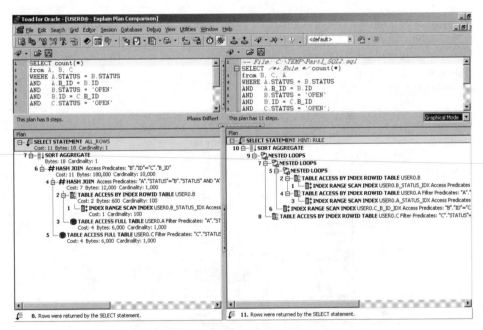

Figure 6.5   TOAD Explain Plan: Compare to Another Plan Panel

Statistics Using Auto Trace

The auto trace facility in Oracle provides run-time statistics for a particular SQL statement; TOAD can also display these statistics. To calculate and display these data, right-click on the SQL being investigated and then click the "Auto Trace" option, as shown in Figure 6.6. When you re-execute the SQL, the run-time statistics will populate the "Auto Trace" tab; see Figure 6.7. If this tab does not appear in your SQL Editor window, right-click on the SQL Editor, select "Desktop Panels," and then click the "Auto Trace" option.

Figure 6.6   Enabling Auto Trace

 The Auto Trace facility (as well as SGA Trace and Oracle Trace) requires that the user have access to the Oracle dictionary views *V$Sesstat*, *V$Session*, and *V$Statname*. Special privileges will need to be granted to the TOAD users to perform some of these features.

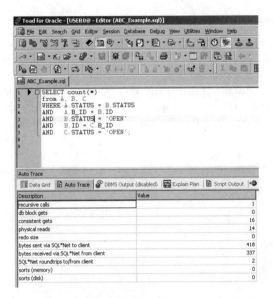

Figure 6.7   Displaying SQL Statement Statistics

Statistics Using SGA Trace

TOAD can also display SQL statistics via the SGA Trace facility, using the $V\$$ tables. To access this feature via the menu bar, select Database → Monitor → SGA Trace/Optimization (see Figure 6.8). TOAD will display similar SQL statistics for SQL that is currently in the library cache; see Figure 6.9.

Figure 6.8   Accessing SGA Trace

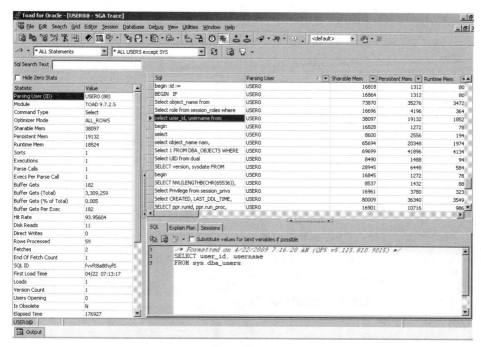

Figure 6.9   Displaying SQL Statement Statistics via SGA Trace

Notice that the data can sorted based on the various columns that appear on the upper-right side of this panel. Selecting a SQL statement in this area will then display the individual statistics on the left side of the panel as well as the SQL statement itself and an explain plan.

Oracle Trace Facility

Oracle's Trace facility (also known as SQL Trace or 10046 SQL Trace) captures the SQL statements generated by an application and places them in a single file called a trace file or a .trc file. This trace is turned on before a test commences (or prior to when a problem will be encountered) and must be turned off after the test is complete or the problem has surfaced. The resulting trace file contains raw information about every SQL statement, both application SQL and dictionary SQL (called recursive SQL), and their associated explain plans, statistics, and wait event information.

The "Creating Trace Files" section discusses how to turn on and off this facility and describes where the trace file is created. The "Analyzing Trace Files" section focuses on how the raw SQL data are transformed into meaningful information.

Creating Trace Files

SQL Trace can be turned on for the following types of sessions:

- The current user session (typically used during testing by developers)
- Other user sessions (typically used to troubleshoot a problem)
- Across the entire database (typically requested by Oracle Support)

The Session Browser (see Figure 6.10) is the best way to turn SQL Trace on and off for a specific user account. The Session Browser can be accessed via the fourth button on the first toolbar (as discussed in Chapter 3).

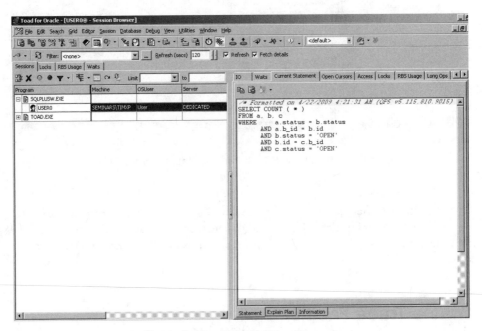

Figure 6.10   TOAD Session Browser

 To use the Session Browser, TOAD users will need special privileges allowing them access to the DBMS_SESSION package.

The Session Browser shows a variety of information. On the left side of the screen is a list of the logged-in users and the applications they are running. When an application is selected, useful information, such as the current SQL statement, is displayed on the right side of the screen, as shown in Figure 6.10.

The Session Browser toolbar includes two key buttons:

Start Trace

Stop Trace

When in the Session Browser, highlight the user session (as illustrated in Figure 6.11) and click the "Start Trace" button. A dialog box will appear, as shown in Figure 6.12. This dialog box contains various options that can be applied when capturing the SQL statement information. Click "OK" on this panel to initiate a SQL trace session.

Figure 6.11   A SQL*Plus User Session

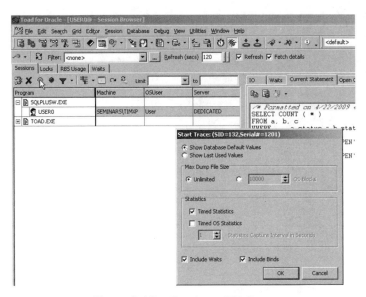

Figure 6.12   Starting a SQL Trace

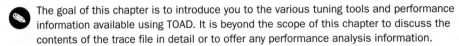

The goal of this chapter is to introduce you to the various tuning tools and performance information available using TOAD. It is beyond the scope of this chapter to discuss the contents of the trace file in detail or to offer any performance analysis information.

The author always captures wait and bind variable information in these trace files.

The SQL trace file will be created in the location determined by the Oracle initialization parameter *USER_DUMP_DEST*. TOAD can show this location via Oracle Parameters, which is accessed via the menu bar: Database → Administer option (see Figure 6.13). The resulting display shows the values of all the initialization parameters; see Figure 6.14. TOAD can also display this information via the menu item TOAD Report Manager → Oracle Initialization Parameters, as shown in Figure 6.15.

Figure 6.13   Displaying Oracle Initialization Parameters

Figure 6.14   Oracle Initialization Parameters

Name	Value
star_transformation_enabled	FALSE
statistics_level	TYPICAL
streams_pool_size	0
tape_asynch_io	TRUE
thread	0
timed_os_statistics	0
timed_statistics	TRUE
tracefile_identifier	
trace_enabled	TRUE
transactions	187
transactions_per_rollback_segment	5
undo_management	AUTO
undo_retention	900
undo_tablespace	UNDOTBS1
user_dump_dest	C:\ORACLE\PRODUCT\10.2.0\ADMIN\ORAXP10G\UDUMP
use_indirect_data_buffers	FALSE
utl_file_dir	c:\temp\
workarea_size_policy	AUTO

Figure 6.15   Oracle Initialization Parameters
Report via TOAD Report Manager

Figure 6.16 shows the SQL*Plus session running a couple of SQL statements with the SQL trace initiated.

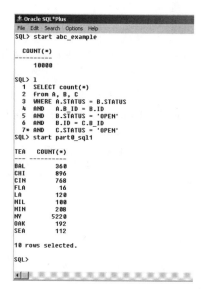

Figure 6.16   SQL Trace Initiated on a SQL*Plus Session

After the test has been completed, click the "Stop Trace" button in the Session Browser to stop the SQL Trace process. TOAD will pop up a box indicating that the SQL trace has been stopped.

Figure 6.17 shows the SQL Trace file in the *USER_DUMP_DEST* location. Notice the name of the file contains the Oracle SID, the text "_ora_", and the process identifier for that particular user session. The file carries a ".trc" suffix as well.

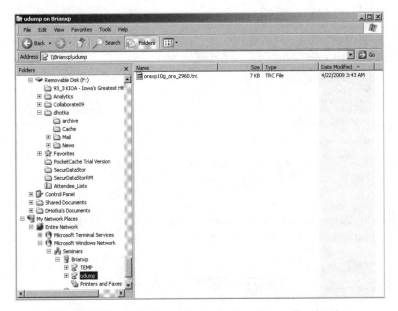

Figure 6.17   SQL Trace File in the User Dump Destination

Analyzing Trace Files

Oracle supplies the character-mode TKProf tool to organize and display the contents of trace files. TOAD's Trace File Browser organizes the contents of these trace files a bit differently and displays the information in a somewhat more attractive format.

The TKProf interface from TOAD is accessed via the menu bar: Database → Diagnose → TKProf Interface (see Figure 6.18).

Figure 6.18   Accessing TKProf Interface

This menu item starts the TKProf Wizard. Within this wizard, you click on the arrow next to the files button and select "Browse Windows Files" to find the desired files; see Figure 6.19.

 The author always copies or FTPs these trace files to his local workstation for analysis. TKProf needs to create an output file and usually the UDUMP folder is not amenable to write access.

Figure 6.19   Starting the TKProf Wizard

In Figure 6.20, the trace file that was generated in the prior section is selected. Highlight the trace file of interest, and click "Open" to open this file.

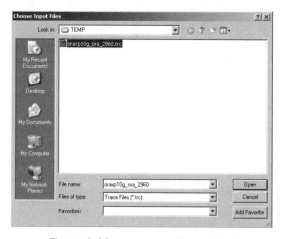

Figure 6.20   Accessing Trace Files

Figure 6.21 shows the trace file name and location appearing in the TKProf Wizard. Click "Next" to continue.

Figure 6.21   Trace File in TKProf Wizard

Figure 6.22 shows the sort options. TKProf can organize the SQL statements so that they will be displayed for any of these statistical categories.

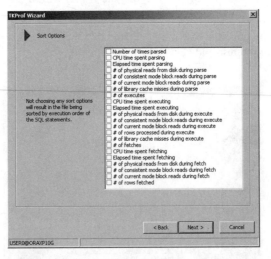

Figure 6.22   TKProf Wizard Sort Options

Figure 6.23 illustrates a key panel in the TKProf Wizard. Using this panel, you can specify a certain number of SQL to be displayed (typically used in conjunction with the sort options), prevent the display of recursive SQL, and implement various execution options. The output of the TKProf Wizard will be displayed in the TOAD default text editor—in this example, using Notepad. Figure 6.24 shows the TKProf output from the trace file generated in this series of examples.

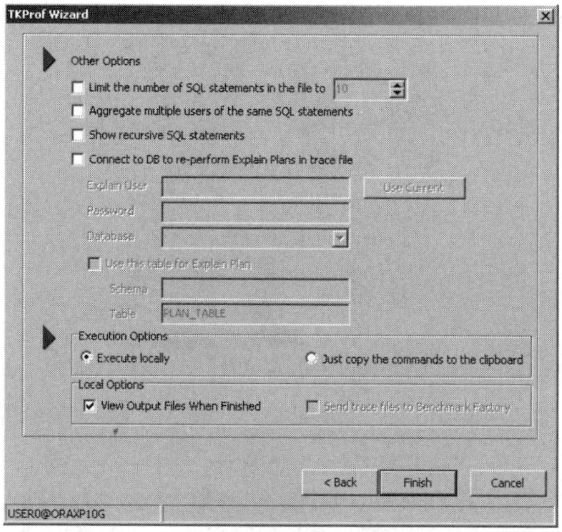

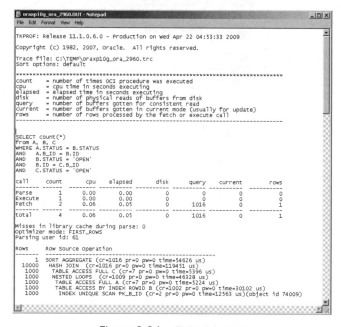

Figure 6.23   TKProf Wizard Output Control Panel

Figure 6.24   TKProf Output

The Trace File Browser is a TOAD enhancement intended for processing SQL trace files. Figure 6.25 shows the menu item needed to access this interface: Database → Diagnose → Trace File Browser. Click the "Open" button (the leftmost button on the Trace File Browser toolbar) to open the SQL trace file for processing; see Figure 6.26.

Figure 6.25   Accessing TOAD's Trace File Browser

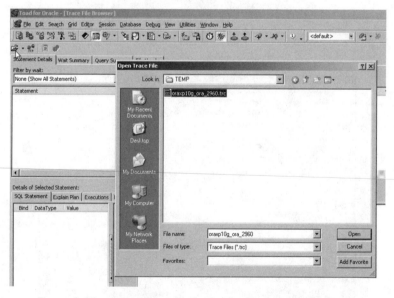

Figure 6.26   Accessing SQL Trace Files via Trace File Browser

Figure 6.27 illustrates all of the options available for drilling into the SQL trace file. In the upper area of the interface, the Trace File Browser allows you to change the view of the contained SQL based on a variety of useful areas of interest; in the lower section of the interface, you view the associated statistics and other related information on a per SQL statement basis. Tabs conveniently organize all of this information.

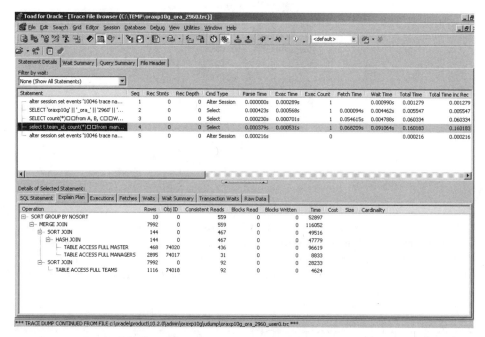

Figure 6.27   Viewing SQL Trace Files Using Trace File Browser

StatsPack Reporting

StatsPack is a snapshot statistical collection facility that most shops working with TOAD run. The DBA staff is typically charged with maintaining this environment. StatsPack output can be useful for the tasks:

- Diagnosing database performance issues
- Database growth trend analysis
- General monitoring

 This feature is available only in conjunction with TOAD's "Admin" option.

TOAD contains a convenient method for displaying this information, without requiring the help of your DBA or other IT staff members. Figure 6.28 shows the menu item used to access this interface: Database → Monitor → StatsPack Browser.

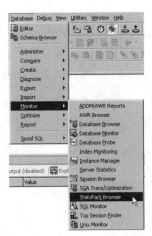

Figure 6.28   Accessing StatsPack Browser

Figure 6.29 shows the StatsPack Browser. The upper-left part of this panel displays the various statistical snapshots available for the data. StatsPack reporting always involves a comparison of two of these snapshots. Select two of these collections by clicking on the box (checking the box), and then click on the specific reports that are of interest for the type of analysis desired.

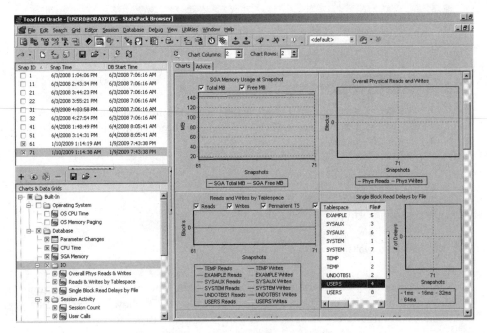

Figure 6.29   StatsPack Browser

If you select multiple snapshots, the details in all of the selected snapshots can then be graphed. This technique is a convenient way to discover trends in the graphs.

You can also right-click on two selected snapshots to compare them. Figure 6.30 shows the various options, including the highlighted option of running the StatsPack Report for the selected snapshots. The resulting character-mode report appears in Figure 6.31.

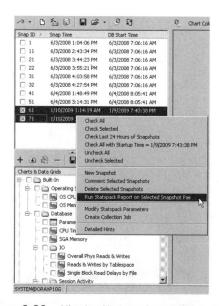

Figure 6.30 Viewing Various StatsPack Options

sp_report_ORAXP10G_61_71 - Notepad

File Edit Format View Help

```
STATSPACK report for

Database    DB Id    Instance     Inst Num Startup Time    Release     RAC
~~~~~~~~ ----------- ------------ -------- --------------- ----------- ---
           1694157431 oraxp10g           1 09-Jan-09 19:43 10.2.0.1.0  NO

Host  Name:   BRIANXP          Num CPUs:    1        Phys Memory (MB):      495
~~~~

Snapshot       Snap Id     Snap Time      Sessions Curs/Sess Comment
~~~~~~~~    ---------- ------------------ -------- --------- -------------------
Begin Snap:         61 10-Jan-09 01:14:19       64       4.0
  End Snap:         71 10-Jan-09 01:14:38       64       4.4
   Elapsed:                0.32 (mins)

Cache Sizes                       Begin        End
~~~~~~~~~~~                  ---------- ----------
               Buffer Cache:        80M              Std Block Size:         8K
           Shared Pool Size:        68M                  Log Buffer:     2,832K

Load Profile                            Per Second       Per Transaction
~~~~~~~~~~~~                       ---------------       ---------------
                  Redo size:             38,607.58            733,544.00
              Logical reads:                350.53              6,660.00
              Block changes:                 58.47              1,111.00
             Physical reads:                 11.79                224.00
            Physical writes:                  0.00                  0.00
                 User calls:                  1.58                 30.00
                     Parses:                 53.16              1,010.00
                Hard parses:                  5.68                108.00
                      Sorts:                 26.63                506.00
                     Logons:                  0.00                  0.00
                   Executes:                 97.11              1,845.00
               Transactions:                  0.05
```

Figure 6.31 Character-Mode StatsPack Report

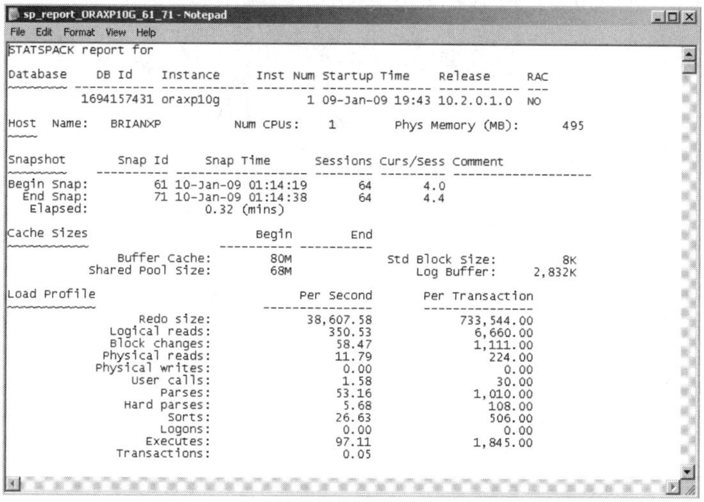

Automated Workload Repository Reporting

Oracle database versions 10 and 11 both maintain a variety of near-real-time statistics. These statistics are known as the Automated Workload Repository (AWR) and are used by a variety of Oracle processes for performance monitoring, among other things. TOAD has a convenient interface that organizes and displays this collected information as well.

 This feature is available only in conjunction with TOAD's "Admin" option.

Figure 6.32 shows the menu item Database → Monitor → ADDM/AWR Reports. Figures 6.33 through 6.35 illustrate the variety of information that is available using this interface.

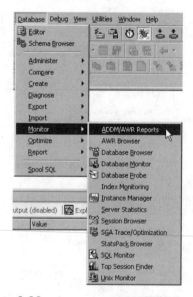

Figure 6.32   Accessing ADDM/AWR Reports

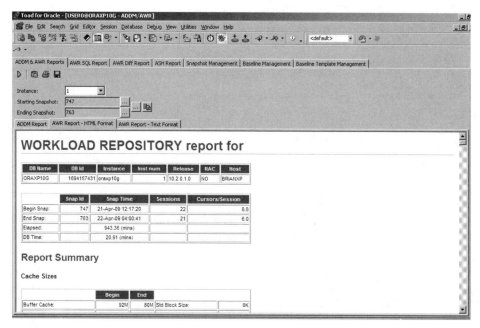

Figure 6.33   Workload Repository Report

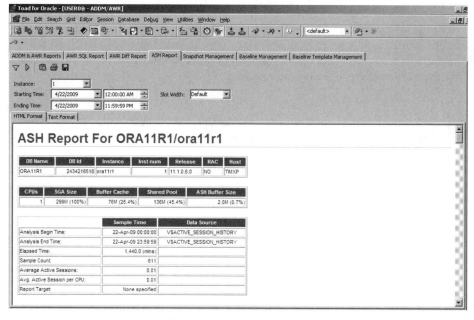

Figure 6.34   ASH Report

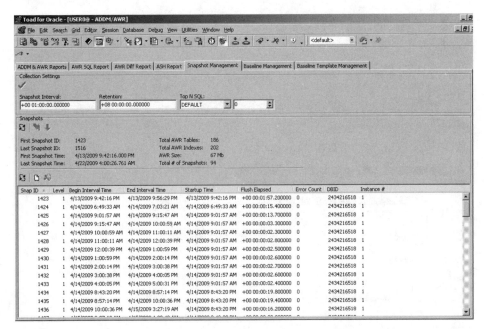

Figure 6.35   AWR Snapshot Management Report

The next menu item visible in Figure 6.31 is the AWR Browser. Figure 6.36 illustrates the type of analysis performed by this interface, which works similarly to the StatsPack Browser. Specifically, you select two snapshots of interest (usually based on time intervals) and then click on the graphs to compare them.

 If you select multiple snapshots, the details in all of the selected snapshots can be graphed. This technique is a convenient way to discover trends in the graphs.

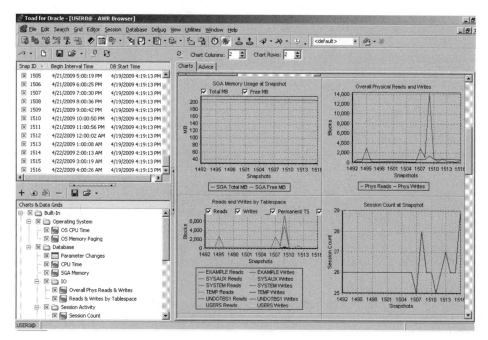

Figure 6.36   AWR Browser

Summary

This chapter covered various tuning topics. TOAD offers a nice explain plan area that can be adjusted to the database environment in which TOAD is running. It can also display individual SQL statistics using Oracle's auto trace feature. TOAD has the ability to start and stop Oracle SQL traces and provides a nice GUI interface to TKProf (a command-line tool). In addition, TOAD has a comprehensive trace analyzer feature, can generate StatsPack reports, and can display AWR information as necessary.

## 7

Database Management

Although TOAD began its life and has historically been regarded as the Tool for Oracle Application Development, it has evolved into so much more over the past few years. TOAD has features for data or business analysts, database application developers, more senior or professional database application developers, and so on, up to and including database administrators (DBAs). In fact, informal polls conducted at TOAD user group meetings and other Oracle conferences suggest that approximately 40% of TOAD users are truly DBAs or routinely perform various and often complex database management tasks. Clearly, TOAD has become much more than just a SQL and PL/SQL developers' tool. It is now a legitimate database management offering, often complementing or sometimes supplanting tools such as Oracle's Enterprise Manager (OEM) and Embarcadero's DB Artisan.

Regardless of whether your job title includes the three letters "DBA," you can and should use TOAD to perform any database administrative tasks required to support your organization databases and database applications. For example, some companies hire database consultants and expect them to do everything, whereas other shops segregate "developers" and "DBAs," considering them to be separate job titles. From TOAD's perspective, it really does not matter. If you need to do any database administrative tasks, then TOAD is the tool of choice. Thus references to the term "DBA" in this book really mean anybody who's doing database administrative tasks, regardless of his or her actual job title. In fact, the DBA moniker was such a highly galvanizing term that the optional TOAD DBA Module has been renamed the DB Admin Module.

Be aware that many capabilities covered in this chapter are not part of the standard or basic TOAD product. To see which TOAD options you have bought (i.e., which license type you possess), simply choose Help → About from the main menu. The pop-up dialog will list your TOAD bundle and options. Most of the database administrative capabilities discussed in this chapter will require the previously mentioned optional DB Admin Module. When in doubt, you can generally check TOAD's online help in two places for instant clarification. First, look for help on a given feature (such as the Database Health Check), which will include the following note just under the help topic headline:

 Note: This TOAD feature is only available in the commercial version of TOAD with the optional DB Admin Module.

The second and often best place to look is the help topic for the DB Admin Module itself, which in turn sends you to toadsoft.com/DBA/dba.html.

A complete list of the TOAD DB Admin Module feature additions appears at the end of this chapter's summary. The items pointed out should make much more sense once you have read this chapter.

Database Health Check

There will be numerous times where you either wonder or get asked about the relative health of your database. In other words, "Is your database okay?" While that may seem like a highly subjective question, there are some guidelines by which a database can be statically reviewed and rated. We say statically, because the TOAD Database Health Check reports on those metrics at a given point in time. It's very much like a physician's report on a person's health. The doctor (i.e., TOAD) looks at the patient (i.e., the database) and measures many key metrics, such as height, weight, temperature, pulse, and blood pressure. These initial observations plus automatic scanning for numerous other common symptoms formulate the TOAD Database Health Check. Often the resulting report will diagnose what ails your database. It's covered first in this chapter because it should be your first line of defense. A "clean bill of health" from this report is a welcome sanity check to prevent wasting time. Why monitor a database looking for trouble when the basic configuration might be the issue—and an issue that can be fixed upfront?

To launch the Database Health Check, from the TOAD main menu select Database → Diagnose → DB Health Check. You will see the screen shown in Figure 7.1.

The left-hand side (LHS) of the screen lists all of your known databases, with the current database connection entry highlighted. You can select multiple items here, but note that such a choice will run the report for each and every selected database, and that could take a long while. Think back to the prior physician metaphor: You're asking for initial consultations with multiple doctors.

The remainder of the screen offers four tabs. The first tab ("Checks and Options") is where you will select the database heath checks to perform. There are 91 checks available. Again, the more you select, the bigger the report will be and the longer it may take to run. Note that some of these database checks possess to their immediate right a "Params" option. For example, rule #30 lists tablespaces with less than 10% free space remaining. Clicking the "Params" option will open the pop-up window shown in Figure 7.2, which lets you customize that threshold value. Note that the various checks and their parameters vary, so the pop-up windows are necessarily different.

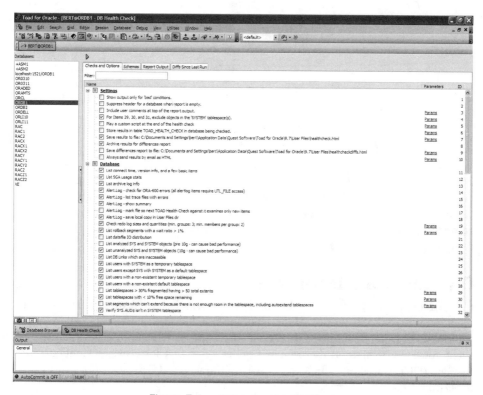

Figure 7.1   Database Health Check

Figure 7.2   Database Health Check: Params Pop-up

The second tab ("Schemas") offers a simple interface for filtering the schemas upon which the health checks will be run. Once you've selected your checks and schema filters, you simply click the green arrow toolbar icon. That will run the database health check report and display its output on the third tab ("Report Output"). The output here will be a tree view, with the health check findings or exceptions raised shown in bold and highlighted in red, as shown in Figure 7.3.

Figure 7.3   Database Health Check: Report Output

The fourth tab ("Diffs Since Last Run") is very useful when you are performing iterative health checks. This tab simply displays the same tree-view information as in the
"Report Output" tab, but with one major difference: It shows just those values that differ
between run N and $N + 1$. This feature allows you to perform iterative health checks,
thereby verifying that incremental improvements were, in fact, effective.

Creating New Databases

On occasion, you may want or need to create a new and fresh database. For example, you
might want to test some portion of the application, and it might be desirable to do so on
your local PC rather than using a database server. If you have the full Oracle database
client installed with all tools, then you may prefer to use Oracle's Database Configuration
Assistant (DCBA) to create a new local database. If not, then TOAD provides a very capable Database Creation Wizard.

To launch the Database Creation Wizard, from the TOAD main menu select Database →
Create → New Database. You will see the screen shown in Figure 7.4.

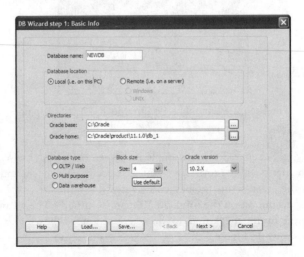

Figure 7.4   Database Creation Wizard: Step 1

Note that the first page of the wizard asks a few simple high-level questions, such as the database name, nature, block size, and Oracle version. The wizard can create new databases either locally or remotely. and for either Windows or UNIX. That's because the resulting output is either a Windows .BAT or UNIX .SH file, which are simply operating system command-line script files containing all the commands needed to create a database.

The TOAD Database Creation Wizard has six steps or pages. The second and third steps ask you questions about the target database server, such as how many CPUs, how much memory, how many users, and so on. TOAD will transform all these high-level environmental answers into corresponding detailed Oracle configuration parameter settings.

The fourth step asks you whether to use automatic or manual tablespace allocation. If you choose the automatic tablespace allocation option (recommended), then all you have to do is specify which disks can be used and how big the database should be, as shown in Figure 7.5.

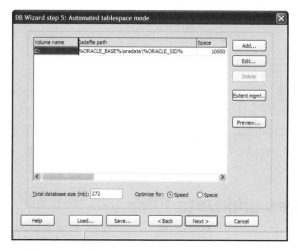

Figure 7.5   Database Creation Wizard: Step 5

If you choose the manual tablespace allocation method, then you will be presented with a more detailed screen where you must specify detailed information for each tablespace. Given that most users are not hard-core DBAs with intimate Oracle insight into optimal tablespace design and construction, you probably would be better served by sticking with the automatic method.

The final step in the Database Creation Wizard asks you for choices about two major options: Oracle components and script generation (see Figure 7.6). First, do you want things like the Oracle Spatial option supported and sample users created? Second, should TOAD create your database or generate the database creation script files? Regardless of the generation option you select, note the three buttons under the script generation location. This wizard will create three types of files that you can preview: the .BAT or .SH operating system command file to drive the process, the .SQL file for SQL*Plus for actually creating the database, and the "init.ora" file for the database parameter settings. You should preview all three files to verify your comfort with them. If there are things you dislike, click the "Back" button (shown in Figure 7.6) and revisit the prior Database Creation Wizard steps to effect any desired changes. Otherwise, just click the "Finish" button to complete the database creation script generation and optional execution of those scripts.

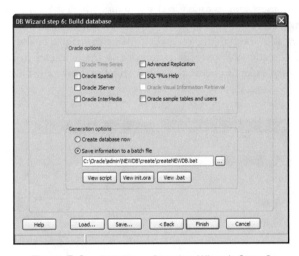

Figure 7.6　Database Creation Wizard: Step 6

Tablespaces and Data Files

Oracle tablespaces are the basic "logical" containers where users place all database objects that require or consume disk space. For example, basic tables and indexes consume disk space, so they must reside within a tablespace. Other database objects such as directories and external tables don't consume space, so they merely require an entry in the data dictionary. For those objects that consume space, a key database management task is to make sure that sufficient room exists for both today's and tomorrow's needs. You want to avoid Oracle error messages such as "cannot allocate extent." Thus tablespace and data file management are key, routine administrative tasks.

Because TOAD originally began as a developer's tool and then evolved into more, its tablespaces offerings are a little disjointed. We hope to see that inconsistency corrected in the future, but for now there are four locations within TOAD for performing tablespace administrative type tasks (which are explained in the following text):

- Database Browser → Space Usage
- Database Browser → Tablespaces

- Schema Browser → Tablespaces
- Main Menu → Administer → Tablespaces

The TOAD Database Browser (covered in Chapter 2) offers two ways to view and work with tablespaces. First, when the LHS focus is on the database instance, the right-hand side (RHS) offers the "Space Usage" tab. It provides simple "one-stop shopping" for seeing the 50,000-foot overview of your tablespace allocations and current consumptions (see Figure 7.7). Note that this tablespace management interface lacks a bar chart representation of the percentage consumed per tablespace. Even with this omission, it's a good first step along the way.

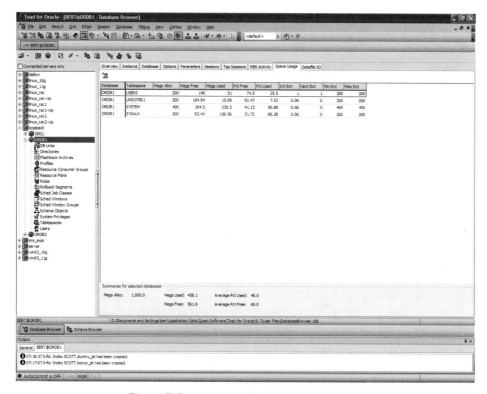

Figure 7.7   Database Browser: Space Usage

Second, when the Database Browser LHS focus is on the Tablespaces node under the database instance itself, the RHS offers a Tablespaces portion of the Schema Browser (the third way to work with tablespaces). Figure 7.8 shows this interface, which also lacks a bar chart representation of the percentage consumed per tablespace. A bar chart indicating the space consumed per data file for that specific tablespace is available, but you have to visit each tablespace to see the total or cumulative tablespace space consumption picture. Nevertheless, this interface does offer all the right-hand mouse (RHM) options and toolbar icons for numerous tablespace administrative tasks. Thus this tablespace interface will be one that you'll need to use frequently.

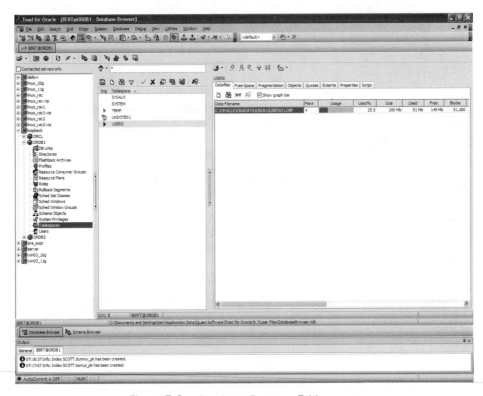

Figure 7.8   Database Browser: Tablespaces

Finally, TOAD offers a screen called "View Tablespaces" that presents much the same 50,000-foot view of tablespace information as the Database Browser "Space Usage" tab provides. To launch this screen, from the TOAD main menu select Database → Administer → Tablespaces. You will see the screen shown in Figure 7.9. Note that this screen offers three unique features not found in the other three tablespace interfaces: a bar chart representation of the percentage consumed per tablespace, plus the ability to record the history for both the space used over time and the IO bandwidth or load. When you first visit either the "Space History" or "IO History" tabs, a pop-up window will remind you to create the server-side tables and database jobs to track this information. You simply connect as the TOAD schema and click the "Create Space Manager Tables" icon on that tab.

Of special note is that the "Space History" tab offers the ability to forecast or predict your space needs. Based on your recent space usage history, it applies proven statistical models to predict your disk space needs over the next user-specified time interval (with 30 days being the default).

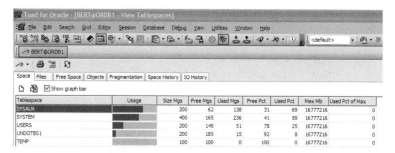

Figure 7.9   View Tablespaces Screen

Start-ups and Shut-downs

Just as in Windows, there are certain database administrative tasks that you might perform with TOAD that may not take effect until the next database restart. As a consequence, you will need a way to shut down and start up your databases. TOAD offers two ways to accomplish this task.

The TOAD Database Browser (covered in Chapter 2) offers a very simple way to manage your database instances. When the LHS focus is on the database instance, the RHM menu offers choices for database instance start-up, shut-down, and modification, as shown in Figure 7.10.

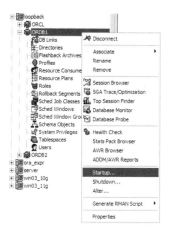

Figure 7.10   Database Browser: Instance Management

Performing these types of instance management operations requires you to supply parameters. For example, will the shut-down take place in normal, immediate, or abort mode? A pop-up window will prompt you for these values before any such operation is actually attempted. Once you supply your choices and click "OK," then the instance management operation will be initiated.

Unfortunately, this approach does not work well for those users who need a dashboard onto all their databases, with the ability to see their contents at a glance and then change multiple databases all at once. For that, TOAD offers the Instance Manager, a screen for observing and managing many instances.

To launch the Instance Manager, from the TOAD main menu select Database → Monitor → Instance Manager. You will see the screen shown in Figure 7.11.

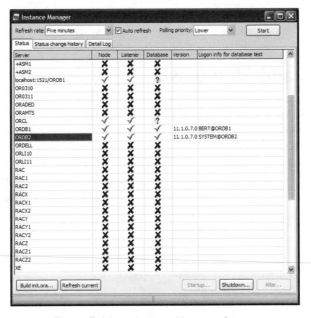

Figure 7.11   Instance Manager Screen

The Instance Manager provides a much more thorough instance management facility. Note that the LHS displays all the databases available for management, but you *cannot* select multiple databases for action. If you've provided a connect string for an instance (as two of ours have), then this dashboard will auto refresh every *N* minutes to display key instance metrics. The "Node" column represents the status of a network PING operation to the database server node (i.e., is the node up). The "Listener" column represents the status of an Oracle TNSPING operation to the database instance (i.e., is the listener up). The "Database" column represents the status of a connection to that database instance (i.e., is the database up). Sometimes just seeing these three pieces of information for all your databases at a glance can be of huge value.

Notice that the Instance Manager screen in Figure 7.11 has three buttons in the lower-right corner for the "Startup," "Shutdown," and "Alter" operations. As with the Database Browser, clicking one of these buttons to request the operation will evoke a pop-up for that operation's parameters. Also note the button called "Build init.ora". In today's world of Oracle "pfiles" and "spfiles," "init.ora" files may seem like a throwback. However, sometimes having a simple text file of all your current instance parameter settings can be useful, so this button might occasionally come in handy.

The Instance Manager also has two other screen tabs ("Status Change History" and "Detail Log") that might be of use. These tabs maintain client-side history information about when instance management commands and/or instance management status changes occur. While this information may already be available on your database server, sometimes the local copies are useful for a fast and centralized review.

Oracle and NLS Parameters

Often when working with a database instance, users need to review and revise certain database configuration parameters. For example, you might want to turn on or off a certain Oracle feature or behavior, such as the Star Transformation query optimization. These abilities are often referred to as the Oracle parameter settings, the "pfile" or "spfile" settings, or even the "init.ora" file settings. Some of these parameter settings can be changed without restarting the database, while changes to others won't take effect until a restart is initiated. If you just need to review these settings, then the Database Browser (covered in Chapter 2) offers the "Parameters" tab for viewing this information, as shown in Figure 7.12. Note that you cannot modify these parameter settings, as this screen is read-only. TOAD offers the "Oracle Parameters" screen if modifications are necessary.

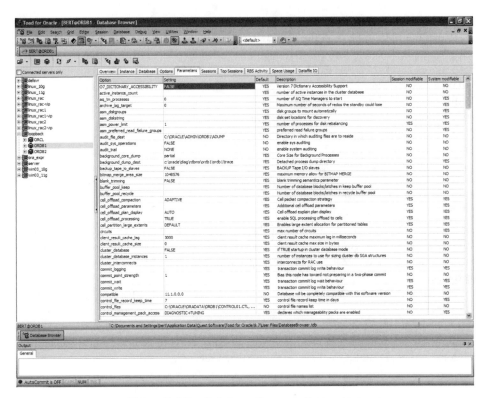

Figure 7.12   Database Browser: Parameters

To launch the "Oracle Parameters" screen, from the TOAD main menu select Database → Administer → Oracle Parameters. You will see the screen here in Figure 7.13.

The "Oracle Parameters" screen is very similar to the Database Browser's "Parameters" tab, but offers some additional benefits. First, it has the ability to filter by the default value setting and/or the name of the parameters (with use of wildcards permitted, similar to the situation with the Schema Browser's quick filter, covered in Chapter 2). More importantly, the "Oracle Parameters" screen offers the ability to modify the instance's parameters settings (where permitted). For example, if you wanted to change the previously mentioned parameter for enabling star transformations, you would simply filter or scroll to the row containing that setting and double-click on it. A pop-up window like that shown in Figure 7.14 would then be displayed.

There's actually quite a bit to observe and mention here. First, you do not generally have to know all the parameters' specifics, as the pop-up screens' content will vary to accommodate their different data types and allowable values. That alone is a huge time saver. But look again at Figure 7.14: The pop-up windows also allow you to specify

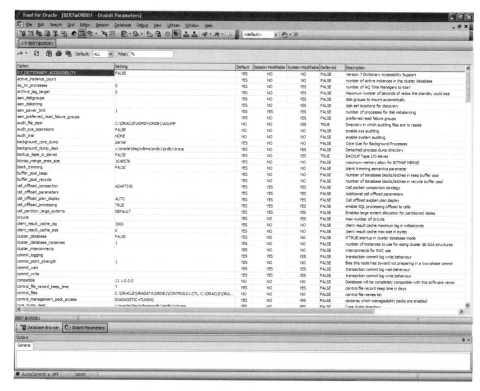

Figure 7.13   Oracle Parameters Screen

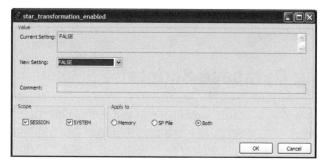

Figure 7.14   Oracle Parameters Screen: Params Pop-up

whether the change is for just the current session or the entire system, and whether the system change should take effect immediately (i.e., memory) or after the next restart (i.e., spfile). Basically the "Oracle Parameters" screen's pop-up for parameter modification supports the entire range of the *ALTER SYSTEM SET* syntax.

Another area focuses on the National Language Settings (NLS) parameters. These parameters determine how Oracle will handle character set information. For example, you might be working with data that must include language-specific characters and markups. If so, then you'll need a way to review and revise these settings. TOAD provides the "NLS Parameters" screen for that task.

To launch the "NLS Parameters" screen, from the TOAD main menu select Database → Administer → NLS Parameters. You will see the screen shown in Figure 7.15. It includes tabs for "Session," "Instance," and "Database," which are the three levels where such settings can be defined. Only the session-level NLS settings are modifiable; double-clicking on one of these entries will display a pop-up to help you choose your settings.

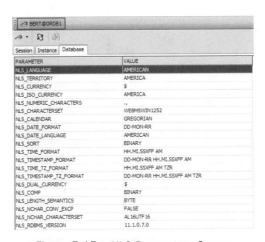

Figure 7.15   NLS Parameters Screen

Generating Database Scripts

On occasion, you may have a need to generate a script for all your database level objects (i.e., those not owned by a schema, but rather required to build the database itself). For example, you may want to create your development and test databases to provide the same basic foundation as your production database server. Thus you want the same tablespaces, roles, profiles, users, resource plans, resource consumer groups, and so on. Hence you need an easy way to generate the Data Definition Language (DDL) for that collection of database-level objects. TOAD offers the "Generate Database Script" screen for that purpose.

To launch the "Generate Database Script" screen, from the TOAD main menu select Database → Export → Generate Database Script. You will see the screen shown in Figure 7.16.

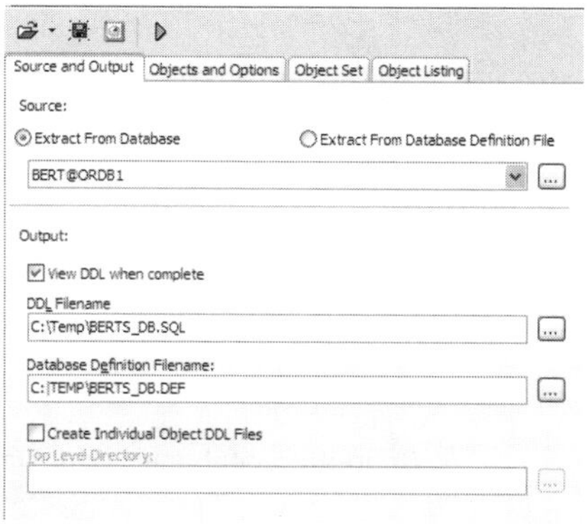

Figure 7.16   Generate Database Script: Tab 1

This screen has four tabs; three are present initially, and the fourth is displayed after you click the green arrow ("Execute" button). The first tab ("Source and Output") allows you to specify two critical pieces of information: the source and the output.

Before going any further, we need to explain what a TOAD database definition (DEF) file is. TOAD can capture an offline copy of your database dictionary and store that metadata in a binary file on your PC. This DEF file can be used either as a super-fast copy of your data dictionary or as a historical and version control system of sorts for your data dictionary. TOAD can process DEF files hundreds of times faster than even local database data dictionaries. As a consequence, DEF files are an extremely useful tool for working with large databases when doing various compare and generate operations.

Returning to the "Generate Database Script" screen shown in Figure 7.16, the first tab's options permit you to use either a database connection or a previously captured DEF file as the source. The target can be a SQL text file, a DEF file, or both. In our case, we chose to capture both in the C:\Temp directory. The "Source and Output" table also offers you the option to view the SQL file once it has been generated, and an option to create a SQL file per object under a user-specified directory structure.

The second tab ("Objects and Options") allows you to choose those database-level objects that will have their DDL generated, plus a few DDL generation syntactical options. The more database-level objects you pick, the longer the run time and the larger the generated script.

Once you click the green arrow ("Execute" button), the fourth tab ("Object Listing") will appear. It presents a tree view showing the object types, their counts, and their object names generated, as shown in Figure 7.17.

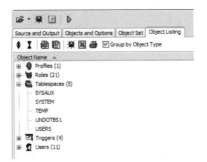

Figure 7.17   Generate Database Script: Tab 4

Generating Schema Scripts

A fairly common database administrative task is to generate a script for all of the schema-level database objects (i.e., those owned by a schema, and not by the database or PUBLIC). For example, you may want to copy the "SCOTT" tables, indexes, sequences, views, procedures functions, and packages from the development environment to the test environment. To do so, you want an easy way to generate the DDL for that collection of schema-level objects. TOAD offers the "Generate Schema Script" screen for that purpose.

To launch the "Generate Database Script" screen, from the TOAD main menu select Database → Export → Generate Schema Script. You will see the screen shown in Figure 7.18.

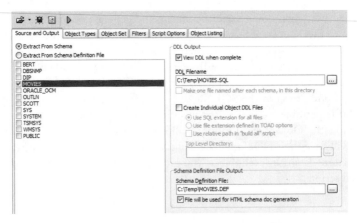

Figure 7.18   Generate Schema Script: Tab 1

This screen includes six tabs; five are presented initially, and the sixth is displayed after you click the green arrow ("Execute" button). The first tab ("Source and Output") allows you to specify two critical pieces of information: the source and the output.

The "Source and Output" tab's options permit you to use either a database connection or a previously captured DEF file as the source. (See the discussion of DEF files in the preceding section.) When using a database connection, you can select multiple schemas to reverse engineer. The target can be a SQL text file, a DEF file, or both. In our case, we chose to capture both in the C:\Temp directory. The "Source and Output" tab also provides the option to view the SQL file once it has been generated, as well as an option to create a SQL file per object under a user-specified directory structure. Note, too, that there is a check box for indicating whether this DEF file will later be used for TOAD HTML Schema Doc report execution, in which case TOAD captures some extra information necessary for that purpose.

The second tab ("Objects Types") allows you to choose those schema-level objects that will have their DDL generated. The more schema-level objects you pick, the longer the run time and the larger the generated script.

The fourth tab ("Filters") lets you further restrict the processed list by name and table-space location. The fifth tab ("Script Options") allows you to control numerous DDL or SQL syntactical options. For example, do you want storage options? How do want to code the various constraints? You should spend ample time reviewing the options here, as they radically affect the resulting code.

Once you click the green arrow ("Execute" button), the sixth tab ("Object Listing") will appear. It presents a tree view showing the object types, their counts, and their object names generated, as shown in Figure 7.19.

Figure 7.19   Generate Schema Script: Tab 6

Comparing Database Differences

Sometimes you may need to compare and synchronize all your database-level objects (i.e., those not owned by a schema, but rather required to build the database itself) between two different databases. For example, you may want to compare your test database to a production version to verify that both have the same basic foundation. Thus you want the same tablespaces, roles, profiles, users, resource plans, resource consumer groups, and so on. In this situation, you want an easy way to compare and sync the database-level objects. TOAD offers the "Compare Databases" screen for that purpose.

To launch the "Compare Databases" screen, from the TOAD main menu select Database → Compare → Databases. You will see the screen shown in Figure 7.20.

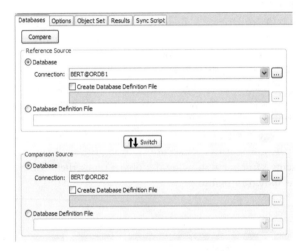

Figure 7.20   Compare Databases: Tab 1

This screen includes five tabs; three are presented initially, and the fourth and fifth are displayed after you click the green arrow ("Execute" button). The first tab ("Databases") permits you to specify two critical pieces of information: the reference or source database, and the comparison or target database. The order you choose here matters greatly, which explains why a button in the middle of the page allows you to switch or reverse these selections (more about this later). You can specify either a database connection or a previously captured DEF file for both the reference and comparison database sources (refer to the earlier discussion for more information on DEF files).

The second tab ("Options") allows you to choose those database-level objects that will have their DDL generated, as well as where you would like the synchronization SQL script written. The more database-level objects you pick, the longer the run time and potentially the larger the generated script.

Once you click the green arrow ("Execute" button), the fourth and fifth tabs will appear. The fourth tab ("Results") presents a tree view showing the three types of objects: objects in the source and not in the target, objects in the target and not in the source, and objects that differ between the two databases. (See Figure 7.21.)

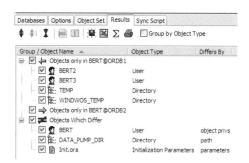

Figure 7.21   Compare Databases: Tab 4

The fifth tab ("Sync Script") shows the DDL necessary to sync the source to the target. If you feel the results are backward (a common error), then simply go back to the first tab and click the "Switch" button. Don't worry—the results are simply reversed within TOAD, and no reprocessing is necessary.

On some occasions, you may need to compare and synchronize all of your schema-level objects (i.e., those owned by a schema, and not by the database or PUBLIC) between two different databases. For example, you may want to compare your test database to a production version to verify that two "SCOTT" schemas are identical. Thus you want the exact tables, indexes, sequences, views, procedures, functions, and packages. To complete this task, you want an easy way to compare and sync these schema-level objects. TOAD offers the Compare Schemas screen for that purpose.

To launch the "Compare Schemas" screen, from the TOAD main menu select Database → Compare → Schemas. You will see the screen shown in Figure 7.22.

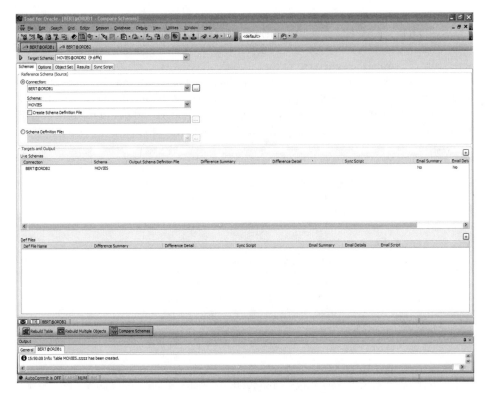

Figure 7.22   Compare Schemas: Tab 1

This screen includes five tabs; three are presented initially, and the fourth and fifth are displayed after you click the green arrow ("Execute" button). The first tab ("Schemas") permits you to specify two critical pieces of information: the reference or source schema, and the comparison or target schema. Both schema sources permit you to specify either a database schema or a previously captured DEF file as the reference and comparison schema sources (refer to the earlier discussion of DEF files for more information).

The second tab ("Options") allows you to choose those schema-level objects that will have their DDL generated. The more schema-level objects you pick, the longer the run time and potentially the larger the generated script.

Once you click the green arrow ("Execute" button), the fourth and fifth tabs will appear. The fourth tab ("Results") presents a tree view showing the three types of objects: objects in the source and not in the target, objects in the target and not in the source, and objects that differ between the two schemas. (See Figure 7.23.) The fifth tab ("Sync Script") shows the DDL necessary to sync the source to the target.

Starting with Oracle 10g, the database query optimizer has switched to being entirely "cost based" (instead of "rule based," as was the case in Oracle 9i and earlier versions). That

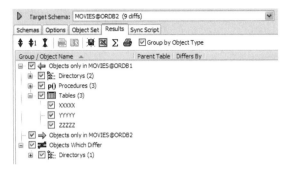

Figure 7.23   Compare Schemas: Tab 4

means that gathering accurate and up-to-date statistics and histograms has never been more critical than it is now. Whether the focus is your application's queries, third-party database applications, or even a tool like TOAD, obtaining proper statistics is now a high-priority database administrative task. Luckily, TOAD offers the "Analyze All Objects" screen to simplify that duty.

To launch the "Analyze All Objects" screen, from the TOAD main menu select Database → Optimize → Analyze All Objects. You will see the screen shown in Figure 7.24.

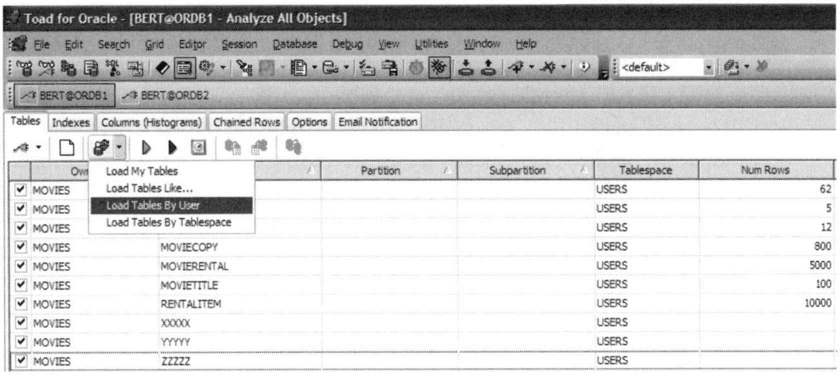

Figure 7.24   Analyze All Objects: Tables

By default, this screen launches with no data (i.e., the tables, indexes, and columns tabs all contain empty data grids). In Figure 7.24, we have chosen to load the tables for the MOVIES schema by using the drop-down list and selecting "Load Tables by User." A pop-up window then displays the schemas that we can choose. You can follow the same steps on the indexes and columns tabs if you want to gather index statistics and histograms as well.

You should take time to investigate the fifth tab ("Options") and its complex offerings. When you use the default statistics collection method of the "Analyze" command (which Oracle has deprecated), there's not too much to decide. However, when you specify the use of DBMS_STATS, that opens up a whole new range of possibilities—and adds both additional tabs and sub-tabs (i.e., tabs under tabs) to the "Analyze All Objects" screen, as shown in Figure 7.25.

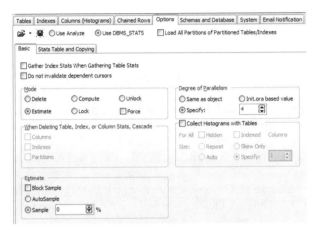

Figure 7.25   Analyze All Objects: Options

This approach supports the use of extended concepts such as statistics collection in parallel, gathering index statistics while processing a table, sampling, simplified histogram specification, exporting statistics to a user-defined table, copying statistics between schemas and/or databases, doing multi-schema statistics collections, gathering statistics for data dictionary and internal fixed tables, and partitioning statistics collections options. You should spend sufficient time and exercise care when selecting the options here for your specific needs—this is one place where blindly accepting the default values will not suffice.

Note that in Figure 7.25 that the "Options" tab contains toolbar icons for saving and loading your options settings. This is an important aspect of the "Analyze All Options" feature, and you should learn to make use of these icons. Spend as much time as necessary to identify and select the correct options for your system, and then save them to a named file that you'll remember. That way you can expedite your use of this screen when you return to it in the future. Once you've clicked the green arrow ("Execute" toolbar icon), you'll see a message listed under each select object that says "Normal Successful Completion."

You may never actually need to run the "Analyze All Objects" screen via the main menu in the manner described in this section. Many users actually arrive at this point via the Schema Browser (covered in Chapter 2). When you are browsing database objects for which statistics may exist, the Schema Browser offers a RHM menu item to automatically take you to this screen with all the proper objects already selected. For example, if you were browsing tables as shown in Figure 7.26, the "Analyze Table" option would send you to this screen for the selected tables.

Figure 7.26   Schema Browser: Analyze Tables

Rebuilding Multiple Objects

One task that always seems to need doing at some point in any database is rebuilding or reorganizing objects. In fact, Oracle has provided a powerful PL/SQL package for handling this task. Unfortunately, the DBMS_REDEFINITION package is far too complex for casual use. And remember, it will re-create your objects—which means a wrong step could lose actual data as well as the objects. What you really need is a simple, effective, and safe interface into this complex package. TOAD offers its "Rebuild Multiple Objects" screen for this purpose. With this facility, even the greenest novice can quickly and safely rebuild database objects like a pro.

To launch the "Rebuild Multiple Objects" screen, from the TOAD main menu select Database → Optimize → Rebuild Multiple Objects. You will see the screen shown in Figure 7.27.

Owner	Load My Tables		Subpartition	Tablespace	% Incr	Size (Mb)	# Extents	Initial (Kb)	Next (Kb)	Logging	Degree	Instances	Max Extents
MOVIES	Load Tables Like...			USERS	0	1	1	1024	1024	NO	1	1	2147483645
MOVIES	Load Tables By User			USERS	0	1	1	1024	1024	NO	1	1	2147483645
MOVIES	Load Tables By Tablespace			USERS	0	1	1	1024	1024	NO	1	1	2147483645
MOVIES	MOVIECOPY			USERS	0	1	1	1024	1024	NO	1	1	2147483645
MOVIES	MOVIERENTAL			USERS	0	1	1	1024	1024	NO	1	1	2147483645
MOVIES	MOVIETITLE			USERS	0	1	1	1024	1024	NO	1	1	2147483645
MOVIES	RENTALITEM			USERS	0	1	1	1024	1024	NO	1	1	2147483645
MOVIES	XXXXX			USERS	0	1	1	1024	1024	YES	1	1	2147483645
MOVIES	YYYYY			USERS	0	1	1	1024	1024	YES	1	1	2147483645
MOVIES	ZZZZZ			USERS	0	1	1	1024	1024	YES	1	1	2147483645

Figure 7.27   Rebuild Multiple Objects: Tables

You may have noticed that the "Rebuild Multiple Objects" screen (Figure 7.27) looks a lot like the "Analyze All Objects" screen (Figure 7.24). That's by design: The two look and function quite similarly, so review the prior section for additional insights into this screen's operation and behavior.

There are two areas where there are significant differences between the "Rebuild Multiple Objects" and "Analyze All Objects" screens—more specifically, where TOAD's "Rebuild Multiple Objects" screen offers some highly specialized capabilities. Figure 7.28 shows the fourth tab ("Thresholds and Performance Options") for specifying key rebuild thresholds and behaviors. We've chosen to rebuild only those objects whose size is 1GB or greater, that have 1000 or more extents, and that have indexes whose b-trees are probably

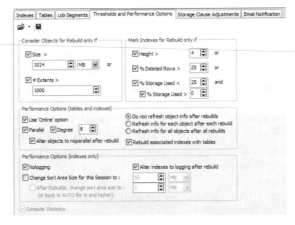

Figure 7.28   Rebuild Multiple Objects: Tab 4

imbalanced. Furthermore we've chosen to perform the rebuild online using eight-way parallel processing and no logging for speed, with both being reset back to the normal defaults after the object rebuild operation is complete.

The fifth tab ("Storage Clause Adjustments") is even more complicated, and possesses sub-tabs. Here you can define small, medium, large, and huge tables, and then scale object storage clauses or place objects in tablespaces based on those definitions. Suppose you want to create standard object sizes and place such objects in tablespaces designed and optimized for an object of that size. This utility will completely automate the entire rebuild process to accomplish that goal.

You should take great care to review and carefully select from these two tabs' numerous offerings. You can generate very complex and valuable SQL scripts for performing amazing object reorganizations if you are willing to invest the time.

Top Session Finder

All database sessions consume some amount of database resources. Often, a few isolated sessions may consume more than their fair share of the shared resources. These sessions will, therefore, become general performance drags on the entire database and all other database sessions. TOAD offers the "Top Session Finder" screen to help you identify these outlier sessions.

To launch the "Top Session Finder" screen, from the TOAD main menu select Database → Monitor → Top Session Finder. You will see the screen shown in Figure 7.29.

The stored profiles drop-down box lists some predefined search filters intended to help identify resource hogs. The default "Overall" profile looks across many different session resource consumption aspects to find unusually resource-intensive areas, whereas other profiles (e.g., "CPU," "IO," and "Memory") focus on other common causes of bottlenecks.

In addition, you can define custom profiles as necessary. Simply click the "Create New Profile" toolbar icon and give your new profile a name, and then review and set the thresholds that you want to filter through the session. When you click the green arrow ("List Sessions" icon), you will see only those sessions that exceed the thresholds specified in the custom profile.

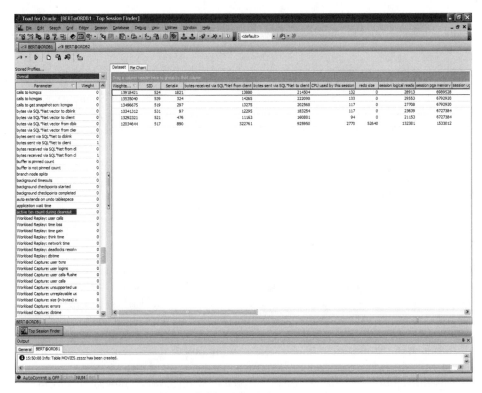

Figure 7.29   Top Session Finder

SGA Trace/Optimization

The Oracle System Global Area (SGA) contains many data structures and caches, including the Shared Pool. One thing the Shared Pool holds is those SQL statements that have been parsed and retained (i.e., statements that have not yet aged out of the cache due to recent use). Thus, if session 1 and session 2 issue the same query, that query will take up only one slot in the Shared Pool. It will be shared by those sessions, but Oracle needs to record it only once.

What if you would like to identify all those queries that are executed many times, executed by multiple sessions, consume lots of CPU or elapsed time, and experience lots of waiting time? TOAD provides the "SGA Trace/Optimization" screen for this purpose; it will help you to identify these kinds of SQL statements.

To launch the "SGA Trace/Optimization" screen, from the TOAD main menu select Database → Monitor → SGA Trace/Optimization. You will see the screen shown in Figure 7.30.

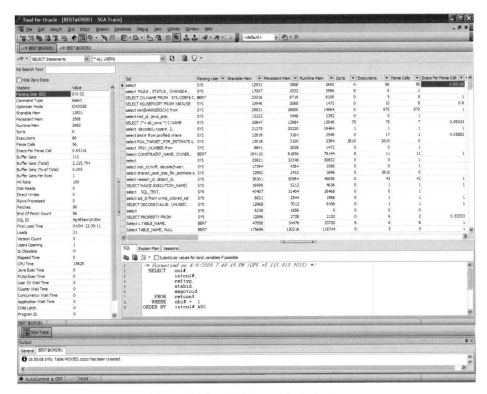

Figure 7.30   SGA Trace/Optimization

Note the filter drop-down boxes in which you can restrict the results produced by statement type and by users. In Figure 7.30, we chose just SELECT statements and all users. Once you've set your filters appropriately, simply click the double arrow ("Refresh" icon) to repopulate the screen. The LHS presents the shared SQL statement's global performance properties, such as the total number of sessions sharing this statement and the total number of times it has been executed by all sessions. On the RHS, the top data grid shows the individual statements associated with their specific session context, as well as the relevant performance statistics for that session's execution. The bottom panel displays the SQL statement and its associated explain plan.

Whereas the "Top Session Finder" feature looks for those sessions consuming too many resources, the "SGA Trace/Optimization" screen looks for the shared SQL statements that cumulatively add up to excessive resource consumption. Of course, sometimes you need to look at resource bottlenecks from both angles to truly find and fix a performance problem.

Session Browser

The single most common database administrative task that many people do is to investigate sessions. You may need to look into a session's overall status, its locks, blocking locks, waits, current statement, explain plan, long operation status, and numerous other status or performance metrics. Sometimes this will result in sessions having traces initiated or even being killed. In fact, earlier versions of TOAD called this facility "Trace/Kill." Once it was augmented to handle all these scenarios and many others, however, this feature was renamed Session Browser. It's quite probably one of the most used administrative-nature features in TOAD—and fortunately for many it's part of the standard product (i.e., it does not require the optional DB Admin Module).

To launch the Session Browser, from the TOAD main menu select Database → Monitor → Session Browser. You will see the screen shown in Figure 7.31.

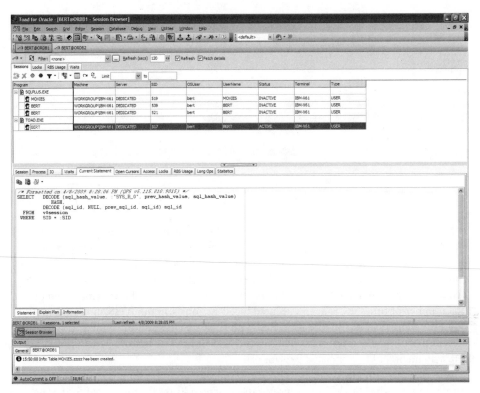

Figure 7.31   Session Browser

The Session Browser presents a very powerful screen both in terms of what it shows and how it shows it. In fact, it's probably one of the most user-configurable screens in TOAD. You should spend a few minutes to review what you can set for this screen, because you can radically improve its readability and usability for your purposes. That, in turn, can increase your own productivity when working with sessions.

The Session Browser includes four tabs. The first tab ("Sessions") is the primary focus—that is, the functionality most often used. It shows all the sessions within your database. If you perform a RHM click in the data grid showing the sessions, three key customization options appear. First, you can decide whether to display the data in a top and bottom panel style versus a side-by-side panel view. Second, you can select which columns to group by in the session's tree view. Third, you can choose which columns to display for each session in that tree view.

Eleven tabs are shown in the bottom portion of Figure 7.31, each of which displays radically different information. Thus you will need to visit each tab and learn what it has to offer. Some tabs provide simple displays of information, while others present a series of sub-tabs. Take enough time to learn and master them all.

Once you find a session of particular interest, the "Sessions" tab's session data grid offers you some options on managing them. For example, if you open the RHM menu for a session, you will see that you can kill or trace that session. These options are also available on the toolbar located just beneath the "Sessions" tab heading. When you choose one of these session management functions, you will see a pop-up parameter setting screen like that shown in Figure 7.32. Even though you may issue a command to trace or kill a session, that action will not actually be carried out until you see this pop-up and click "OK."

Figure 7.32   Session Browser: Params Pop-up

The second tab ("Locks") shown in Figure 7.31 is the other most frequently used part of the Session Browser. It lists all sessions that are holding locks or are being blocked by locks. Furthermore, it indicates which types of locks have been implemented and whether they are exclusive. The blocked locks section even shows the SQL statements that are awaiting execution. This information is critical when you try to troubleshoot database lock problems, including the dreaded "dead lock" scenario. On a high-volume transactional system, this tab may take a long time to refresh. That's because these queries are not cheap, and on a busy system their overhead is even worse. Given this fact, be careful when setting any automatic refresh intervals while working with locks.

The third tab ("Waits") shown in Figure 7.31 also proves useful in many situations. It displays key database wait event information. There has been a major shift over the past decade to move away from performance metrics such as hit ratios in favor of wait event analysis. The idea is that it's better to know what's holding things up rather than how efficiently an internal operation is performing. An analogy may help to clarify this point. If we needed to know why a trip to the grocery store took too long, which information is more useful: the average miles per hour the car drove during the trip or the fact you stopped for an ice cream cone on the way?

The "Waits" tab has three sub-tabs: waits during the past minute, waits by session, and waits for the entire system. In Figure 7.33, some wait times are highlighted in blue similar to a Web URL. That simply means that if you double-click on the wait, a pop-up will appear with a description of what the wait means, along with some possible solutions to resolving it.

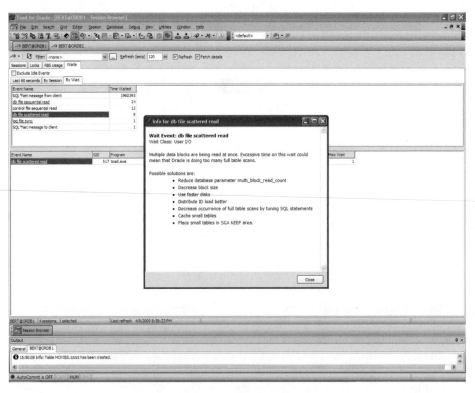

Figure 7.33   Session Browser: Waits

Summary

In recent years, TOAD has emerged as much more than just a developer's tool; it has grown into something that offers numerous database administrative capabilities. Whether you're a DBA or just someone tasked with performing database administrative work, TOAD now has much to offer you as you deal with these duties. You may need the optional TOAD DB Admin Module to get many of the features covered in this chapter. Once you have those features available, you will find that TOAD can expedite all your various database administrative tasks—from the most mundane and routine to the most complex and unusual. For some people, TOAD may well complement or even supplant other database administrative tools. TOAD has gown up into a true one-stop, do-it-all tool.

Here's the current, complete listing of optional features provided by the TOAD DB Admin Module, many of which were covered in this chapter (others are covered in Chapters 6 and 8 on tuning and exporting data, respectively):

- ADDM/AWR Report Generator
- Analyze All Objects
- ASM Manager
- Audit Objects
- Audit SQL/Sys Privs
- AWR Browser
- Code Road Map and ER Diagram
- Compare Databases
- Compare Schemas
- Control Files
- Database Browser
- Database Health Check
- Database Monitor
- Database Probe
- DataPump Import/Export Wizards
- DBMS_FLASHBACK Interface
- DBMS_REDEFINITITION Wizard
- Export File Browser
- Generate Database Script
- Generate Schema Script
- Identify Space Deficits
- Index Monitoring
- Instance Manager

- Log Switch Frequency Map
- LogMiner Interface
- New Database Wizard
- NLS Parameters
- Operating System Utilities
- Oracle Parameters
- Pinned Code
- Redo Log Manager
- Resource Plan Scheduling
- Schema Browser
- Segment Advisor
- StatsPack Browser
- Tablespace Map
- Top Session Finder
- Trace File Browser
- Undo Advisor
- View Tablespaces

Exporting Table Data

While TOAD may offer hundreds of features and capabilities, we realize that just three are used most frequently by the typical user: simple data browsing (see Chapter 2's coverage of the Schema Browser), basic queries (see Chapter 3's coverage of the Editor), and exporting data for use in other tools or databases. In fact, people "move" data more often than they realize—and that's why this chapter on exporting data is important. TOAD makes data extraction from your Oracle tables and views a very simple process. With TOAD, you can easily move data to wherever you need to work on it. Thus, no matter whether you need the data in Microsoft Excel, Access, text files in numerous formats, or even XML, TOAD can quickly perform all of your required data extractions.

Saving Grid Contents

The data grid is a key component or feature within TOAD. In fact, numerous screens within TOAD present their output as a data grid—that is, as a tabular display that looks like a mini-spreadsheet of sorts. For example, here are some of the many places within TOAD where data grids are important:

- Database Browser: right-hand side; all tabs have a data grid
- Schema Browser: right-hand side, "Data" tab
- Session browser: bottom panel; most tabs have a data grid
- Editor: bottom panel, "Data Grid" tab (when pressing F9 or clicking the "Execute" button)
- Editor: bottom panel, "Script Output" tab, "Grid N" sub-tab (when pressing F5 or clicking the "Execute" button to execute a script)
- Oracle Parameters: screen contents
- Master Detail Browser: right-hand side; all data grids
- Top Session Finder: right-hand side, "Dataset" tab
- Query Builder: bottom half, "Query Results" tab

What's important for you to know is that all of these data grids have inherent, identical, and very simple facilities for saving their data either to your PC or directly to other PC applications. Moreover, the TOAD data export or extract interface is standardized such that if you know how to use one screen, you know how to use them all. In most cases, you simply need click the right-hand mouse (RHM) and choose "Save as." In a few cases, the data grid may not have the RHM available, but there is generally a screen toolbar icon provided that allows you to perform the same action. In some cases, as shown in Figure 8.1, both a toolbar icon (upper-left corner, first icon on the screen toolbar before the VCR navigation buttons) and the RHM menu item for "Save as" are available.

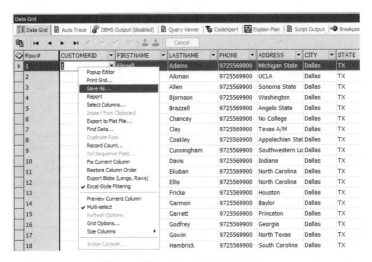

Figure 8.1   Data Grid Save As

Once the "Save as" operation is chosen, TOAD will display the pop-up screen shown in Figure 8.2. Most of the options found on the pop-up are obvious or self-explanatory, but a few require further explanation. Basically, this "Save As" screen offers the ability to extract the current data grid's content to some external location.

The first and most important option is which format to export the data to. In Figure 8.2, we've selected an Excel spreadsheet file. There are numerous other options available as well, including the following:

- Microsoft Access database file (.mdb).

- Delimited text file.

- Microsoft Excel spreadsheet file (.xls). If Excel is not already running, TOAD creates a file that can be opened by Excel.

- Microsoft Excel spreadsheet instance. If Excel is already up and running, TOAD creates a new worksheet tab within the current workbook.

Figure 8.2   Save As Pop-up

- Fixed file spacing.
- HTML table.
- SQL INSERT statements.
- SQL MERGE statements.
- Oracle SQL*Loader file.
- XML: plain
- XML with XSL style sheet.

Of these, the Microsoft Excel spreadsheet instance is the least obvious choice, and a little more complex than the other options. This option does not create a file per se, but rather exports the contents of the data grid into a live and already open Excel workbook as a new worksheet (i.e., tab). You would subsequently create an Excel file from your data when you save the Excel worksheet. If you just want to save your data as an Excel file to work on later, select "Excel File" from the "Save As" pop-up list. Note, too, that as you select among the different export format types, the options in the lower half of the screen will change.

The second, often quite important options are those found in the "Output" section. Here you specify where the file (if one is being produced) will go, whether it should automatically be zipped (TOAD has built-in zip capabilities, so you don't have to purchase or install zip software to get this feature), and whether to launch the file after creation. The clipboard output option works only for those file formats that are textual in nature (such as delimited text, fixed field, HTML, SQL statements, and XML).

Of the remaining "Save As" options, just the following three check boxes in Figure 8.2 require additional explanation:

- "Include column headers" indicates whether the column headers will be included as part of the output. The key point here is that when doing an import (covered at the end of this chapter), you may need to start at the second row of the data grid because the first row may consist of headers and not data per se. Thus, if you plan to do just data imports, perhaps you don't need to include the headers at all.

- "Export selected rows" permits you to specify the extraction of just those rows from the data grid that are currently highlighted (i.e., selected). This is probably one of the most useful and often overlooked features of the "Save As" operation. You can and should select and export the rows you're interested in rather than the entire data set. Be aware that this very useful check box is not selected by default.

- "Include null text" permits you to specify whether to include null values as empty strings or to instead use the keyword NULL. This choice can be very important based on where you might need to use the data or if you have to import it. For example, some non-Oracle databases might not accept the SQL reserved word NULL.

Flat File Export

The data grid "Save As" operation is probably the most useful and easy-to-use method for exporting and extracting table data. But what if you wanted to create your own special-ized export format, something like an Oracle SQL*Loader file, but with your own special syntax for saying what the content looks like? That's where the "Export Table as Flat File" capability comes into play. You'll find it in many data grids as the menu item "Export to Flat File…" as shown in Figure 8.1. You can also access this feature through the main menu: Database → Export → Table as Flat File. When it is activated, you'll see the screen shown in Figure 8.3.

The underlying concept is quite simple. The first tab ("Spec File") deals with the export format specification. You can type your specification from scratch, click the "Gen-erate Columns" button to jump-start the process, or click the "Load Spec File" button to reload an existing file. There are basically just four syntactical options for these spec file lines, as highlighted in Listing 8.1.

Figure 8.3   Exporting Data to a Flat File

Listing 8.1   **Four Basic Spec File Commands**

```
TABLENAME=table_name
OWNER=owner_name
LINESPERRECORD=number
COL#=column_name, # occurrence, starting position, length
```

The second tab ("Options") allows you to specify options such as the owning schema, the table name, and whether to copy the data to the clipboard or create a user-specified file. The third tab ("SQL Loader") lets you preview (and optionally save) the Oracle SQL*Loader control file that corresponds to your TOAD file export spec file.

We've seen limited use of this feature given the constant user enhancement requests related to TOAD and, therefore, evolving improvements to the "Save As" options. You may find little or no use for this screen, especially given that no other software can process the TOAD spec file.

Creating Inserts

The Schema Browser data grid has one more RHM menu item than all the other data grids—"Create INSERT for Selected Rows." It launches the "Data Export" window shown in Figure 8.4.

Figure 8.4   Data Export

The first tab ("Options") lets you specify which rows to include (by row ID), whether to export the data to the clipboard or a user-specified file, and how often to add COMMIT commands to the generated INSERT statements. The second tab ("Columns") lets you choose which columns to include and select additional options such as whether to include null or primary key columns.

We've seen limited use of this feature given the constant user enhancement requests related to TOAD and, therefore, evolving improvements to the "Save As" options. You may find little or no use for this screen, especially given that the "Save As" screen offers both SQL INSERT and MERGE command file options.

Schema Browser Script

The Schema Browser (see Chapter 2) offers a method for exporting or extracting data that might not conceptually be the best or right place to do so, but that nonetheless seems to be used quite often. When using the Schema Browser's "Script" tab, you have numerous options available with which to control the behavior related to DDL generation. If you click the toolbox toolbar icon in the upper-left corner of the screen as shown in Figure 8.5, the "Script Options" pop-up window's third tab ("Tables") offers an option to add INSERT statements to the DDL generated.

This approach is highly useful because it allows you to produce a totally self-contained or packaged table definition file, one that contains the DDL to define the table and the SQL to populate it. Plus, because this capability is found on a very popular screen in the Schema Browser (remember, we said earlier that browsing is a key activity), it appears in a place that many users already like to use.

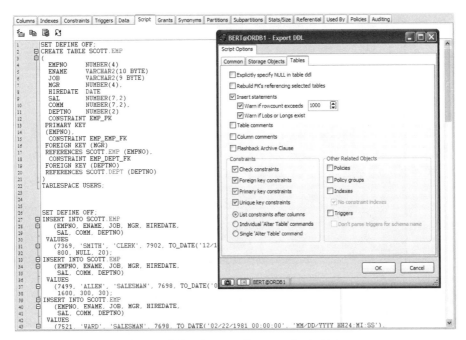

Figure 8.5   Schema Browser: Script Tab

Oracle Export

Oracle has historically favored its command-line export utility (i.e., EXP) for exporting database objects. This utility can be run on either the database server or a client machine such as your PC, and it creates a proprietary binary file that contains the selected database objects' definitions and data. Using such command-line tools has always been troublesome, however, because you need to be familiar with so many commands. As a result, many people end up having to code the calls to EXP with their *Oracle Utilities Manual* in hand—and that is not nearly as productively as most of us like to work. TOAD offers a wonderful GUI front end to the Oracle utility that can totally eliminate the need for the Oracle manual.

To launch the Export Utility Wizard, from the TOAD main menu select Database → Export → Export Utility Wizard. You will see the screen shown in Figure 8.6.

The export wizard presents a multistep interface whose content fully depends on the selections that you make on its screen. For example, we've chosen to perform a user- or schema-level export. Hence the following comments and screen snapshots will highlight the process and options for that selection. The other options are not much more complicated, so if you understand this example you'll be more than adequately prepared for the other user cases not presented here.

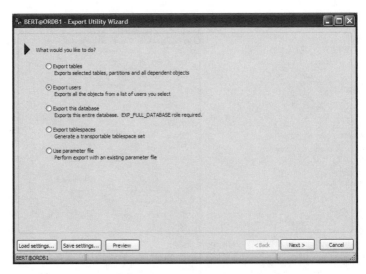

Figure 8.6   Export Utility Wizard: Step 1

The second step of the Export Utility Wizard lets you select the schemas to export. Here we set the filter check box to say that the results should display only selection schemas that own objects and should be presented as a simple LHS versus RHS display that shows the schemas available and selected, with buttons available to move them back and forth between panels.

The export wizard's third step displays the most common command-line parameters for the Oracle export utility, as shown in Figure 8.7. Of these, the only one that affects what you see on the screen is "Feedback." When a feedback count is specified, you will see a dot (.) displayed every time that number of rows has been processed.

In the Export Utility Wizard's fourth step, you specify the locations for the export file, log file, and bad records file. When you first enter a value for just the export file, the other values are filled in by default. Thus all of these files will, by default, end up in the same directory and with the same name, differing only in terms of their file extensions. For many people, that's good enough.

The export wizard's fifth and final step lets you select how to actually run or execute the export process. As shown in Figure 8.8, you can run it immediately (with or without the feedback being displayed), schedule it to run at a later time using the Microsoft Window's scheduler, or create the export parameter file with all your selections. If you choose to execute the export process now, TOAD will display an "Export Watch" window for monitoring the export utility's execution. This watch window is nonmodal, which means you can initiate an export and then go off and do something else within TOAD while the process continues in the background.

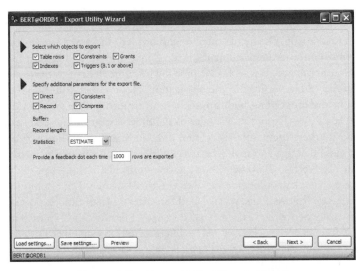

Figure 8.7   Export Utility Wizard: Step 3

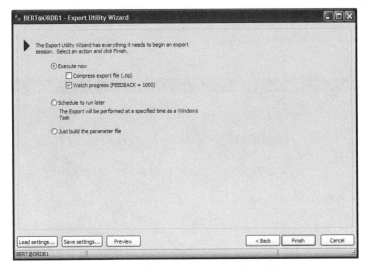

Figure 8.8   Export Wizard: Step 5

Data Pump Export

Starting with Oracle 10g, Oracle has offered (and favored) the new Data Pump utility as a general and much improved replacement for the Oracle Import and Export features. Thus the information in the previous section is probably of more benefit to those people who use Oracle 9i and earlier versions of this application. Nonetheless, you should read the prior section before proceeding with this section on exporting data via the Data Pump, because the Data Pump Export is so similar to the older Export utility that many of the same options, and therefore wizard navigation directions, will apply. Furthermore, Oracle is moving to close that gap and make the two utilities interchangeable in terms of syntax (starting with 11g Release 2), so that knowing one utility will mean knowing the other. However, there is one key difference between the two—namely, Data Pump is purely a database server-side feature. Thus, when TOAD initiates a Data Pump export operation, the work is actually performed on the database server. Likewise, the export output file will reside on that same database server. TOAD will create and manage that Data Pump Export processing request, but all of the activity actually takes place on the server side.

To launch the Data Pump Export Wizard, from the TOAD main menu select Database → Export → Data Pump Export Wizard. You will see the screen shown in Figure 8.9. Note that while it presents the same basic options as the Export screen shown in Figure 8.6, the choices for tables, users, tablespace, and databases have been grouped into a drop-down list box. You will see some other, very minor cosmetic differences along the way as well. Some major differences will also be apparent, as the Data Pump offers features and capabilities not found in the older Export utility.

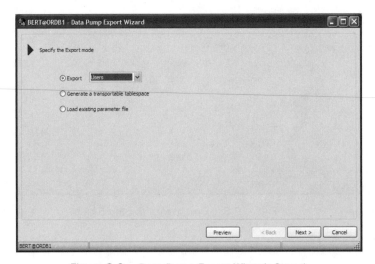

Figure 8.9   Data Pump Export Wizard: Step 1

The Data Pump Export Wizard presents a multistep interface whose content fully depends on the selections you make on its screens. For example, we've chosen to perform a user- or schema-level export. Hence the following comments and screen snapshots will highlight the process and options for that selection. The other options are not much more complicated, so if you understand this example you'll be more than adequately prepared for the other user cases not presented here.

The second step of the Data Pump Export Utility Wizard lets you select the schemas to export. Here we set the filter check box to say that the results should display only selection schemas that own objects and should be presented as a simple LHS versus RHS display that shows the schemas available and selected, with buttons available to move them back and forth between panels.

The third step offers you the ability to add a filtering query to the export process. For example, you might add something like "export data for only those customers who reside in the state of Texas and who have active accounts." This type of filter can greatly reduce both the export run time and the export file size.

The Data Pump Export Wizard's fourth step displays all of the most common command-line parameters for the Oracle export utility as shown in Figure 8.10. Of these, the only one that affects what you see on the screen is "Feedback." When a feedback count is specified, you will see a dot (.) displayed every time that number of rows has been processed.

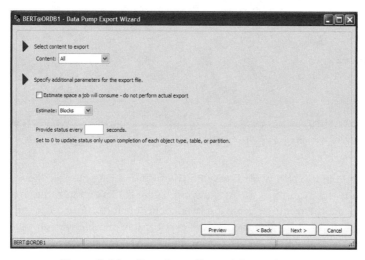

Figure 8.10   Data Pump Export Wizard: Step 4

The Data Pump export wizard's fifth step allows you to specify some meta-data filters—specifically, which database objects types to include or exclude. For example, you could check the options to exclude procedures, functions, package headers, and package bodies. The wizard presents an extensive list of all database objects that can be filtered this way.

In the Data Pump Export Utility Wizard's sixth step, you specify the locations for the export file, log file, and bad records file. When you first enter a value for just the export file, the other values are filled in by default. Thus all of these files will, by default, end up in the same directory and with the same name, differing only in terms of their file extensions. For many people, that's good enough. But there is one major difference here as opposed to the simple export described in the previous section: With the Data Pump, you must specify the name of the Oracle directory object where these files will be located, as shown in Figure 8.11. Also, you have to provide a job name for the export process. This is the database server-side job name that the task will be run under—whether it's run immediately or scheduled for later execution.

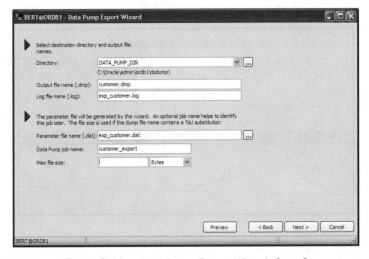

Figure 8.11   Data Pump Export Wizard: Step 6

The Data Pump Export Wizard's seventh and final step lets you select how to actually run or execute the export process. As shown in Figure 8.12, you can run it immediately (with or without the feedback being displayed), schedule it to run at a later time using the Microsoft Window's scheduler, or create the export parameter file with all your selections. If you choose to execute the export process now, TOAD will display an "Export Watch" window for monitoring the Data Pump Export utility's execution. This watch window is nonmodal, which means you can initiate an export and then go off and do something else within TOAD while the process continues in the background.

If and when you schedule Data Pump jobs to run at a later time, or if your TOAD session somehow gets disconnected from the Data Pump process while it's running (e.g., TOAD or Windows crashes), then you can always have TOAD reconnect to the prior sub-

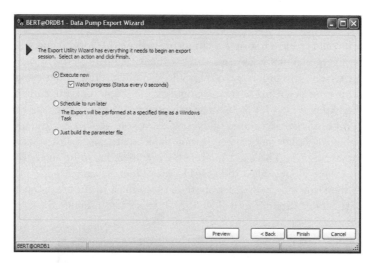

Figure 8.12   Data Pump Export Wizard: Step 7

mitted Data Pump jobs because they run on the database server. TOAD provides a simple Data Pump job process monitoring screen so that you can watch the execution of those jobs. To launch the Data Pump Job Manager, from the TOAD main menu select Database → Import → Data Pump Job Manager. You will see the screen shown in Figure 8.13. With this screen, you can stop or start Data Pump jobs as necessary, as well as reconnect to those jobs that are already running.

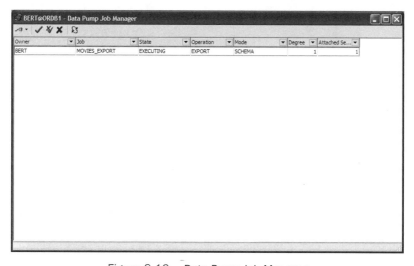

Figure 8.13   Data Pump Job Manager

Data Subset Wizard

Ever wish you could create a test or development database that looked and felt just like the production version, but with, say, just 10% of the data? There are many ways in which one might try to solve this problem. For example, you might think about using the Data Pump Export process described in the previous section. If you took this path, however, you would have to provide a lot of less-than-trivial filters to reduce the data size while still capturing a relationally correct subset of the data. Also, you would have to remember to manually disable constraints and triggers during the load process, and then reactivate them once the data was in place. That's just too much work; there has to be an easier and better way. Of course, there is—it's called the TOAD Data Subset Wizard.

To launch the Data Subset Wizard, from the TOAD main menu select Database → Export → Data Subset Wizard. You will see the screen shown in Figure 8.14.

Figure 8.14   Data Subset Wizard Step 1

The Data Subset Wizard is intended for copying a subset of data from a source database to a different target database; that explains why the wizard's first screen has two connections that you must specify. Alternatively, you can copy data from one schema to another within the same database.

The second step of the Data Subset Wizard presents you with just one question: Do you want to copy the data into truncated existing tables, or do you want to create all the objects in the target as part of the subset process? There are also options for you to specify which database objects to copy (or not).

The third step of the Data Subset Wizard is where you specify the subset or percentage reduction of the data transfer, as shown in Figure 8.15. The percentage slider is very simple; it represents the percentage of the data to capture from each table. The minimum number of rows per lookup table is a little challenging. For lookup tables, you might always want the whole table or most of it. You can control that aspect of the copy using this option. Finally, some key Oracle database scripting options in the third step can be selected that make for highly efficient SQL to perform large transfer operations. For example, the parallel and no logging options, when set properly, can reduce run times by many orders of magnitude.

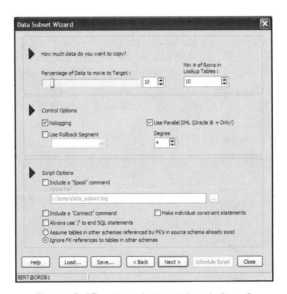

Figure 8.15   Data Subset Wizard: Step 3

The fourth step of the Data Subset Wizard is a little more complicated, as it includes a series of sub-tabs. Here you can define small, medium, large, and huge tables, and then scale object storage clauses or place objects in tablespaces based on those definitions. Suppose you want to create standard object sizes and place such objects in tablespaces designed and optimized for objects of that size; this utility will automate the entire rebuild process to accomplish that goal. In fact, these subset options are just like the fifth step of the Rebuild Multiple Object Wizard (see Chapter 7).

You should take great care to thoroughly review and carefully select among these two tabs' numerous offerings. You can generate very complex and valuable SQL scripts for performing amazing object reorganizations if you invest the time.

When you finally click the "Generate Script" button, this wizard will create all of the efficient and relationally accurate logic needed to perform the data subset operation.

Import Table Data

It may seem odd to cover the process of importing data into a table in a chapter labeled "Exporting Table Data," but we often cover the two capabilities side by side during live demos. Namely, we export the table data using the "Save As" feature and then turn right around and import that same exported data right back into a database—often into another database or even right back into the original table.

With TOAD, the entire export and import process is very simple, as the following example illustrates. First, we open the Schema Browser and choose the SCOTT schema EMP table; we save it as a comma-delimited text file as described earlier in this chapter. That's it—we now have a text file with our table's content that we wish to load. Remember, too, that we could have saved the data in a format other than text—for example, as a Microsoft Excel spreadsheet or an Access database file.

Now we simply navigate to another user in the Schema Browser that has an empty copy of the EMP table and choose the RHM menu item titled "Import from text, Excel or Access." This action launches the import wizard shown in Figure 8.16. This wizard was patterned after the Microsoft Excel import data wizard and works very much just like the Microsoft utility.

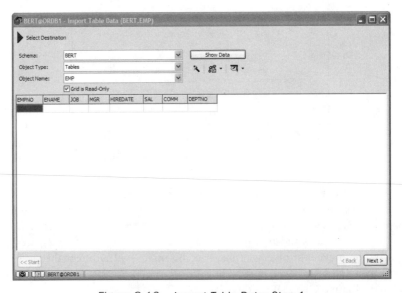

Figure 8.16   Import Table Data: Step 1

This first screen requires that you click the "Show Data" button before proceeding. The rationale behind this requirement is simple: You need to know which table you're working on and which data (if any) it already possesses before trying to load more data into it.

The second screen allows you to choose the format of the source data that you're going to import. The following options are supported:

- Dbase database file (.dbf)
- Text file (.txt)
- Excel file (.xls and .xlsx)
- Access database file (.mdb)
- Clipboard

The third screen, shown in Figure 8.17, lets you specify how the source and target entities map to each other. For example, when importing a text file, this screen lets you map the import file's fields to the target database columns. This is a critical step, and you need to spend sufficient time here to make sure that what you specify is really what you want. You don't have to map things in any special or implied order. For example, you can reverse the fields-to-columns mapping order if you like. It's all up to you; there are no limitations in terms of mapping.

	EMPNO	ENAME	JOB	MGR	HIREDATE	SAL	COMM	DEPTNO
1	7369	SMITH	CLERK	7902	12/17/1980	800		20
2	7499	ALLEN	SALESM	7698	2/20/1981	1600	300	30
3	7521	WARD	SALESM	7698	2/22/1981	1250	500	30
4	7566	JONES	MANAGE	7839	4/2/1981	2975		20
5	7654	MARTIN	SALESM	7698	9/28/1981	1250	1400	30
6	7698	BLAKE	MANAGE	7839	5/1/1981	2850		30
7	7782	CLARK	MANAGE	7839	6/9/1981	2450		10
8	7788	SCOTT	ANALYS	7566	12/9/1982	3000		20
9	7839	KING	PRESID		11/17/1981	5000		10
10	7844	TURNER	SALESM	7698	9/8/1981	1500	0	30
11	7876	ADAMS	CLERK	7788	1/12/1983	1100		20
12	7900	JAMES	CLERK	7698	12/3/1981	950		30
13	7902	FORD	ANALYS	7566	12/3/1981	3000		20
14	7934	MILLER	CLERK	7782	1/23/1982	1300		10

Figure 8.17   Import Table Data: Step 3

The fourth and final screen lets you specify database-centric behavior options, such as how often to commit the changes, whether to append the data, whether to disable constraints and triggers before carrying out the import, and whether to enable constraints and triggers after completing the import.

Summary

This chapter dealt with what very often ends up being one of the most common tasks for database users: extracting or exporting data from the Oracle database where it originally resides. After browsing and querying the data, you will often want to move that data somewhere else for further massaging or combining with other non-Oracle data. TOAD makes this process very straightforward and simple. You just need to know which capabilities TOAD offers, and when it's best to use each feature. That should now be clear from the content within this chapter.

9

Other Useful Tools

This book has been organized to focus primarily on the major TOAD features and/or functionalities that appeal to the most people and that are used most frequently. However, TOAD offers substantially more than what can be crammed into a few chapters and their centralized topics. Thus this chapter attempts to cover a smattering of unrelated features that don't easily fit into the prior chapters, yet whose functionality is still compelling and worth exposure. In baseball parlance, this chapter represents the entrance of the "closing pitcher." It attempts to bring together all the final major topics worth reading about and using (other than the final chapter's coverage of TOAD's new App Designer).

Master-Detail Browser

You might well wonder why the Master-Detail Browser was not covered in Chapter 2, where we covered both the Database Browser and the Schema Browser. The reason is simple: Those browsers are more focused on learning about the structure (with some emphasis in browsing the data), whereas the Master-Detail Browser is clearly 100% about browsing the data. Furthermore, even though the Database browser and the Schema browser possess options that affect their appearance and basic function, both start out by default with something visible and usable. In contrast, with the Master-Detail Browser, you have to define what is to be shown—and for multiple tables, what their connection is (whether defined in the database or provided by you). Thus the Master-Detail Browser is a much more interactive screen, where you must provide input and direction as to its basic operation.

Just what does the Master-Detail Browser screen do? Ever wished that you could navigate a specific table's data, and at the very same time see all the associated records from other related tables? For example, have you ever wanted to browse the ORDER table data and for each order also see the LINEITEMS for that specific order? That's what the TOAD Master-Detail Browser offers—intelligent data browsing for related tables. It lets you "*see*" your data in a much less database-centric and much more human-readable format. Both business/data analysts and database application developers have found this screen highly useful, because it truly humanizes and increases the readability of their businesses' data.

To launch the Master-Detail Browser, from the TOAD main menu select Database →
Report → Master-Detail Browser. You will see the screen shown in Figure 9.1. Note that
this screen is empty when it first launches. You must define what's to be displayed—a
process that is fully explained in the following paragraphs.

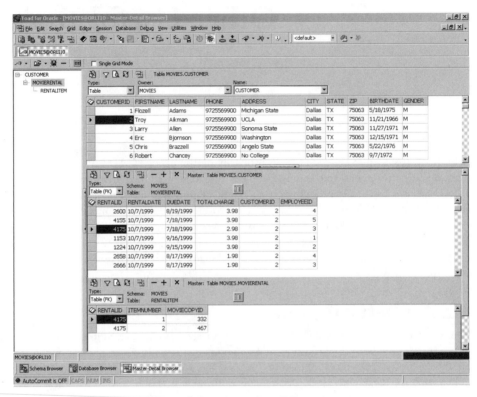

Figure 9.1   Master-Detail Browser

Before explaining just how we got the information displayed in Figure 9.1, let's first
look at what we see in such a completed screen. On the left-hand side (LHS), TOAD displays a panel showing a tree view of the relationships between parent and child tables. In Figure 9.1, we can see that the CUSTOMER table has a child table called MOVIERENTAL,
which has a child table called RENTALITEM. Furthermore, all child tables are related to
their parents by database foreign key constraints (i.e., the type for each child is shown as
Table FK). But the best part is how this screen works once the information has been provided. When you select a row in the data grid for any table, the children of that table have
their contents refreshed to correspond to the parent. Thus, when we selected the Troy Aik-
man CUSTOMER record, only the MOVIERENTALS for him are shown. The same is
true with the MOVIERENTAL and RENTALITEM records: When you select the parent
rows, the child rows match those of the parent.

But how did we get this specific information to display? Recall that when you first launch this screen, the LHS navigator and the central display area data grids are empty. Remember, that's the key difference with this screen—you must configure it for your data and browsing needs. First you need to choose the base object upon which to build the screen, as shown in Figure 9.2. Here we're selecting the CUSTOMER table as our base object.

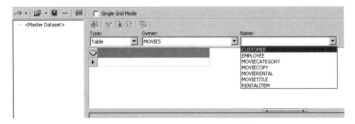

Figure 9.2   Master-Detail Browser: Choose Base Object

Of course, that action merely results in the display of a single data grid with the selected table's data, which is not too different from what happens when you use the Schema Browser or Editor. Now, however, we will add in the child tables with their automatically synchronized data. In Figure 9.3, note that the cursor shows we've clicked the "Add Detail Under This Dataset" toolbar icon. Because our database has foreign key constraints defined and enabled for the base object, the child was automatically added. Thus the MOVIERENTAL table was mechanically added as a type of "Table (FK)." We did not have to do a thing. If we repeat this process by clicking the "Add detail ..." option for this new table, the third data grid will be added for the RENTALITEM table, as shown in Figure 9.1.

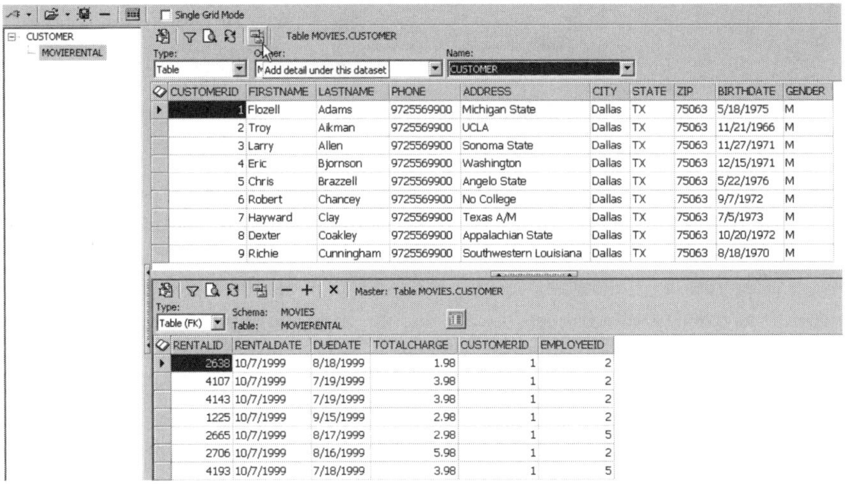

Figure 9.3   Master-Detail Browser: Add Child Object

There are three toolbar icons in the child data grid areas that you should use. Clicking the minus sign (−) will decrease the data grid size, whereas clicking the plus sign (+) will increase it. As you add more children, you'll need to use these options to manage the limited real estate available on the screen. Clicking the X toolbar icon removes the child, its data grid, and all the children below it; this function allows you to remove items from the tree view displayed on the LHS navigator. Note that you can also remove items by selecting the tree node for that item, performing a right-hand mouse (RHM) click to access the RHM menu, and selecting "Delete Current Node."

But what happens when our database does not have convenient foreign keys already defined for the automatic "Add detail …" option? How do we get the same end result? Many developers and analysts work with big third-party applications such as ERP and CRM packages, and we cannot modify the database design to get TOAD features to work with those applications. Don't worry: TOAD can handle this scenario as well. When you choose "Add detail …" and there are no preexisting database foreign keys, TOAD requires you to use the "Define Master/Detail Relationship" toolbar icon to add them, as shown in Figure 9.4. Until you perform this step of manually defining how the parent and the child relate, the data grid remains empty (i.e., TOAD has no idea of how to initially populate the data grid or how to keep it in a synchronous state).

Figure 9.4   Master-Detail Browser: Empty Child Added

When you click the "Define Master/Detail Relationship" toolbar icon, a pop-up window for manually defining the parent–child link is displayed, as shown in Figure 9.5. Of course, the top portion of this pop-up is prefilled with your base object. In our case, DEPT did not have a primary key, so only the left quadrant was prefilled with data. We then chose to have TOAD use the DEPTNO column as the parent's key, chose the EMP tables to serve as the child, and selected the DEPTNO column to serve as the child's key. *TOAD is not creating any database keys nor constraints* here; rather, we are simply telling TOAD how to auto-sync these tables (i.e., instructing TOAD what the join conditions are for the related data grids). Also note that the "Type" for the child will be "Other" and not "Table (FK)"; this notation is used for any object with user-selected criteria that explain how to link parent and child.

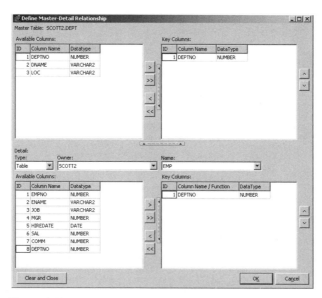

Figure 9.5   Master-Detail Browser: Manually Defining Links

No matter which method (auto versus manual) you used to construct your Master-Detail Browser screen, you will want to save your work so that you can later reopen the screen and have it appear exactly as you have defined it. To do so, click the floppy disk toolbar icon, which saves the complete current screen definition as an ".MD" file. When you restart the Master-Detail Browser, you can choose to open that prebuilt screen. Also, be aware that your screens where you define manual master/detail relationships (i.e., links) between tables are stored in this file.

ER Diagram

Ever wanted a diagram of some of your tables, so that you can visualize their structure while writing either SQL or PL/SLQ code? Or maybe you need to attend a code review, and you want a picture to refer to while assessing code. There are many such occasions where a small physical data model of the important tables would be handy—the key word here being "small." TOAD offers a very basic ER diagramming feature for just such purposes. It's not meant to replace a full-featured data modeling tool, but rather to fill this gap for those smaller and isolated needs. For example, if you need to work with roughly two dozen or fewer tables and would like a picture of them plus their relationships, TOAD's ER Diagram can do the trick.

To launch the ER Diagram, from the TOAD main menu select Database → Report → ER Diagram. You will see the screen shown in Figure 9.6. Note that this screen will be empty when it first launches. You must define what is to be displayed and how—a process that is fully explained in the following paragraphs.

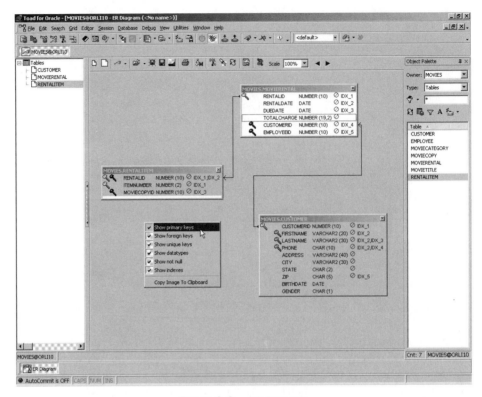

Figure 9.6   ER Diagram

Before explaining just how we got the information displayed in Figure 9.6, let's look at what we see in such a completed screen. On the LHS, TOAD displays a panel showing a tree view of the tables in this diagram. When you select an object in this tree-view display, the matching object in the diagram will be brought into view and highlighted; this option should be your main quick-navigation tool for these diagrams. Also, the tree-view objects offer the same RHM menu options as are available with the Schema Browser. Thus you can drop and alter objects, or perform any other TOAD action on those objects directly from inside the ER Diagram. Furthermore, if you access the RHM menu for a diagram object, you will see all the same options. Thus the diagram itself can function as a graphic Schema Browser of sorts. Finally, as you can see in Figure 9.6, when we access the RHM menu on just the drawing canvas area, we can choose the key display options.

But how did we get this specific information to display? When you first launch this screen, the LHS navigator and the central drawing canvas area will all be empty. To add (and remove objects) from an ER Diagram drawing canvas area, we must use TOAD's Object Palette, which is found on the right-hand side (RHS) fly-out panel in Figure 9.6.

To display the Object Palette, from the TOAD main menu select View → Object Palette. Now you can drag and drop objects from the Object Palette to the ER Diagram.

The ER Diagram feature also offers a much less manually oriented, quick-start method for creating models with a group of related objects already imported. When you click the "New ER Diagram" toolbar icon (upper leftmost choice), the screen shown in Figure 9.7 appears. This wizard permits you to make four choices that automatically create a complete model: the schema, a starting table, the levels of foreign keys to automatically traverse, and any tables to exclude along the way. The third item is especially powerful, as it tells TOAD how many levels of foreign keys to follow and whether to include all those objects found. But be careful: If you start at one of your central tables and choose a high level (e.g., > 5), then you might end up with hundreds of items in your ER Diagram. (Remember, we stressed that this feature is best for limited-use scenarios.)

Figure 9.7   ER Diagram: New Diagram

Finally, there's another way to launch the "New ER Diagram" pop-up screen in an interesting way. The Schema Browser RHM menu offers an "ER Diagram" option, which launches the New ER Diagram screen with the schema and table already set based on where you were in the Schema Browser. Be careful when selecting the recursion level here as well.

No matter which method (auto versus manual) you used to construct your ER Diagram, you will want to save this work so that when you later reopen the diagram, it will appear exactly as you have defined it. To do so, click the floppy disk toolbar icon, which saves the complete current screen definition as an ".ERD" file. When you restart the ER Diagram at a later time, you can simply choose to open that prebuilt model.

Code Road Map

Ever wanted a diagram of some of your PL/SQL objects, so that you can visualize their interdependencies relative to other coded objects or even the tables that they reference? Some people refer to this process as impact analysis, as it reveals everything that will be affected by coding or database structural changes. Or maybe you need to attend a code review, and you want to take along a picture to refer to while assessing the code. How does the new code fit into the overall project and with which components does it interact? TOAD offers the Code Road Map for just such purposes. Like the ER Diagram (see prior section), this feature is not meant to construct mammoth models; rather, it's better for specific and isolated or limited purposes.

To launch the Code Road Map, from the TOAD main menu select Database → Report → Code Road Map. You will see the screen shown in Figure 9.8. This screen is empty when it first launches. You must define what's to be displayed and how—a process that is fully explained in the following paragraphs.

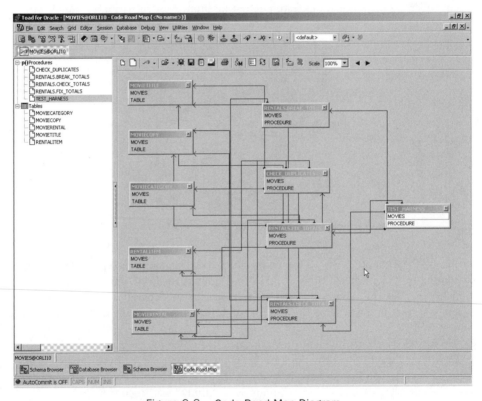

Figure 9.8   Code Road Map Diagram

Before explaining just how we got the information displayed in Figure 9.8, let's look at the completed screen. On the LHS, TOAD displays a panel showing a tree view of the code objects and optional tables in this diagram. When you select an object in this tree-view display, the matching object in the diagram will be brought into view and highlighted;

this should be your main quick-navigation tool for these diagrams. Also, the tree-view objects offer all of the same RHM menu options as are available in the Schema Browser. Thus you can drop and alter objects, or perform any other TOAD action on those objects directly from inside the Code Road Map. Furthermore, if you access the RHM menu for a diagram object, all of the same options will be available. Thus the diagram itself can function as a graphic Schema Browser of sorts.

But how did we get the specific information to display? Unfortunately, TOAD's Object Palette works for database structural objects such as tables and views, but not for coding objects such as procedures and packages. Thus, unlike in the ER Diagram (discussed earlier in this chapter), we cannot use the Object Palette to incrementally build the model based on specific selections. That's a major shortcoming in TOAD, and one that we hope to see corrected in a future release.

The Code Road Map offers only the automated quick-start method for creating models with a group of related objects already imported. When you click the "New Code Road Map" toolbar icon (upper leftmost choice), you will see the screen shown in Figure 9.9. This wizard permits you to make six choices that automatically create a complete model for you: the schema, the code object type, the starting code unit, the levels of program interdependencies to automatically traverse, the items to display (code only versus both code and tables), and some display options/filters. The fourth item is especially powerful, as it tells TOAD how many levels of program interdependencies to follow and whether to include all those objects found. But be careful: If you start at one of your central tables and choose a high level (e.g., > 5 with data or > 10 without data), then you might end up with hundreds of items in your Code Road Map. Also, remember that this feature is best for limited-use scenarios.

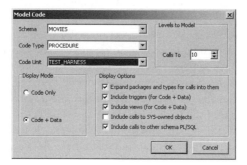

Figure 9.9   Code Road Map: New Diagram

Finally, there's another way to launch this "Code Road Map" pop-up screen in an interesting way. The Schema Browser RHM menu offers a "Code Road Map" option, which launches the "New Code Road Map" screen with the schema, object type, and code object already set based on where you were in the Schema Browser. Again, be careful when selecting the recursion level here.

There's one final note worth mentioning here: The Code Road Map does a lot more than just follow the Oracle table for code dependencies. The real value here is that TOAD scans the code and finds a plethora of hidden or less obvious dependencies. For example, the Code Road Map includes and handles triggers in its traversal. For example, if procedure X calls procedure Y, and procedure Y updates table A, which then fires trigger B, which now calls procedure Z, then TOAD's Code Road Map will include X, Y, and Z. Many other tools would have missed procedure Z, because they don't handle triggers properly. Thus the Code Road Map can eliminate many impact analysis mistakes that might be overlooked due to obscured trigger side effects. That comprehensive quality makes the Code Road Map highly useful.

Once you've assembled a Code Road Map diagram that you like, you will want to save this work so that when you later reopen the diagram, it will appear exactly as you have defined it. To do so, click the floppy disk toolbar icon, which saves the complete current screen definition as an ".CRM" file. When you restart the Code Road Map, you can then choose to open that prebuilt model.

One last thought: The Code Road Map diagram probably doesn't fully stand all by itself (i.e., as your only working documentation). We recommend that you combine the Code Road Map with the output from either the TOAD HTML Schema Doc Generator or the Generate Schema Script. That way, you have both the 50,000-foot view (i.e., Code Road Map) and the 5,000-foot detailed perspective for all the database objects.

Query Builder

For a lot of business or data analysts, writing SQL is not their idea of fun and quite often not their forte. They would much rather (and rightly so) focus just on what "needs to be done" rather than the SQL code required to get there. Even experienced database application developers find SQL writing tedious at times, and would welcome a way to jump-start or streamline writing complex statements. Thus TOAD offers the Query Builder—a graphical user interface that allows you to draw your way to the SQL code. It's a great tool; we could easily write a whole chapter on just this one feature. In this section, we will expose the major portions of the Query Builder that are used most frequently so as to get you up and running with this feature. You should then research and experiment with the Query Builder further, because you might find that it becomes your preferred method for writing SQL.

If you've already read about the TOAD ER Diagram (a few sections back), then you can consider the Query Builder to be essentially an ER Diagram that adds SQL generation to the picture. The key difference is that for the ED Diagram the picture is the end result, whereas for the Query Builder the key output is the SQL code for the picture.

To launch the Query Builder, from the TOAD main menu select Database → Report → Query Builder. You will see the screen shown in Figure 9.10. This screen will appear empty when it launches. You must define what should be displayed and how—a process that is fully explained in the following paragraphs.

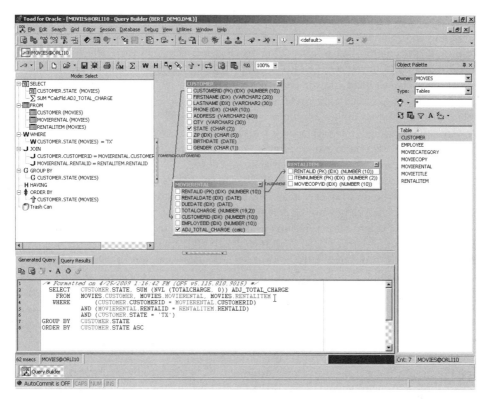

Figure 9.10   Query Builder

Before explaining just how the information displayed in Figure 9.10 got there, let's look at the completed screen in its entirety. On the LHS, TOAD displays a panel showing a tree view of the major SELECT statement syntactical components. This tree view supports drag-and-drop arrangement of pieces, so you can copy items from one section of the code to another (e.g., you can copy SELECT columns to the ORDER BY section). The central drawing canvas displays the database objects or portions of objects that you've selected, and the bottom offers two tabs: the generated query and the data grid containing the results when that query is executed. As you perform operations in either the tree view or the canvas drawing area, the generated query tab updates the code to reflect those changes. Clearly, there's a lot going on in this screen.

But how did we get the specific information to display in this screen? As mentioned earlier, when you first launch this screen, the LHS navigator and the central drawing canvas area will be empty. To add and remove objects from a Query Builder drawing canvas area, we must use TOAD's Object Palette (the RHS fly-out panel in Figure 9.10). To display the Object Palette, from the TOAD main menu select View → Object Palette. Now you can drag and drop objects from the Object Palette to the Query Builder.

Adding objects to the drawing canvas via the Object Palette generates updates to the LHS only in the FROM and JOIN sections (and, of course, in the SQL shown at the bottom of the screen). In other words, adding or removing tables and views affects only the FROM and JOIN operations. The FROM is pretty simple: There's a one-to-one correspondence between what you add and what is added to the list. The JOIN is more complex, as it adds any and all join conditions required for the selected tables. Thus, if the table's primary key has multiple columns, several join condition lines will be added. This feature alone is a huge time-saver, and is worth using before you resort to the Editor simply because it allows you to avoid coding complex and lengthy joins. You'll need to do other things to cause changes to the remaining sections.

How do we add columns to the SELECT section? The easiest method is to drag and drop them from the drawing canvas to the SELECT section. But did you notice in Figure 9.10 that each table's box on the drawing canvas has check boxes next to every column? They allow you to select which items should be added to the SELECT section of the LHS. We chose to select the CUSTOMER table's STATE column (a practice that relational theory calls "projection"). But what if we had a table with lots of columns and we wanted to select all of them for projection? Look at Figure 9.11, where we clicked the RHM menu option to display the options available; we can choose the Select All option. Note, also, two other key options: the alias for the table and the column. These two options will display simple pop-up screens that permit you to provide an alias for table and column names, which in turn affects the SQL code generated. For example, perhaps you would prefer to see CUSTOMER abbreviated as "CUST" in all your SQL code. Or perhaps you want to specify whether the SQL's table names should be prefixed by their schema—that is, whether the table name should be MOVIES.CUSTOMER or just CUSTOMER.

Figure 9.11   Query Builder: Right-Hand Mouse Menu

Next we need to place some items into the WHERE section (which relational theory calls "restriction"). We can use either of two approaches to accomplish this task. First we can select multiple items and then drag and drop columns from the SELECT section to the WHERE section. But what if the columns we want to use as constraints are not something that we want to project? That leads us to the second approach: We can drag and drop columns from the drawing canvas to the WHERE section. Note the key difference between these two methods. When we use the first method, the columns are added to the WHERE section as empty columns (i.e., without any details); you then need to double-click on them to launch the WHERE Definition screen shown in Figure 9.12. In contrast, when we use the second method, the screen pops up automatically. In our case, we kept matters very simple; we chose STATE = 'TX'. Such a simple WHERE clause condition is doable using the screen's "User" mode tab at the bottom (which we think really means "easy," as opposed to the "Expert" mode).

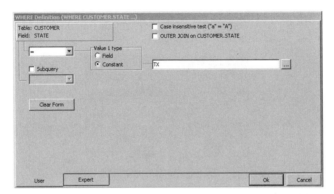

Figure 9.12   Query Builder: Basic WHERE Definition

Sometimes you may want to build queries that cannot be handled by the simple "User" tab. At that point, you'll need to investigate the "Expert" tab. When you click that tab, TOAD first displays a pop-up warning stating that you may not be able to go back to user mode depending on what you do. Then you'll see the screen shown in Figure 9.13. This screen has three areas (SQL Functions, SQL Operators, and Data Fields and Defined Calculated Fields) that you can double-click to select and add those items to the top field where you construct the complex WHERE clause syntax.

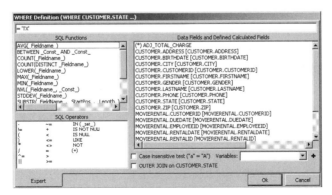

Figure 9.13   Query Builder: Expert WHERE Definition

For the ORDER BY and GROUP BY sections, the development process is fairly easy. As with the WHERE section, you can select multiple columns for a drag-and-drop operation down from the SELECT section, or you can drag and drop the columns from the drawing canvas area. Of course, both of these SQL operations require internal sort operations, so there are performance ramifications for adding either. Remember, too, that when you add GROUP BY columns, SQL requires all non-GROUP BY columns to be covered by a grouping function. Thus you may need to double-click on those columns in the SELECT section to display the screen shown in Figure 9.14, where you can add the required grouping functions. Otherwise, Oracle will generate an error when you try to execute the query: "ORA-00979: not a GROUP BY expression."

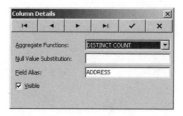

Figure 9.14   Query Builder: Grouping Functions

There's one final point related to the use of Query Builder for SQL construction that we need to cover. In Figure 9.10, notice that the MOVIERENTAL table has a column called ADJ_TOTAL_CHARGE whose data type is "(calc)." In fact, there is no such column in the table because this is a calculated field. Figure 9.15 zooms in to better show this calculated field. In the SELECT section, it's prefixed with an asterisk and an alias of "CalcFld"; in the table box shown on the drawing canvas, it has the previously mentioned data type of "calc." How did it get there? In Figure 9.10, the screen has 18 toolbar icons, most of which we don't have time to cover. The "Sigma" (Σ) toolbar icon, however, deserves further explanation.

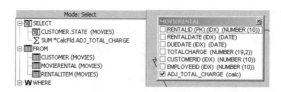

Figure 9.15   Query Builder: Calculated Field Example

When we want to define calculated fields, we click the "Sigma" (Σ) toolbar icon, which brings up the pop-up shown in Figure 9.16. In this dialog box, you will either define or update any calculated fields that you need. Whether you click the plus (+) sign button to create a new calculated field or the three ellipses (...) button to update an existing calculated field, initiating an action here launches the "Calculated Field Definition" screen shown in Figure 9.17. Note that it's almost identical to the WHERE Definition screen shown in Figure 9.13; thus, if you know and understand one, then you will be able to use both screens effectively.

Figure 9.16   Query Builder: Calculated Field Editor

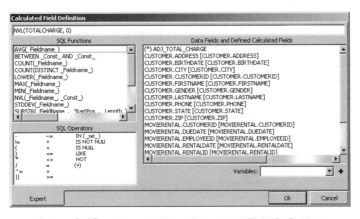

Figure 9.17   Query Builder: Calculated Field Definition

We have now covered most of the Query Builder's construction aspects. Once you have a query built, your focus should move to the bottom third of the screen and its two tabs: "Generated Query" and "Query Results." Instead of executing the query at this point, you might instead choose to send it to the Editor by clicking the "Generated Query" tab's second toolbar icon. That way you can elaborate on or just work with the generated query manually. Many people use the Query Builder this way—as a shortcut that builds 70% of their query quickly and easily; they then complete the remaining 30% of the work manually in the Editor. If you are happy to run the query in the Query Builder, then you would click the green arrow icon on this window's main toolbar to execute it. This will cause the focus to switch to the "Query Results" tab and you will see your data displayed.

Once you've assembled a Query Builder query that you like, you will want to save this work so that when you later reopen the query, it will appear exactly as you have defined it. To do so, click the floppy disk toolbar icon, which saves the complete current query definition as a ".DML" file. When you restart the Query Builder at a later date, you can then choose to open that prebuilt query.

There's one final Query Builder feature that we will cover here that many people are unaware of—and yet it's one of the most useful features. Ever wished you could take a preexisting text file containing a SELECT statement and reverse-engineer it into the Query Builder? Well, you can. This feature was added a few versions ago in TOAD and has improved with each subsequent release. Simply choose the "Open Existing Model" toolbar icon, change the file type from ".DML" to ".SQL", and then choose your SQL text file. TOAD will reverse-engineer that command into Query Builder, ensuring that you have a graphical version of your query to work with.

External Tools

Sometimes while you're in TOAD, you may need to jump into another program, such as Quest Software's Script Runner or Oracle's SQL Plus. You may not want to use the Windows Start menu to bring up these applications, because you would have to repeat information, such as your database connection user ID and password. TOAD has an intelligent and customizable program launcher that makes opening other programs a very clean and simple process.

To launch the External Tools Options configuration screen, from the TOAD main menu select Utilities → External Tools. You will see the screen shown in Figure 9.18. The window will initially be empty because TOAD, by default, does not come with any external tools knowledge predefined.

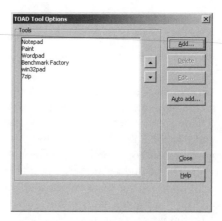

Figure 9.18   External Tools: Configuration

To jump-start the process of defining external tools, TOAD offers the "Auto add…" button, which automatically discovers several key programs you are likely to want to use (if they are installed). When you click this button, the screen shown in Figure 9.19 will appear. Simply highlight the entries you find useful and click "OK." Those programs will then appear as available options on the main External Tools screen.

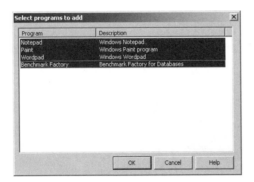

Figure 9.19   External Tools: Auto Add

You may also want to add your own entries so that you can specify various aspects of the program launch, such as the working directory, Oracle user ID and password, and other parameters. For that, you will need to click the "Add …" button, which launches the pop-up shown in Figure 9.20. Here we've set it to launch the Oracle SQL*Plus utility in the C:\Temp directory, and to pass our current connection's Oracle user ID and password.

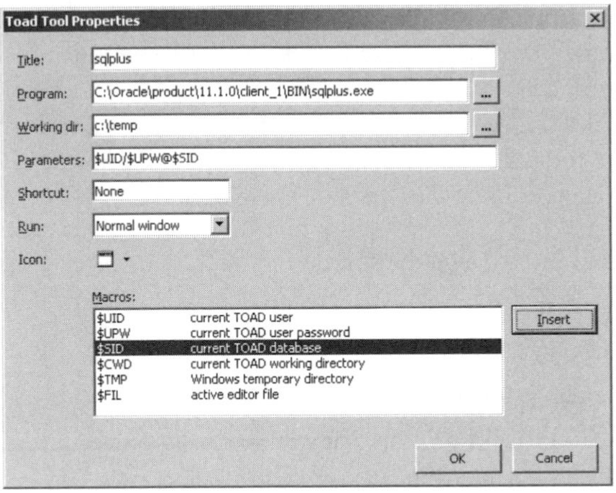

Figure 9.20   External Tools: Manual Add

With these choices, anytime and from anywhere in TOAD when we want to launch into Oracle's SQL*Plus for the same database connection, we can choose the drop-down menu off the TOAD main toolbar as shown in Figure 9.21. That's all there is to it. Perhaps at this point you're saying, "So what—TOAD already offers a similar capability to invoke SQL*Plus from within the Editor." In fact, now you can choose which applications can be easily invoked and how they're called. Plus those applications are now callable from anywhere within TOAD.

Figure 9.21   External Tools: Launch an Application

Compare Files

One fundamental task that nearly everyone needs to do is to compare text files for differences. Windows offers the COMP command for that purpose, and UNIX has the diff command. Both of these commands are command-line utilities that lack advanced GUIs or reporting capabilities. In contrast, TOAD offers the Compare Files utility—an advanced GUI for simplifying all comparison tasks and review.

To launch the Compare Files utility, from the TOAD main menu select Utilities → Compare Files. You will first be prompted to choose both the source and target files for comparison. After you make your selections, you will see the screen shown in Figure 9.22.

The Compare Files screen offers quite a bit of useful information, so take the time to learn and use all the toolbar icons found on this screen. The primary choices among this screen's toolbar icons worth knowing include these options:

- Switch Sides: to interchange the source and target
- Prior/Next Difference: to move backward and forward
- Just Show Regular/Major Differences
- Just Show Matching Lines
- Comparison Summary: a pop-up that summarizes the overall results
- Options: a pop-up for controlling numerous appearance items
- File Comparison Rules: a pop-up that provides extensive control over the comparison process (i.e., what actually constitutes a difference)

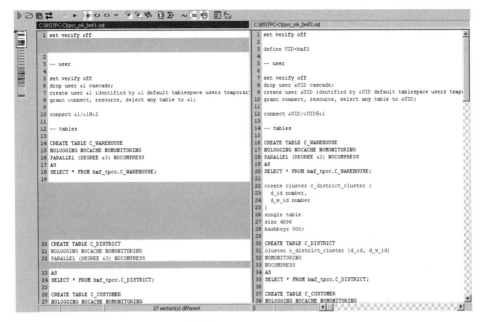

Figure 9.22   Compare Files: Result

TNS Editor

Any developer or DBA who works with multiple Oracle databases on many different servers will invariably end up at some point with a need to modify his or her Oracle TNS Names file. Some people will just open the file in a text editor and have at it. Others will use Oracle's Java utilities: Net Manager or Net Configuration Assistant (NETCA). But either of those approaches requires leaving TOAD and its user-friendly and highly productive GUI. Thus TOAD offers the TNS Names Editor screen for making short work of modifying even the most complex TNS Names file.

To launch the TNS Names Editor screen, from the TOAD main menu select Utilities → TNS Names Editor. You will see the screen shown in Figure 9.23. You might wonder why it offers a split screen or two panels for working with TNS Names files. The reason is quite simple: Very often you'll need to copy entries back and forth between files. That's exactly why the "VCR" buttons (i.e., >, <, >>, and <<) are provided.

The base screen offers some very useful toolbar icons that you should know about and use. The green check mark performs a TNS Names file syntax check for the entire file. The lightning bolt performs a database ping (i.e., *tnsping*) for the selected entry. But it's the "New Service" and "Edit Service" (F2) toolbar icons that are of the most interest. Both launch the pop-up screen shown in Figure 9.24, which makes defining or updating services straightforward and easy. In fact, this screen very much mimics, in both look and capabilities, Oracle NETCA.

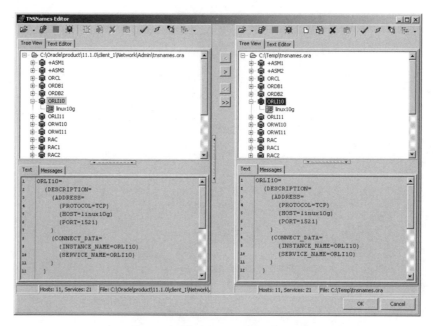

Figure 9.23   TNS Names Editor

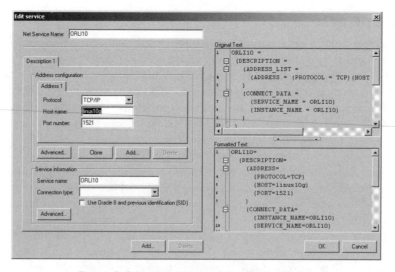

Figure 9.24   TNS Names Editor: Edit Service

Script Manager

Over time almost anyone doing serious Oracle work—DBAs and developers alike—will collect numerous SQL scripts. Moreover, there are always those hard-core DBAs and developers who simply prefer SQL scripts to any GUI, period. Wouldn't it be nice if TOAD could help you create, organize, manage, and execute your collections of SQL scripts? For those users who are opposed to GUI tools like TOAD, such a script library management interface might possibly pique their interest as well. Actually, TOAD offers a handy feature to meet these users' needs—the Script Manager.

To launch the Script Manager, from the TOAD main menu select Utilities → Script Manager. You will see the screen shown in Figure 9.25.

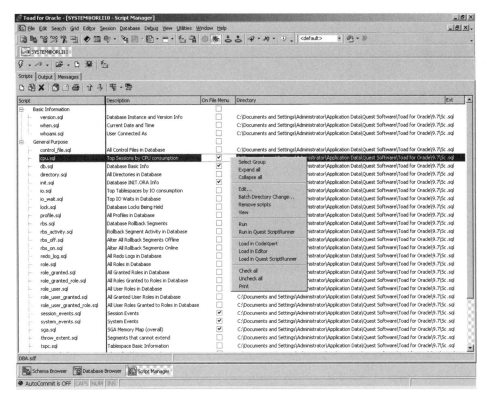

Figure 9.25   Script Manager Screen

The TOAD Script Manager uses special ".SDF" files that record the meta-data for your script libraries. TOAD ships with three highly useful predefined categories of scripts: DBA, Schema Objects, and Oracle Data Dictionary. Of course, you can create additional categories for your own collections of scripts as well as modify these prebuilt ones. In Figure 9.25, we've chosen to open the DBA library of scripts. The next few paragraphs will first talk about setting up the SQL libraries, which may not seem particularly exciting. But then we'll show the true power of the Script Manager—which is revealed when we begin working with those script libraries once they're defined.

There's quite a bit going on in Figure 9.25, so let's examine it in more detail. We begin by examining the more important RHM menu options:

- Edit: opens a pop-up window for modifying the properties (i.e., the script category or use, the script description and its location).

- View: opens (i.e., launches) your external text editor option for the highlighted script.

- Run: sends the script contents to the TOAD Editor and then executes it as a script (i.e., F5); thus you will see the output.

- Load in Editor: sends the script contents to the TOAD Editor.

We also need to examine the first five toolbar icons under the "Scripts" tab. The first and second are simple enough: "Add Scripts" and "Edit Scripts." They open pop-up windows much like the "View" RHM choice. The third icon (the red X) enables you to remove a script entry from the library. It's the fourth and fifth icons that offer some interesting potential. If you select multiple script entries and then click the fourth icon ("Combine Scripts"), TOAD will create a new script (which you can give a unique name) that calls all the selected scripts in the order you selected them. Hence you can select scripts A, B, and C and create a new script called D that calls scripts A, B, and C, in that order. Don't laugh: Many DBAs and developers build scripts incrementally. This practice also enables you to build portions for basic reusability. In fact, whenever you select multiple scripts and request an action to be performed, TOAD asks if you want to combine and name them. The fifth and final icon under the "Scripts" tab ("Schedule Script") lets you schedule via your Windows Task Manager.

In Figure 9.25, what do the scripts denoted with a check mark in the "On File Menu" do? That's where the real power of the Script Manager emerges. These checked scripts, which are known as "Quick Scripts," appear in the main menu toolbar for the Script Manager drop-down menu, as shown in Figure 9.26. Choosing a Quick Script from this drop-down menu causes that script to be loaded into the Editor and then executed as a

Figure 9.26   Script Manager: Quick Scripts

script (i.e., as if you had pressed F9). Thus you can run your scripts anytime you need them, from anywhere within TOAD. That is, TOAD is serving as nothing more than a script management and execution facility—which should make it attractive even to those anti-GUI people.

Summary

TOAD is the amazing "Swiss army knife" of Oracle database tools, offering more "blades" than any other utility. TOAD offers an enormous number of useful features and capabilities, many of which do not nicely fall into the basic themes covered in prior chapters of this book, but which nevertheless deserve discussion. This chapter attempted to cover the remaining smattering of important and useful features. Some capabilities covered here are full-featured enough to warrant their own chapters. Given that TOAD offers more features than any book could cover completely, we've simply attempted here to provide adequate coverage for a large group of topics you should be aware of and investigate further on your own. Because when the question is, "Can TOAD do that?" you should just remember the old Ragu spaghetti sauce commercial catch-phrase: "It's in there."

TOAD App Designer

TOAD is first and foremost an Oracle productivity tool—and as we said back in Chapter 1, productivity is its mantra. Most of this book's content, however, requires a person to launch TOAD and perform manual labor or tasks (except for those few screens that offer an option to schedule the final step for execution). Of course, many of you have a need to perform some database task on a regular basis, and you don't want to have to do anything in TOAD except to instruct it to perform that exact same operation with zero user input. What you're basically asking for is something like a TOAD "record" and "playback" macro mode of operation. Furthermore, the playback should be callable via the command line so that you don't have to do anything at all in TOAD. Guess what? That capability has been available in TOAD for many years now, although it has certainly evolved over time. In this chapter, we'll explain both the older TOAD command-line mechanism and the new TOAD App Designer.

Before reading on, note that the TOAD Command Line mode, which has been available for some time, is being gradually (and, in time, completely) replaced by the much more powerful TOAD App Designer. For this reason, you should embrace the new facility, which debuted in TOAD 9.7. A preliminary attempt was made to provide this capability in TOAD 9.6 that was called the Action Console, but it quickly evolved into the App Designer. Thus, depending on which TOAD version you're currently using and the status of the App Designer progress to fully provide such capabilities, you may find that you have multiple choices presented under several terminologies. Rest assured, however, that very soon the App Designer will be only method available within TOAD.

TOAD Command Line

The old TOAD Command Line feature works fairly simply. When you launch certain screens, they will possess two icons on their toolbar, as shown in Figure 10.1. "Load All Settings from File" and "Save Settings to File" will generally (but not always) be in the first two toolbar icon positions. When you choose the save icon, it creates a text file that contains all of the information that you set every screen control. In Figure 10.1, we have

asked the "Generate Schema Script" option to create a file called C:\Temp\SCOTT.sql. If
we were to now click the green arrow toolbar button to execute the task, we would find
the requested SQL file in the temp directory. We will not execute this task, however, but
rather will click the save toolbar icon and ask TOAD to create a command-line file called
C:\Temp\gen_scott_schema.txt.

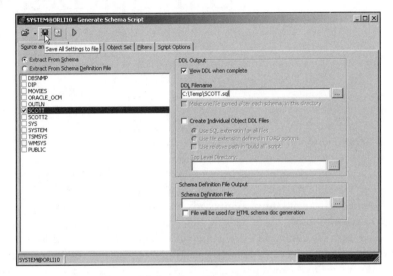

Figure 10.1   Save/Load Settings

What does a TOAD command line file look like? It is a human-readable file (well, kind
of), and you can set some options in terms of how you make decisions or program for further control. Listing 10.1 shows the simple C:\Temp\gen_scott_schema.txt file that was
generated for Figure 10.1. Look this entire listing over, but realize there are only two very
minor portions that you'll really need to understand and work with—they're covered
next. Most of the lines are just screen control settings that reset the screen to the desired
state during execution and, therefore, can be safely ignored.

Listing 10.1   **Command-Line Settings File**

```
#
#  You can create a schema script from a command line
#  using this file with a few modifications.
#
#  Lines that start with a # are comments.
#
#  Calling TOAD like this will invoke the generate schema script screen
#  from the command line:
#
```

```
#   "C:\Program Files\Quest Software\Toad for Oracle\toad.exe" -c "SYSTEM/
#   <7,0,0,0,162,120,216,188,161,190,36,227,159,16,143,48,222,8,104,199>@ORLI10"
#   GSS="c:\temp\gen__scott_schema.txt"
#
#   Obviously, your path to TOAD may differ, along with your connect info.
#   The file name after "GSS=" is the name of this file.
#
#   To disable the Team Coding login prompt,
#   add "TC=NO" (without the quotes) in the command-line string.
#
#   You can also generate a schema script from a command file like this:
#
#   "C:\Program Files\Quest Software\Toad for Oracle\toad.exe" -c SYSTEM/
#   <7,0,0,0,162,120,216,188,161,190,36,227,159,16,143,48,222,8,104,199>@ORLI10
#   CMDFILE=c:\mycommandfile.txt
#
#   qhere mycommandfile.txt might look like this, after first generating a schema
#   script, then performing an index rebuild, doing a schema comparison, and
#   finally building some HTML schema documentation.
#
#   GSS=c:\schemascript.txt
#   RMI=c:\indrebuild.txt
#   COMP=c:\schemacomp1.txt
#   GENHTML=c:\html1.txt
#
#
#   When you start TOAD with the GSS command-line option, the generation of the
#   schema script will start automatically. There are only two possible commands:
#   one to close the Generate schema script window, and one to close TOAD after the
#   script is created. Do not put more than one command per line. Do not leave
#   spaces before the commands.
#
#   Command Summary:
#   -----------------
#   CloseGSS
#   CloseTOAD
#
#
####################################
#         Begin Settings           #
####################################
cbPctAlways|0
sePctAlways|0
cbInitialNext|0
cbScaleBy|0
seScaleBy|25
seMinSize|4
cbMinSize|KB
```

Listing 10.1   **Command-Line Settings File,** *continued*

```
seMaxSize|200
cbMaxSize|MB
rgBasedOn|0

. . .
```

First, we need to decide how TOAD will play back this command file. When we run a command-line file, the steps are as follows: The TOAD application launches, opens the requested command file, calls or opens the screen for that command file, sets all the screen's controls, and then executes that screen (e.g., you click the green arrow toolbar icon). But what should happen after that? Look at the second bolded set of lines in Listing 10.1. The comment describes two commands that you can uncomment: *CloseGSS* to close the open Generate Schema Script screen, and *CloseTOAD* to close the TOAD application itself. It's been our experience that you'll typically want to uncomment both of these lines, because you'll most often just use the TOAD Command Line facility to automate the process of performing a single task.

The second and more important issue is now that we've recorded a screen's settings to a file and possibly edited that file for the desired close action, how do we use it (i.e., how do we run TOAD and execute the command-line file)? Look again at Listing 10.1. The first bolded set of lines details the screen-specific command-line parameter to pass to TOAD to invoke this command file. We need to run TOAD while passing the parameter "GSS=", where GSS stands for "Generate Schema Script." We also need to pass a database connection parameter, because this screen requires a database connection. We can accomplish this via the TOAD "−C" parameter, which provides connection information. The resulting invocation looks like the Windows command-line (".BAT") script shown in Listing 10.2. If we now double-click on this command file from Windows Explorer, TOAD will launch, perform this task, shut down, and leave us with the desired output file.

Listing 10.2   **BAT File Using the TOAD Command Line**

```
SET DB_ID=bert
SET DB_PWD=bert
SET DB_SID=ORCL
"C:\Program Files\Quest Software\Toad for Oracle\toad.exe" -c
%DB_ID%/%DB_PWD%@%DB_SID% gss="c:\temp\gen_scott_schema.txt"
EXIT
```

Remember, the TOAD Command Line feature is being phased out in favor of the newer and more powerful TOAD App Designer, so you are likely to see fewer screens with the save and load settings options going forward. Even the screens that now offer this ability soon will not. Put simply, your collection of command files will be useless someday soon. If you are not already using the TOAD Command Line, now is probably not the time to start doing so. If you are already using the TOAD Command Line, now is the time to start changing your process so that you switch to the TOAD App Designer.

TOAD App Designer

There were many problems with the old TOAD Command Line feature, most of which are in the process of being corrected by the new TOAD App Designer. For example, the TOAD Command Line suffers from the following shortcomings:

- It is not consistently offered throughout TOAD screens.
- It can perform only a single screen's tasks or operation.
- It cannot chain together tasks or operations into streams.
- It does not provide conditional logic for complex processing.
- It does not provide loop constructs for complex processing.

Basically both the feature set and the foundation for TOAD Command Line proved to be a dead end. Consequently, something new and more capable was needed. The new TOAD App Designer meets all these challenges—and many more.

The App Designer feature is relatively easy to use. When you launch certain screens, two icons will appear on the lower-left corner of the window, as shown in Figure 10.2. The first icon, the camera, is the "Save/Load Window Snapshot." It's the primary interface we'll examine here. In Figure 10.2, we have asked HTML Schema Doc Generator to create an HTML report of the SCOTT schema with an HTML index file called C:\Temp\scott.html. If we were to now click the green arrow toolbar button to execute this task, we would find the requested HTML report in the temp directory. However, we will not execute this task, but rather will click the camera icon ("Save/Load Window Snapshot") to build our new application.

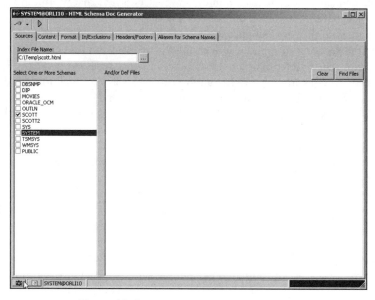

Figure 10.2   App Designer: From Screens

Clicking the camera icon brings up the screen shown in Figure 10.3. What's happening here is that we have started to construct a TOAD application. An application has both a name and actions (i.e., operations or tasks) that belong to it. In Command Line parlance, an "action" is much the same as the command file. It represents a single screen's record settings selection for execution. We can either assign the action to an existing application or create a new application by entering a currently nonexistent application name. Once we click the "OK" button, this new action will be added to the chosen application. That's it. No command file is generated, but rather a facility within TOAD itself manages the application and their actions.

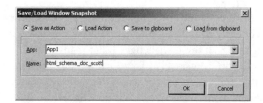

Figure 10.3   App Designer: Save Snapshot

To launch the TOAD App Designer, from the TOAD main menu select Utilities → App Designer. You will see the screen shown in Figure 10.4. There's a lot going on here, so let's dissect all of the options. Once you master this screen, you can actually create all of your applications and their actions right from this screen—with no real need to go to each screen and click the camera icon in the lower-left corner. That will mean you'll be able to build applications much more quickly and easily.

Let's begin with the App Designer screen's main toolbar icons. The first three toolbar icons support executing an application (i.e., all of its actions), just the action selected, or everything from the selected action in an application to the final one, respectively. The next two toolbar icons are also very straightforward: create a new application or delete one. They are followed by a schedule application icon, which defines the Windows Task Manager scheduled job required to run the TOAD application. Figure 10.5 shows what this screen looks like, including the corresponding Command Line invocation. The App Designer syntax is much simpler than the Command Line syntax, because now there is just a single parameter to pass. The "–a" parameter followed by the application name— that's it. The final two toolbar icons worth mentioning are the export and import the application to and from a file. Basically TOAD can save and load application definitions to text files. Note, however, that this capability is *not* meant to serve as a bridge between the old command-line text files and applications and the App Designer.

Can we see what a TOAD action really looks like under the covers? You bet—just execute a right-hand mouse (RHM) click on an action and choose "Copy" from the resulting menu. Next, open a text editor and paste in the clipboard contents. You should see text like that produced by our "html_schema_doc_scott" action in Listing 10.3. But unlike

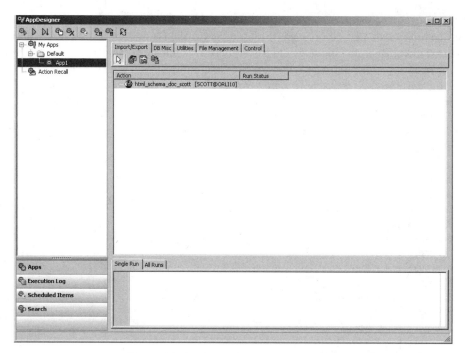

Figure 10.4   App Designer: Main Screen

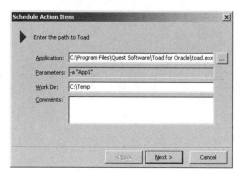

Figure 10.5   App Designer: Scheduling

when you are working in Command Line mode, you don't have to edit or even care about the contents of this file. However, there is a tremendously useful feature available for cutting and pasting the action contents. You can now easily email or copy them to a flash disk to hand out to your coworkers. This same concept applies to any applications you want to export to text files as well.

Listing 10.3 provides the entire App Designer code that is generated by this action. While it may look like a lot of code, this listing is actually far shorter than what the old TOAD Command Line mode would have generated; compare Listing 10.3 to Listing 10.1 to prove it to yourself. Yet it accomplishes the same things: It runs the TOAD screen or wizard with the chosen settings, but now you don't have to scan that code for command-line parameter name settings or add close commands for either the screen or TOAD.

Listing 10.3   **App Designer Action Code**

```
object TarSchemaDoc
  Enabled = True
  ID = 3
  ParentID = 1
  UserName = 'html_schema_doc_scott'
  ActionSetID = 0
  SchemaList.Strings = (
    'SCOTT')
  SumCluster = False
  SumDBMSJob = False
  SumDimension = False
  SumIndex = True
  SumFunction = True
  SumLibrary = False
  SumSnapshot = True
  SumSnapLog = True
  SumPackage = True
  SumProcedure = True
  SumPolicy = False
  SumPolGroup = False
  SumQueue = False
  SumQueueTable = False
  SumRefreshGroup = False
  SumSchedJob = True
  SumSchedProgram = True
  SumSchedSchedule = True
  SumSequence = True
  SumSynonym = True
  SumTable = True
  SumTrigger = True
  SumType = True
  SumView = True
  SumUserBasic = True
  SumUserProfile = True
  SumUserObjPriv = True
  SumUserSysPriv = True
  SumUserQuota = True
  SumUserRole = True
```

```
SumMViewTable = True
SumObjectCount = True
SumStorage = False
SumComment = False
DescCluster = False
DescClusterIndex = False
DescClusterTable = False
DescDBMSJob = False
DescDimension = True
DescDimensionRef = False
DescFunction = True
DescFunctionSource = False
DescFunctionGrant = False
DescFunctionRef = False
DescLibrary = False
DescLibraryGrant = False
DescLibraryRef = False
DescPackage = True
DescPackageSpecSource = False
DescPackageBodySource = False
DescPackageGrant = False
DescPackageRef = False
DescProcedure = True
DescProcedureSource = False
DescProcedureGrant = False
DescProcedureRef = False
DescRefreshGroup = False
DescRefreshGroupSnapshot = False
DescRole = True
DescSchedJob = True
DescSchedProgram = True
DescSchedSchedule = True
DescSequence = True
DescSequenceGrant = False
DescSequenceRef = False
DescSystemTrigger = True
DescType = True
DescTypeSource = False
DescTypeGrant = False
DescTypeRef = False
DescTable = True
DescTableDefault = True
DescTableIndex = True
DescTableFKConstraint = True
DescTableOtherConstraint = True
DescTableGrant = False
```

Listing 10.3　**App Designer Action Code,** *continued*

```
DescTableTrigger = False
DescTablePolicy = False
DescTableRef = False
DescView = True
DescViewSource = False
DescViewGrant = False
DescViewTrigger = False
DescViewRef = False
DescNoSysRef = False
FileOption = 2
CSS = False
IndexFileName = 'C:\Temp\scott.html'
BackgroundMode = 0
BackGroundColor = 14286335
TableBorder = 0
HeaderColor = 16776960
TransparentRows = True
RowBackgroundColor = 8421504
IndentHTML = False
PageBreaksBeforeTables = False
LowercaseTables = False
TOCEntries = 100
CharacterSet = 'windows-1252'
TableHeaderFontName = 'MS Shell Dlg 2'
TableHeaderFontSize = 8
TableHeaderFontStyle = 'bold'
TableHeaderFontColor = 0
TableRowFontName = 'MS Shell Dlg 2'
TableRowFontSize = 8
TableRowFontStyle = 'normal'
TableRowFontColor = 0
BodyFontName = 'MS Shell Dlg 2'
BodyFontSize = 12
BodyFontStyle = 'bold'
BodyFontColor = 0
UnvisitedLinkColor = 16711680
VisitedLinkColor = 8388736
HoverLinkColor = 255
UseObjectSet = False
ObjectSet = 'chk'#9'ObjType'#9'ObjName'#9'Status'#9'LastDDLTime'
rbFilter = False
UseTableInclusionFile = False
UseTableExclusionFile = False
UseViewInclusionFile = False
UseViewExclusionFile = False
```

```
ProcDeps = False
UseHeader = False
Header1FontName = 'MS Shell Dlg 2'
Header1FontSize = 18
Header1FontStyle = 'bold'
Header1FontColor = 0
Header2FontName = 'MS Shell Dlg 2'
Header2FontSize = 18
Header2FontStyle = 'bold'
Header2FontColor = 0
Header3FontName = 'MS Shell Dlg 2'
Header3FontSize = 12
Header3FontStyle = 'bold'
Header3FontColor = 0
Header4FontName = 'MS Shell Dlg 2'
Header4FontSize = 18
Header4FontStyle = 'bold'
Header4FontColor = 0
UseFooter = False
Footer1FontName = 'MS Shell Dlg 2'
Footer1FontSize = 18
Footer1FontStyle = 'bold'
Footer1FontColor = 0
Footer2FontName = 'MS Shell Dlg 2'
Footer2FontSize = 18
Footer2FontStyle = 'bold'
Footer2FontColor = 0
Footer3FontName = 'MS Shell Dlg 2'
Footer3FontSize = 12
Footer3FontStyle = 'bold'
Footer3FontColor = 0
Footer4FontName = 'MS Shell Dlg 2'
Footer4FontSize = 18
Footer4FontStyle = 'bold'
Footer4FontColor = 0
Aliases = 'SourceType'#9'SourceName'#9'Alias'
RunData = {
```
```
  545046300A54617252756E44617461000B416374696F6E536574494402FF0249
  4402FF084661696C4D6F6465070A666D436F6E74696E75650653746174757307
  09617353756363657373730000}
```
```
Logins = {
```
```
  545046300A544C6F67696E5265566573737300054974656D730A630100005450463009
  544C6F67696E5265566530011456E6372797074656450617373776F7264067D3230
  2C302C302C302C3234372C3134362C3133312C39382C38352C3137372C323338
  2C39322C3135302C37362C3232322C38312C3139332C3139332C39352C313035
  2C3133312C3230382C382C3234332C3130362C35332C3234362C3138342C3139
```

Listing 10.3   **App Designer Action Code,** *continued*

```
312C3131382C36302C3230322C3138302C38362C3138312C3139310455736572
060653595354454D0653657276657206064F524C4931300850726F746F636F6C
0603544E53064E756D62657202010B4C617374436F6E6E6563740500A8A8ABD9
87FA9B0E4009436F6E6E656374417306064E4F524D414C05436F6C6F72038000
0A4F7261636C65486F6D650621433A5C4F7261636C655C70726F647563745C31
312E312E305C636C69656E745F310B4175746F436F6E6E656374080C53617665
50617373776F72640808084661766F7269746508064D6574686F64020000000000}
```

end

So far we've covered just the most basic mechanics of creating applications in the App Designer, corresponding to the way those tasks were carried out using the old Command Line approach, where the construction process begins from the individual screens. But as we've said there's a much better way to define actions that is natively available on the App Designer screen. Furthermore, this approach nicely answers a very important question: Where within TOAD is this feature implemented? Look at Figure 10.6. The first four tabs across the top right-hand side (RHS) of the screen show all the places where the App Designer has been implemented. As you can see, the HTML Schema Doc Generator is available and placed under the "DB Misc" category/tab. What's critical for you to note is that when each TOAD screen finally gets App Designer support, a notation of its availability will show up somewhere here.

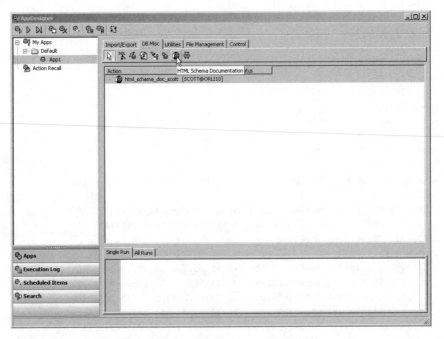

Figure 10.6   App Designer: Availability

You can simply click on one of these screen toolbar icons to add an action to an application. Also, when you execute a RHM click and choose "Properties," or when you double-click on an existing or new action, TOAD will display the "Action Properties" pop-up window, as shown in Figure 10.7. Note that this screen is essentially the same one that would appear if you had invoked it via the menu system, although the save snapshot and schedule toolbar icons are no longer visible in the lower-left corner. TOAD knows that you're calling the screen from the App Designer, so it removes these icons.

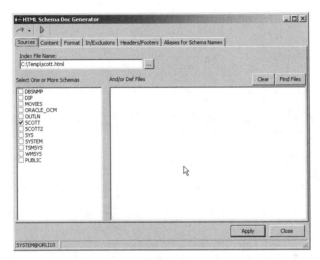

Figure 10.7   App Designer: Action Properties

At this point, we've covered how to create and manage applications and their actions from within the App Designer main screen. Now it's time to add application advanced "programmatic control"—including variables, conditional logic, and looping or iteration constructs—to your arsenal of weapons. That takes us to the fifth and final tab found at the top RHS of the screen, labeled "Control." Here you'll really be limited only by your imagination and programmatic skills. In our case, we want to perform a TNS ping operation to verify that the database is up and running before we attempt to generate our HTML Schema Doc report. We double-click on the highlighted "IF THEN ELSE" toolbar icon, and then drag and drop our actions to the specific syntactical portions we desire. Each action returns an action code of pass or fail—so we can place almost any action into any conditional logic expression. Now when we click the "Execute Application" button, TOAD runs everything to completion as expected, as shown in Figure 10.8. Had the TNS ping failed, however, TOAD would have skipped over the report creation action.

You should spend time exploring all that the "Control" tab has to offer. The conditional logic, looping constructs, and variables are relatively straightforward. Three other very powerful constructs make even more wonderful things possible: the file iterator, the folder iterator, and the list iterator. Suppose you wanted to perform an action on every file

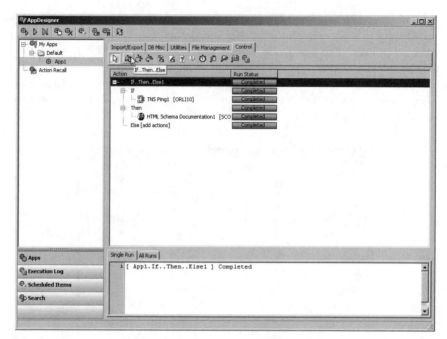

Figure 10.8   App Designer: Programmatic Control

in a directory (e.g., import every Excel file into a table); the file iterator provides exactly this capability. Most real-world jobs will require you to take advantage of one or more of the iterators, so it's best to learn them early and use them often.

Summary

TOAD is all about making you more effective and efficient at your job. And it's in terms of this aspect—efficiency or productivity—where TOAD shines brightest. Of course, for many real-world scenarios, you simply need the ability to both record and play back (very much like macros) what you do in TOAD. That way you can automate the execution of those tasks without having to launch and navigate TOAD's many menus and screens each and every time you need to perform those tasks. For that purpose, TOAD offers two facilities: the older Command Line feature and the newer, powerful App Designer. Both make automating repetitive TOAD tasks much easier. The TOAD App Designer is the wave of the future and will soon replace the old Command Line feature, so it's best to use the App Designer for all of your current work.

Index

Bert Scalzo
Dan Hotka

Second Edition

TOAD® Handbook

Developer's Library

FREE Online Edition

Your purchase of **TOAD® Handbook, Second Edition** includes access to a free online edition for 45 days through the Safari Books Online subscription service. Nearly every Addison-Wesley Professional book is available online through Safari Books Online, along with more than 5,000 other technical books and videos from publishers such as Cisco Press, Exam Cram, IBM Press, O'Reilly, Prentice Hall, Que, and Sams.

SAFARI BOOKS ONLINE allows you to search for a specific answer, cut and paste code, download chapters, and stay current with emerging technologies.

Activate your FREE Online Edition at
www.informit.com/safarifree

> **STEP 1:** Enter the coupon code: XIBNZBI.

> **STEP 2:** New Safari users, complete the brief registration form.
> Safari subscribers, just log in.

If you have difficulty registering on Safari or accessing the online edition,
please e-mail customer-service@safaribooksonline.com